A Contest of Faiths

A Contest of Faiths

Missionary Women and Pluralism in the American Southwest

Susan M. Yohn

Cornell University Press
Ithaca and London

First published 1995 by Cornell University Press.

Printed in the United States of America

⊗ The paper in this book meets the minimum requirements
of the American National Standard for Information Sciences—
Permanence of Paper for Printed Library Materials, ANSI Z39.48-1984.

Library of Congress Cataloging-in-Publication Data

Yohn, Susan M. (Susan Mitchell), 1958–
    A contest of faiths : missionary women and pluralism in the American
Southwest / Susan M. Yohn.
        p.   cm.
    Includes bibliographical references and index.
    ISBN 0-8014-2964-1 (cloth: alk. paper)   ISBN 0-8014-8273-9 (paperback:
alk. paper)
    1. Hispanic Americans—Missions—New Mexico.   2. Women
missionaries—New Mexico.   3. Presbyterian women—New Mexico.
4. Pluralism (Social sciences)—New Mexico.   5. Home missions—New
Mexico.   6. Presbyterian Church in the U.S.A. Woman's Board of Home
Missions—History.   7. Presbyterian Church—Missions—New Mexico.
8. New Mexico—Church history—19th century.   9. New Mexico—Church
history—20th century.   I. Title.
BV2788.H56Y64   1995
266'.51789—dc20   94-39195

For my grandmother
Jeannette Rice Stromberg

Contents

Contents

Acknowledgments

This book could not have been completed without the support of many different people and institutions. I owe a tremendous debt to the faculty who served as my teachers, advisers, and mentors at New York University. Thomas Bender, especially, cheerfully served as my graduate adviser even though western, religious, and women's history were not his fields of specialty. He has read draft after draft, providing criticisms and suggestions that have always helped to make the manuscript stronger. In addition, the many conversations we have had about my work and the discipline of history helped me sustain my interest in this project and see it in the broadest context possible. I am grateful for his continuing guidance and friendship. Marilyn Young, whom I value for her uncanny ability to go right to the heart of the matter, was always ready to help me make sense of problems I confronted in my work. In her classes she has a gift for rendering the complexity of human relations with compassion and clarity. I hope that this book lives up to the model she provided. The comments of Molly Nolan, Danny Walkowitz, Paul Mattingly, and Susan Ware have also made this work stronger. Nancy Robertson, Marci Reaven, Annelise Orleck, and Melanie Gustafson, friends and fellow graduate students at New York University, provided valuable comments at critical junctures. I thank Ronald Butchart for sharing his research on missionaries who worked among the freedmen and for supporting my efforts. I am also grateful to Peggy Pascoe, Jane Hunter, and Sarah Deutsch for their careful and thoughtful reviews of the manuscript.

Carolyn Atkins introduced me to the collection at the Menaul Historical Library of the Southwest, in Albuquerque, and helped to get this project under way. I am indebted to the staff of the library for their help and encouragement over the many years of the project. At the Presbyterian Historical Society in Philadelphia, it was a pleasure to work with Fred Heuser and Kristin Gleeson, who cheerfully met my requests and made important suggestions about the collections and materials available at the library. I also thank the many other librarians and archivists who helped me locate materials, including those at the New York Public Library, the Sophia Smith Collection at Smith College, and the New Mexico State Research Center and Archives in Santa Fe.

Several grants helped in the completion of this project. A Charlotte Newcombe Fellowship from the Woodrow Wilson Foundation helped me in the early stages. More recently, a Spencer Fellowship from the National Academy of Education allowed me to take a leave from teaching to complete the manuscript. The Indiana University Center on Philanthropy not only provided financial support but also introduced me to an interdisciplinary group of scholars who provided a range of new perspectives on the missionaries who are the subject of this book. John Moore, former Chair of the Hofstra History Department, and Robert Vogt, Dean of Hofstra College, were instrumental in helping to secure these grants. I also thank the *History of Education Quarterly* for permission to use material from my article "An Education in the Validity of Pluralism: The Meeting between Presbyterian Mission Teachers and Hispanic Catholics in New Mexico, 1870–1912," *History of Education Quarterly* 31 (Fall 1991): 344–64.

My family has proved very patient as I have been promising them this book for many years now. My mother, Gretchen Stromberg, has played several important roles, from morale booster to editor. My grandmother, Jeannette Rice Stromberg, to whom the book is dedicated, has been among the best of teachers and friends. Her roots in northern New Mexico and southern Colorado go back to the 1870s when her grandparents arrived in Trinidad, Colorado, to serve as Methodist missionaries. Her enthusiasm for this project has, at times, served to rekindle my own. I thank her for taking care of me when I was in New Mexico doing research, for sharing her knowledge of the region, and for carefully listening to what were, at times, tedious descriptions of the records I was examining. Valerie Barr has faithfully read multiple drafts, taking time away from her own work as a computer scientist to unravel overly complicated prose and to question parts of the narrative that were not clear (not to mention providing many hours of technical support). I thank her for her gentle criticisms; they have made this a stronger book.

S.M.Y.

A Contest of Faiths

Introduction

This book examines the process by which Anglo-Protestant missionaries attempted to introduce a particular set of religious and cultural values to the Hispano-Catholic population of the area that is now northern New Mexico and southern Colorado in hopes of "Americanizing" these people. The principal actors were Presbyterian women, who, like many other Protestant women in the latter part of the nineteenth century, entered the home mission field for modest personal goals; some wanted to be of greater use to society or to feel closer to God, while others simply desired a change of scenery and some adventure. They found something much larger. Caught in the drama of national expansion, these missionaries were forced to confront the limitations they faced, both in the church and in mission work, to reconsider the nature of the work they were asked to do, and to reevaluate the "mission" of the church.

Today New Mexico advertises itself as the "land of enchantment," stressing both its dramatic landscapes and multicultural population, but the Protestant women missionaries who undertook to convert the Hispano-Catholic population in the late nineteenth century more often saw the land and its peoples as obstacles to the creation of a more perfect United States.[1] Beginning shortly after the Mexican-American War in

---

[1] The Anglo-Protestant missionaries did not use the term "Hispano" to describe the descendants of the Spanish who lived in this territory. They used "Mexican" initially; later, after an

1846, itinerant preachers passed through the newly annexed New Mexico territory, handing out Bibles and extolling the virtues of Protestantism to the largely Catholic population. These informal efforts were followed, after the Civil War, by more organized missions from the mainstream Protestant denominations. Representatives of the Presbyterian Church came to northern New Mexico and southern Colorado, the heart of the Hispano population, first attempting to organize churches and then building small schools. The immediate concern of the missionaries was to convert Catholics to Protestantism, but they felt they had a larger mission than simply to promote their religious principles.

At the heart of this enterprise was a concern about national character. Rather than revel, as people do today, in the wild and rugged character of the landscape and the complex dynamics of the Hispano/Indian population, Anglo-Protestants sought to tame and to control a new frontier. Their efforts to subdue elements they saw as "foreign," that is the Indian, Spanish, and Catholic heritage, and to remake the territory in their own image were only partially successful. Instead of a monument to the hegemony of Protestant ideals, this conquest was marked by a series of ongoing contests that called into question commonly held stereotypes and forced the missionaries and their supporters to reconsider and reassess their goals.

Within the context of the larger contest of faiths taking place in the Southwest, between Protestant and Catholic, Anglo and Hispano, women missionaries confronted a series of personal contests. The Southwest's

---

increase in Mexican migration to the United States caused by the Mexican Revolution in 1910, they employed the term "Spanish-American" to distinguish the longtime residents of New Mexico from Mexican immigrants. Neither did they use the term "Hispanic" to refer to all those of Spanish descent living in the United States; rather, they employed the term "Spanish-speaking." Arthur Campa, in his *Hispanic Culture in the Southwest* (Norman: University of Oklahoma Press, 1979), argues that "Hispano" connotes "cultural characteristics of people from Colorado to Mexico. . . . It means a people having cultural attributes that stem from their Hispanic heritage regardless of nationality. They speak Spanish, they share basically the same cultural values, they have a common philosophy of life, and they have inherited all this from the same source, Spain. It does not mean that they came from Spain or that they do not have any Indian blood or that they have no cultural background of their own. The term simply sets them apart from Anglo-Americans" (p. 6). In this work, I use the term to mean, more specifically, Hispanics who were residing in the Southwest before the area's annexation by the United States and their descendants. I have chosen to use the Spanish word "Hispano" rather than the English "Hispanic" to underscore the point that they had a culture (including a language) distinct from that of Anglo-American settlers. But, unlike Campa, I refer to this one group—not later Mexican immigrants or other nationalities of Spanish descent.

place in the national imagination today differs from that which missionaries originally envisioned. The very dynamics of the contests that ensued from the meeting between missionary and student, as well as among missionaries themselves and among their students, precluded the outcome sought by Anglo-Protestants. What resulted was the elaboration of a process to be repeated again and again in different parts of the country as a dominant Anglo-Protestant class tried to assimilate a growing population of immigrants and others deemed foreign, thereby generating increasing awareness of cultural pluralism. This debate about who was an "American" and what was required to be "American" ultimately called into question the role of the state. Like their sisters in the secular reform movement, women missionaries found that as they expanded their ideas about who could be American, their expectations of the state also changed. The liberal state, they concluded, could adequately address their changing ideas about pluralism only by focusing more attention on issues of social justice and social welfare.

This, then, is the story of how one group of Anglo-Protestant women reformers came to reassess ethnocentric standards of national identity that insisted, for instance, that "good" citizens were Protestant. Their original assumptions about the people who were the subjects of the home mission enterprise, in this case Hispanos, were replaced by a demand for a society more accepting, more tolerant, and more understanding. Yet however their experience as missionaries altered their consciousness, these reformers stopped short of demanding equity for their clients. They did not challenge the race and class structure of this society. That challenge was left to their Hispano students.

† † †

This book is structured so as to elaborate the contest of ideas, or what I have called faiths, that this group of women confronted. I use the term "faiths" in its broadest sense to mean several different things, not all of which have to do specifically with religion. My intention is, rather, to suggest that these women's political self-consciousness was shaped by a series of competing ideas that they confronted simultaneously as missionaries, as women, as Anglos, and as teachers. Chapter 1 begins with an examination of Protestant women's attempts in the late nineteenth century to broaden the range of their responsibilities within mainstream, male-dominated religious institutions such as the Presbyterian Church.

The contest recounted in this chapter is one of gender, as women challenged men's presumed dominance, first in the religious arena but second as purveyors of national identity. This chapter focuses on the emergence of the Woman's Executive Committee of Home Missions of the Presbyterian Church in the U.S.A. when its founding members sought to assert a larger role for women within the church and its attempt to create a more Christian America.[2] This organization was offered as one answer to the failure on the part of male missionaries to convert "foreigners" successfully. Presbyterian women proposed to raise money to build, maintain, and staff missionary schools with women teachers, thus expanding the effort to include a large number of single women. Anglo-Protestant women, they asserted, had a special role to play, as citizens, in safeguarding the "Christian" moral standards they believed to be at the heart of this democratic nation.

Chapter 2 turns to the contest that emerged in the Southwest between Anglo-Protestants, who sought to secure this new territory for the United States, and Hispano-Catholics, who wanted to maintain cultural autonomy as well as political and economic power. The Southwest is one of the fields in which Protestant women hoped to prove to their male counterparts that they could effectively evangelize and Americanize. A simultaneous contest between Hispano-Catholics and the Euro-Catholic hierarchy, which left many Hispanos feeling excluded from or at odds with the Catholic Church, gave them an opening wedge in this area.

In Chapter 3 I examine the women who sought out mission work and discuss the dynamics in their lives that led them to mission work. What emerges is a tension between their need to earn a living and a desire, born of their religious convictions, to do useful work. They were drawn to the movement by a rhetoric that emphasized the spiritual aspects of the work, promising that they would serve a useful purpose, as missionaries but also as citizens. They found, instead, a far more complicated situation that required them to balance the spiritual with the practical aspects of the job. The promise was an enterprise like a large family working in unison, but they confronted a growing bureaucracy, with all

2 The dates of this study are determined by the beginnings of the Presbyterian woman's missionary effort in the New Mexico Territory in 1867, when Charity Ann Gaston arrived to open the first school for Hispano students. In 1924 this separate women's effort officially ended when the Woman's Board of Home Missions was integrated into the larger Board of National Missions. This merger did not, however, mean the end of Presbyterian missionary activities in New Mexico, which continue, in a much diminished form, to this day.

the problems of any national endeavor. They found that they had to juggle their desire for spiritually fulfilling work with the reality that they were employees of an organization professing to have holy goals but unable to escape worldly problems.

The contest discussed in Chapter 3 is not one between different groups. I reiterate that I use the term "faiths" as a metaphor for ideology. It is intended to evoke a sense of how this group of Anglo women responded to the many conflicting ideas they encountered through their lives. Sometimes these conflicting ideas were embodied in encounters between different groups of people—between men and women in Chapter 1 and between Hispanos and Anglos in Chapters 2, 4, and 5. In other situations the ideological conflict is apparently just that, as we will see in Chapter 6, which concerns individuals within the same group who held different ideas about the course the organization's work should take. Chapter 3 is about more general, and hence more difficult to characterize, notions of what constituted "respectable" work for this class of American women. In this chapter I point out the contest between the individual missionary's and the society's expectations of the kinds of work and public activities she should undertake and describe the internal contest a woman considering mission work would have confronted. What were her motivations, how did she decide to join the mission enterprise, and what obstacles did she face in making this choice?

The meeting between Anglo missionaries and their Hispano students and neighbors is the subject of Chapter 4. Once in the field, missionaries were frustrated by their inability to fulfill their spiritual duties, to evangelize and convert. Ultimately they came to realize that most Hispanos were not interested in converting or in leaving the Catholic Church, even though they may have had grievances with the church, but that they wished to avail themselves of other services such as education that mission women provided. The ethnic contest in this meeting was muted by the desire of missionaries to succeed at their work. They came to believe that the goal of useful work, of success in the field they believed to be their calling, could be gained by making alliances with Hispano students. In so doing, however, they moved away from their original religious goals and began to stress the more secular aspects of their work, such as teaching Hispanos to read and write in English.

These changes that individual mission women confronted once in the field provided experiential evidence that moved the organization as a whole to become more committed to issues of social justice. They also sparked a wider discussion among supporters of the mission enterprise about cultural pluralism. I am unwilling to label the mission women who served in this field "cultural pluralists," for they shared no one fixed idea of cultural pluralism. As individuals they developed a variety of different relationships to their clients which expressed their often contradictory ideas about social unity and cultural diversity. Instead, their experience might best be thought of as illustrating a process by which Anglo-Protestants came to reconcile demands made by those who were not Anglo and Protestant to be recognized as full citizens.

Chapter 5 examines their Hispano students, the better to define the limits of mission women's changing sensibility. For many Hispano mission students, but especially for the small number who converted to Protestantism, mission schools were an aid in navigating a larger ethnic and class contest that emerged when Anglo and other Euro-Americans moved into the New Mexico territory. The education offered by mission women helped Hispanos deal with the social and economic changes taking place in New Mexico as the United States imposed its control. In the process, Hispanos who converted battled the ethnocentrism and racism of the Presbyterian Church, demanding that this institution recognize them as legitimate members (much as Anglo women had done a half century earlier). Unlike their teachers, these Hispano students were cultural pluralists. Their demands for justice became part of a persistent call made by minorities within the church for racial and ethnic equity, increasing the awareness of many Anglo-Protestants about the issue of civil rights. In addition, the refusal of Hispano converts to give up cultural traditions rooted in a Catholic heritage forced the church to moderate its anti-Catholicism, further encouraging a growing historical trend toward ecumenism and secularism.

This book is not a true cross-cultural analysis in the sense that the title might suggest. I have not given equal attention to the experience of the missionaries' Hispano clients. For a more finely developed and nuanced analysis of the Hispano experience during this period, one might start with Sarah Deutsch's book *No Separate Refuge: Culture, Class, and Gender on an Anglo-Hispanic Frontier in the American Southwest, 1880–1940.* Certainly there is room for more discussion and analysis of the effects of Protestant mission efforts on Hispanic clients in the Southwest. My intent has been to use this case study, this meeting between Anglo and Hispano, to illustrate the role played by evangelical women in helping to lay a foundation for both the welfare state and later debates about cultural pluralism. In the concluding chapter the focus shifts away from the Southwest, back to the Presbyterian Church, to examine the contest that ultimately led to the demise of the women's mission movement, that between voluntarism and professionalism.

As the work of missionaries in the field took on a more secular tone and conversion was deemphasized, the organizations that constituted the home mission enterprise began to look much like any other social service organization. Religious conservatives would argue in the 1920s that the enterprise had lost sight of its mission to convert or to "save" individuals. To a degree this was correct. The women who ran the enterprise more eagerly embraced the part of the work concerned with social justice (or in the terms of the Social Gospel, "good works") than that concerned with conversion. The resistance missionaries had encountered to their efforts to convert forced them to become more pragmatic and, in response, the leaders of the organization moved in much the same direction. Leaders began to stress the importance of training and of a mission pedagogy. They eagerly sought to streamline the organization and make it more efficient. This process of professionalizing the organization, however, alienated its core of supporters, from among whom missionaries had earlier been recruited. This final contest, which pitted an ethic of voluntarism (which presumed that almost all women could do the work and embraced all women as "sisters" in the endeavor) against one of professionalism, rendered the mission enterprise's constituency largely passive. Their service was not needed, simply their financial support.

These changes might not have mattered but for the fact that mission enterprise was a political endeavor. From the outset the Woman's Executive Committee of Home Missions had fused its religious and political goals. Evangelizing and converting "foreigners" to Protestantism were believed to be fundamental to the making of good American citizens. The work also gave its female supporters the opportunity to act on their convictions and to volunteer their services, thereby redefining the meaning of citizenship for women. As the emphasis shifted to issues of social welfare—largely in response to "foreigners" who would not convert— the leaders justified these changes by arguing that poverty, injustice, and the like spoke poorly of America's Christian leaders and constituted a blight on its Christian heritage. By the 1920s, the nature of the problem had been redefined to require a special class of employee, the social worker. The effect of empowering a particular group of people to address issues of welfare was to separate ideology from action. Mission supporters were called on to aid in the expansion of the welfare state, for example, but middle-class Anglo-Protestants had fewer opportunities to perform "useful" social services for client populations or to go through a process that challenged the stereotypes they held about such people.

My intention is not to glorify the volunteer, or the missionary for that matter, but rather to underscore the point that evangelical Protestantism, and evangelical Protestant women in particular, played a significant part in educating a political constituency about the need for and efficacy of the emerging welfare state. Although historians have shown growing interest in evangelical women's organizations, the discussion about women's role in shaping the welfare state has remained focused largely on secular activists. From Allen Davis's analysis of Jane Addams to Ellen Fitzpatrick's more recent examination of the University of Chicago group —Sophonisba Breckinridge, Edith Abbott, Katherine Bement Davis, and Frances Kellor—much of the discussion has focused on women who played a leading and pivotal role as social activists and policymakers.[3] Other studies have focused on the people who were the clients of the programs developed by these secular activists.[4]

---

[3] Much of this literature takes the form of biography. Allen Davis, *American Heroine: The Life and Legend of Jane Addams* (New York: Oxford University Press, 1973), and Ellen Fitzpatrick, *Endless Crusade: Women Social Scientists and Progressive Reform* (New York: Oxford University Press, 1990), are but two examples. For discussion of other women who were also part of the Progressive elite see Kathryn Sklar, "Hull House in the 1890's: A Community of Women Reformers," *Signs* 10 (Summer 1985): 658–77, and George W. Martin, *Madam Secretary, Frances Perkins* (Boston: Houghton Mifflin, 1976). Robyn Muncy, in *Creating a Female Dominion in American Reform, 1890–1935* (New York: Oxford University Press, 1991), seeks to explain how women's organizations served as the bridge between the Progressive Era and the New Deal. She examines the work of many of these same leading reformers; however, she discusses how the hierarchy, or leaders of this movement, were distanced from the volunteer corps when their programs were taken over by the government. Linda Gordon has also broadened the focus by examining the work and ideas of leading welfare advocates, male and female, so as to further our understanding of the gendering of welfare policy and its implementation. See Gordon, "Social Insurance and Public Assistance: The Influence of Gender in Welfare Thought in the United States, 1890–1935," *American Historical Review* 97 (February 1992): 19–54. She, however, looks specifically at the leaders of the movement and does not include "those who were only the employees of welfare programs or institutions." In addition, her group is composed almost entirely of secular activists. For a general overview of historical work being done on women and the welfare state see Seth Koven and Sonya Michel's review "Gender and the Origins of the Welfare State," *Radical History Review* 43 (Winter 1989): 112–19.

[4] See, for example, Linda Gordon, *Heroes of Their Own Lives: The Politics and History of Family Violence, Boston, 1880–1960* (New York: Viking, 1988), and Rivka Shpak Lissak,

Yet, as Paula Baker has pointed out, as the nineteenth century gave way to the twentieth, a radical shift in American politics was taking place, which she attributes to the rise of women's voluntary organizations. Unable to redress the myriad social problems through their private welfare networks, women reformers decided to pass on "to the state the work of social policy that they found increasingly unmanageable." "Woman's domain" gradually came to define the public domain (a process that Baker calls the "domestication of politics"). No longer were individualism and laissez-faire the central tenets of the "liberal" state. "Liberalism" meant, instead, a "sense of social responsibility coupled with a more activist, bureaucratic and 'efficient' government."[5]

This shift in politics and ideology described by Baker did not take place just among elite women reformers. Implementing the policy initiatives, first in private welfare organizations and later in government, required the financial, moral, and ultimately political support of a much broader group of middle-class Anglo-American women. Despite what we know about women's voluntary work, we have shied away from a closer examination of how this class came to make a commitment to the principles of the new "liberalism" or the ideas of social justice and social welfare. Baker concludes that these political changes also compromised the ability of "woman" to act as a class.[6] Therefore, we must ask too whether these developments might have compromised support for the new "liberalism."

The women's home mission movement was but one part of a much larger evangelical impulse which, as it reemerged in the late nineteenth century, also produced the Woman's Christian Temperance Union and the Young Women's Christian Association, both organizations that coupled religious inspiration with social reform and attracted millions of followers. The organization that employed the women who are the subject of this book, the Presbyterian Church's Woman's Executive Committee of Home missions (later renamed the Woman's Board of Home Missions), was part of a much larger Protestant mission movement with foreign and domestic branches which, at its height in the mid-1910s,

Pluralism and Progressives: Hull House and the New Immigrants, 1890–1919 (Chicago: University of Chicago Press, 1989).

[5] Paula Baker, "The Domestication of Politics: Women and American Political Society, 1780–1920," in *Unequal Sisters: A Multicultural Reader in U.S. Women's History,* ed. Ellen DuBois and Vicki Ruiz (New York: Routledge, Chapman & Hall, 1990), p. 78.

[6] Ibid., p. 82.

numbered an estimated three million women.[7] The interdenominational Council of Women for Home Missions, established in 1908, counted among its constituent boards those of the Baptist, Christian, Congregational, Evangelical Lutheran, Methodist Episcopal, Methodist Episcopal South, Presbyterian, Reformed Church of America, and United Presbyterian denominations.

Although it is difficult to measure the combined resources of the home mission movement, in 1924, before it ceased to exist as an independent agency of the Presbyterian Church, the Woman's Board of Home Missions counted 421,656 members in its women's missionary societies and young people's organizations. It employed 451 missionaries, who worked in Alaska and with the Asians on the Pacific Coast, the Spanish-speaking, American Indians, the Mormons of Utah, and poor whites in the southern mountains, as well as at stations in Puerto Rico, Cuba and the Dominican Republic. Its budget for the 1923–24 fiscal year was $1,120,000, with which it administered twenty-four boarding schools and twenty-one day schools serving 4,000 pupils, twenty-eight community stations from which workers made 18,000 visits to private homes, and eight medical centers which saw 49,000 patients.[8] The approximately 230 women assigned to work among Hispanos in New Mexico between 1870 and 1924 were only one part of a much broader movement.

This movement's principal concern was not to achieve social reform per se but to strengthen the nation by making good citizens. From the outset it addressed the issue of the state's role in this process. The women who found their way into the home mission movement believed it was the state's duty, for instance, to act as a instrument of morality by ensuring all citizens an education. This education was to be both practical and "moral" (rooted in Protestant religious doctrines) and was thought to be fundamental in assuring the welfare of both the individual and the state. Failing this, as was the case in New Mexico, it was the responsibility of private organizations to fill the gap. Women missionaries would build schools and serve as teachers in New Mexico until

---

[7] As Patricia Hill has pointed out in *The World Their Household: The American Woman's Foreign Mission Movement and Cultural Transformation, 1870–1920* (Ann Arbor: University of Michigan Press, 1985), figures on the numbers of women active in the mission movement varied widely. She cites totals of anywhere from 600,000 to three million (see p. 195, n. 1).

[8] "Board Fact and Figures," *Home Mission Monthly* 37 (September 1923): 253.

MAP SHOWING OUR MISSION SCHOOLS IN NEW MEXICO

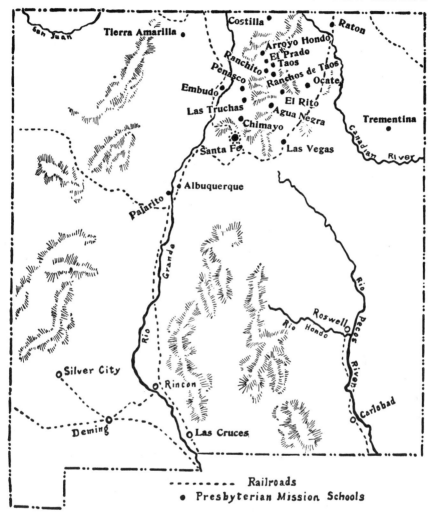

Published in the *Home Mission Monthly,* November 1908 (Department of History and Records Management Services, Presbyterian Church USA)

reforms had been enacted and the public system was deemed adequate. When experience suggested that education alone could not redress the poverty of their Hispano students, missionaries took on additional duties. They provided health care, while urging that this become a public concern. Over the years they came to advocate a more expansive role for the state, which was justified in terms of "social justice" rather than those of "morality." Missionaries welcomed the Sheppard-Towner Act, which enhanced public health efforts in New Mexico. With the advent of the New Deal, those who remained in New Mexico (for the enterprise had shrunk·in the 1920s) embraced the Works Progress Administration and federal relief initiatives.

The women who traveled to New Mexico as missionaries, however, were also suspicious of the state, and therein lies a source of their ambivalence toward the new "liberalism." Like many other women in similar positions, they had not been fully enfranchised until 1920, and as social activists they had often confronted public officials they perceived as recalcitrant and corrupt. Unlike their more elite sisters (including the leaders of their movement), they did not and could not expect to be consulted when the state took over their duties. Although they did not use the language of contemporary theorists (they did not speak of "social democracy" for instance), they did share many of the same doubts expressed by leading Progressives and social democrats.[9] They worried about the loss of individual autonomy, they feared that people would grow passive, they believed (harking back to an earlier era) that without deprivation people would show no initiative. Finally, they were concerned that those who were not worthy would benefit the most from public welfare programs. These last two fears, especially, suggest the continuing influence of evangelical ideas that emphasized the importance of individual salvation.

Today the United States has an incomplete welfare structure and the term "liberal" evokes ambivalent responses. The doubts expressed by

[9] Many of these same doubts were expressed by leading Progressives and social democrats of the day. Clarke Chambers, in *Seedtime of Reform: American Social Service and Social Action, 1918–1933* (Minneapolis: University of Minnesota Press, 1963), has argued that in the 1920s leading settlement house reformers suffered a spiritual crisis when they saw the model of these "centers of contact, understanding, impulse," where "connection springs from personal contact," give way to a more mechanistic style of social service (pp. 148–49). Otis Graham, in *The Old Progressivism and the New Deal* (New York: Oxford University Press, 1967), has argued that many Progressives found New Deal programs of the 1930s to be "coercive." Although they endorsed the need for federal aid to relieve Depression hardships, they worried about the expense, about public officials with excessive power, and about what they perceived to be the undermining of an ethic that championed hard work, thrift, and character. As James Kloppenburg has shown, in *Uncertain Victory: Social Democracy and Progressivism in European and American Thought, 1870–1920* (New York: Oxford University Press, 1986), leading intellectuals such as John Dewey believed that one unfortunate result of expanding the powers of the state to address issues of social welfare was the creation of a bureaucracy that eroded participatory democracy.

home missionaries earlier in this century continue to work to limit the role played by the state. We have a continuing debate about what "welfare" means and the state's role in providing for social welfare, and many of today's policy initiatives have short lives, repealed when it is deemed that individual initiative is being stymied or when it is argued that the "wrong" people are receiving aid (the exceptions, of course, are Social Security and Medicare, but in these cases the recipients have been deemed worthy by virtue of their age).

† † †

When I began this project, my concern was with the role that women home missionaries played in the physical expansion of the nation—hence the focus on New Mexico. I envisioned that my analysis would focus on issues of assimilation and acculturation. As I conducted my research, however, it became clear that these women missionaries were part of a much larger ideological transformation taking place in this society.[10] Their interaction with Hispanos in the geographically isolated towns of the New Mexico territory was not unlike that taking place between settlement house workers and their immigrant clients in Chicago and New York. In both instances, these meetings raised questions about the nature of American pluralism, about Anglo-Protestant dominance, and about the power and influence that Anglo women reformers could wield. The effect of these reformers' activities, whether in rural New Mexico or urban New York, was to provide a national model and to establish a basic infrastructure for the delivery of social services across the country. None of this could take place, however, without a larger shift in the attitudes of the dominant culture.

[10] For historical works that discuss home missionaries but chart social transformation of a different sort, see Peggy Pascoe, *Relations of Rescue: The Search for Female Moral Authority in the American West, 1874–1939* (New York: Oxford University Press, 1990), and Sarah Deutsch, *No Separate Refuge: Culture, Class, and Gender on an Anglo-Hispanic Frontier in the American Southwest, 1880–1940* (New York: Oxford University Press, 1987).

CHAPTER ONE

"A Woman's Club of National Interest": The Emergence of the Female Home Missionary

The dramatic growth of the United States in the nineteenth century, epitomized by booming cities and expansion westward, raised questions about national identity, particularly the relationship between religion and democracy. This was a particular concern for the Protestant religious elite, which was at once inspired by the possibilities created by such growth and profoundly worried that its own power and influence might be eroded in the process. American democracy rested on Protestant foundations, its members argued, and without the extension of Protestantism across the land there could be no expansion of democratic institutions. With this as their rallying cry, they called for a dramatic expansion in missionary efforts and sent hundreds of young men across the country to spread the American gospel among non-Protestant "infidels." A half century later, the home mission work that men had performed would be done by women. Protestant women had successfully challenged the men in their churches to sanction separate women's mission groups, contesting the idea that women had only a limited role to play in the shaping of the religious foundations of the nation.

The establishment of the Presbyterian Church's Woman's Executive Committee of Home Missions (WEC) in 1878 represented one victory in a long struggle by Protestant women for recognition of their efforts in support of missionary activity. Even though by 1811 there had been a proliferation of women's tract, Bible, and "Female cent" societies engaged in raising monies for the cause, women had acted unofficially, not as a formal part of church structure.[1] In his 1891 history of the Protestant mission effort, Edwin Bliss recalled that before the Civil War, women's mission societies had been "circumscribed, lacking in organization, and not recognized by the denominational boards as performing a large service." Women's mission societies, he suggested, "lacked stimulus of responsibility, they pledged no amounts, assumed neither missionaries nor schools."[2]

Those women who served as missionaries were attached to men as wives, sisters, or sisters-in-law. Their labor was so critical to the success of male missionaries that men were advised not to enter mission work without the aid of a woman. Mission women's principal role was to keep house, to provide for the private needs of male missionaries, and, if need be, to enter into and do mission work in arenas inaccessible to men. In the foreign missions, located in cultures that segregated men and women, such work was primarily among women and children.[3] Women who remained at home supported their sisters in the mission enterprise by packing and sending boxes full of clothes, dried foods, and other articles.

These early mission organizations had no place for unmarried or unattached women. Many women seized the only opportunity to become a missionary by hastily marrying men about to embark for the field. They then had to adapt to new environments and different cultures while they struggled to build a relationship and establish a home with a man who was a relative stranger. They were applauded for their role as helpmates to male missionaries but were not given the recognition due them for the larger public duties they performed. Women's work in building and maintaining schools, in recruiting church members and students, and in serving as pastoral counselors seemed to bring few rewards. The boards

---

[1] M. Katherine Bennett, "Mission Agencies of the Presbyterian Church," *Women and Missions* 12 (January 1936): 331–32.

[2] Edwin Bliss, *The Encyclopedia of Missions* (New York: Funk and Wagnalls, 1891), p. 488. For a more contemporary overview of women's mission efforts see R. Pierce Beaver, *American Protestant Women in World Mission: A History of the First Feminist Movement in North America* (Grand Rapids, Mich.: Eerdmans, 1968), pp. 13–57.

[3] For more on the lives of women involved in missions before the Civil War see Patricia Grimshaw, *The Paths of Glory: American Missionary Wives in Nineteenth-Century Hawaii* (Honolulu: University of Hawaii Press, 1989); Julie Roy Jeffrey, *Converting the West: A Biography of Narcissa Whitman* (Norman: University of Oklahoma Press, 1991); Barbara Welter, "She Hath Done What She Could: Protestant Women's Missionary Careers in Nineteenth-Century America," in *Women in American Religion*, ed. Janet James (Philadelphia: University of Pennsylvania Press, 1978), pp. 111–26.

that oversaw mission work continued to exclude women even while they grew increasingly dependent on women to raise money and supplies for the enterprise and to sustain the emotional and financial commitment of Protestants at home.[4]

By the mid-nineteenth century Anglo-Protestant American women had begun to use their evangelical experience to reassess and reform their worlds both in and out of the church.[5] They were joining temperance organizations, advocating more humane treatment of the mentally ill, seeking to reform prostitutes, and petitioning for the abolition of slavery.[6] In church, they constituted the higher percentage of the congregation; they wielded considerable influence in determining the tone and content of religious devotions, even though they continued to be subordinated within the institutional hierarchies.[7] The Civil War served as the turning point, legitimizing, extending, and lending new power to women's benevolent activities. The demand for missionaries in the immediate aftermath of the war drew in larger numbers of women than ever before. The accumulated experience of mission women overseas as well as those who worked as missionaries among freedmen set a precedent and greatly enhanced the opportunities for all women who desired work as missionaries as well as those who sought to support such an effort.[8]

---

[4] See Beaver, *American Protestant Women in World Mission*, pp. 59–86; Grimshaw, *Paths of Glory*, p. 194; Leonard Sweet, *The Minister's Wife: Her Role in Nineteenth-Century American Evangelism* (Philadelphia: Temple University Press, 1982); Lois A. Boyd, "Presbyterian Ministers Wives: A Nineteenth Century Portrait," *Journal of Presbyterian History* 59 (Spring 1981): 3–17.

[5] Joan Jacobs Brumberg argues that mission women's epistolary reports played an especially important role in stimulating religious feminism. See *Mission for Life: The Story of the Family of Adoniram Judson* (New York: Free Press, 1980), pp. 79–108.

[6] See, for example, Barbara Epstein, *The Politics of Domesticity: Women, Evangelism, and Temperance in Nineteenth Century America* (Middletown, Conn.: Wesleyan University Press, 1981), pp. 89–114; Carroll Smith-Rosenberg, *Religion and the Rise of the American City* (Ithaca: Cornell University Press, 1971); Nancy Hewitt, *Women's Activism and Social Change: Rochester, New York, 1822–1872* (Ithaca: Cornell University Press, 1984); Mary Ryan, *Cradle of the Middle Class: The Family in Oneida County, New York, 1780–1865* (New York: Cambridge University Press, 1982); Lori Ginzberg, *Women and the Work of Benevolence: Morality, Politics, and Class in the Nineteenth-Century United States* (New Haven: Yale University Press, 1990).

[7] Barbara Welter, "The Feminization of American Religion, 1800–1860," in *Clio's Consciousness Raised: New Perspectives on the History of Women*, ed. Mary Hartmann and Lois Banner (New York: Harper Torchbooks, 1974), pp. 137–57; Ann Douglas, *The Feminization of American Culture* (New York: Knopf, 1977), pp. 94–139.

[8] For a discussion of the precedent set by women who worked as missionaries among the freedmen, see Jacqueline Jones, *Soldiers of Light and Love: Northern Teachers and Georgia*

The impetus for the Woman's Executive Committee of Home Missions came from a coalition of Presbyterian women, some of whom had national reputations outside of the church and others who had for years served the church faithfully as the wives of ministers or elders. Their efforts were encouraged and aided by a small group of male home missionaries who worried that men's declining interest in ministerial work would mean an end to home missions. These two groups joined forces on behalf of home missions not simply from a concern about their own status within the church but also a shared belief that the Protestant foundations of the national identity were at risk. No longer were Anglo-Protestant women content to remain on the margins of the mission effort. Instead, they encouraged their male counterparts to recognize that women missionaries could, perhaps more successfully, evangelize among groups of people who had proven resistant to the Protestant message.

† † †

In 1874, the Presbyterian Board of Home Missions reported that the General Assembly had cut its apportionment by $122,500 from $475,000 to $352,500 and that church collections had fallen by $25,000.[9] This decline in the church coffers suggests that the middle-class farmers, small businessmen, and self-employed professionals who made up the core of the Presbyterian Church were hurt by the depression of the 1870s and cut back their contributions. The crisis did not abate. In 1875, the Board of Home Missions fell six months behind in paying the salaries of missionaries.[10] In 1877, in its annual report to the General Assembly, the board lamented that church members had "not yet awakened to the realization of the importance of [home missionary] work."[11] As a result of continued poor contributions, twenty-nine ministers could not be fully employed. In 1878, the year the Woman's Executive Committee was organized, more ministers were unemployed, and fewer men

---

Blacks, 1865–1873 (Chapel Hill: University of North Carolina Press, 1980); Ronald Butchart, "Recruits to the 'Army of Civilization': Gender, Race, Class, and the Freedmen's Teachers, 1862–1875," *Journal of Education* 172 (1990): 76–87.

[9] Presbyterian Church in the U.S.A., Board of Home Missions, *Annual Report*, 1874, p. 5.

[10] Florence Hayes, *Daughters of Dorcas* (New York: Board of National Missions, 1952), p. 61.

[11] Presbyterian Church in the U.S.A., *Minutes of the General Assembly*, 1877, p. 438.

were being sent out as missionaries, the annual report concluded that the "fields are growing whiter than ever before."[12] The Board of Home Missions found it increasingly difficult to pay its home missionaries.

The worsening financial situation was compounded by changes in the economic structure, which gave rise to new definitions of "useful" work for men. Henry George ruefully lamented that during this period the mentality of the nation was best described as "get money—honestly if you can, but at any rate get money."[13] These developments heightened competitive pressures, causing greater rationalization of the nation's productive forces and a new emphasis on professional standards.[14] Young men became reluctant to join the home mission effort.[15] There was no shortage of ministers per se, but graduating students of the theological seminaries could not be persuaded to enter the missionary field.[16]

In 1875, Reverend T. Hill reported that he was having difficulty recruiting missionaries. "It is easy enough to find men ready, even eager, for good places," he wrote, "but they are afraid of anything that has missionary connected with it no matter how promising."[17] Young men preferred the larger, established churches with sufficient finances to ensure job security. Ministers sent to the West enjoyed less prestige than those in the East. As Ferenc Szasz has noted, "Society on the turbulent frontier could not be forced into the established categories of the East . . . in the West his [a minister's] status remained undetermined."

[12] See Presbyterian Church in the U.S.A., *Minutes of the General Assembly*, 1878, p. 571.

[13] George worried about the concentration of wealth, the growth of monopolies, and the growth of large factories and businesses that swallowed up small proprietors and individual craftsmen and artisans. He was not opposed to people's making money, but he did foresee dire social consequences for a society in which this became its citizens primary concern and held the church as responsible as other social institutions for this state of affairs. See *The Complete Works of Henry George: Social Problems* (New York: Doubleday Page, 1904).

[14] On the changes in the structure of business see Alfred Chandler, *Strategy and Structure: Chapters in the History of the American Industrial Enterprise* (Cambridge, Mass.: Harvard University Press, 1962); Chandler, *The Visible Hand: The Managerial Revolution in American Business* (Cambridge, Mass.: Harvard University Press, 1977). For a discussion of professionalism see Burton Bledstein, *The Culture of Professionalism: The Middle Class and the Development of Higher Education in America* (New York: Norton, 1976).

[15] Not only was the mission field increasingly less appealing to men, but Ann Douglas has noted the declining popularity of the ministry as a vocation (*Feminization of American Culture*, pp. 17–49).

[16] *Rocky Mountain Presbyterian*, January 28, 1874, p. 3, col. 2.

[17] Reverend T. Hill, "Where Are the Men?" *Rocky Mountain Presbyterian* 4 (September 1875): 2.

The lack of respect these men felt may have been justified; in some denominations accepting a western transfer was to admit failure.[18]

For others, a western assignment meant a future of financial instability. Responding to the Reverend Hill, a young student wrote that he would be willing to go anywhere for the Word but not if it meant "[crushing] my usefulness by incurring debt" and not if the job did not provide stability for his family. The crux of the problem was money: "Do you pay the expenses of a student and his family to his field when he graduates?" this student asked. "Are you prepared to pay a salary sufficient to support him and his family when in the field?" No, he concluded, "the past experience of the Home Mission field gives no encouragement for a young man to give up inferior prospects—it may be—in the East, for a more extended sphere of usefulness which at best is only precarious."[19] This student did not disagree that western mission work might be necessary, even vitally important, but patriotic appeals alone could not convince seminary students to take jobs that demanded many sacrifices with little reward.

The morale of men who had spent their lives doing mission work on the frontier plummeted. In his *Pioneering in the San Juan*, a loosely autobiographical but apocalyptic tale written in the 1890s, George Darley, a Presbyterian home missionary in the San Juan Valley of southern Colorado, wrote about the precarious position of the male home missionary. To fulfill his duty he was required to open churches, but much to his dismay he found that, in the process, he had to go into debt. Assuming that these expenses would be covered by the body that employed him, the Board of Home Missions of the Presbyterian Church in the U.S.A., he dutifully applied for reimbursement only to have his petition denied. He was told that the board's treasury lacked the funds needed to repay him. His small but poor congregation had no money either so the financial burden for the new church fell on the minister. With his wife's help, with the "little money" she had "on hand," the minister "pull[ed] through," thinking that surely the church would come to his aid the following year.[20] Rather than reward the missionary for

---

[18] Ferenc M. Szasz, *The Protestant Clergy in the Great Plains and Mountain West, 1865–1915* (Albuquerque: University of New Mexico Press, 1988), pp. 38–40.

[19] *Rocky Mountain Presbyterian* 4 (November 1875): 1.

[20] George M. Darley, *Pioneering in the San Juan: Personal Reminiscences of Work Done in the Southwestern Colorado during the Great San Juan Excitement*, (New York: Fleming H. Revell, 1899), pp. 108–12.

his sacrifice, the board decided to grant him an even smaller commission. The exasperated man could only surmise that "possibly the Home Board takes it for granted that, since the missionary managed to survive last year on less than the Presbytery voted him, he can do it again." Determined to continue his work but poorer than ever, the minister asked the local grocer to extend credit but discovered that even the grocer had limits. He prevailed on the banker for a loan only to find that, once again, the board had cut back on his commission.

In Darley's view, the Protestant home mission enterprise was dying, the home missionary starved and his work undermined, not for lack of support in the field but by an unappreciative and unsupportive church. He concluded his story by asking his readers, "If some good soul, who has the time, will please figure how a missionary, under these circumstances, can make a church, where his congregation is continuously changing, self-supporting in five years, he will greatly oblige many home missionaries. The process looks to me like Paddy's experience with his horse—'one straw less each day' but when the horse got down to one straw a day it died."[21]

Critics of the board lamented its conduct, the ways it administered the work, and its lack of organization. From the field, missionaries complained about poor supervision and administrative weaknesses. In a letter chastising the board, the missionary Reverend James M. Shields, stationed at Jemez, New Mexico, wrote that the Board of Home Missions had not yet renewed his contract and those of other missionaries in New Mexico. He worried that he and his colleagues would not be officially employed: "These commissions will run out on the last day of this month," he warned, "and even if the Board does continue them they may not send other commissions or let one know for two or three months. This leaves everything in uncertainty and is a peculiar way that the Board has, which . . . is no way for men to do business. . . . It is useless for me to say more to the Board for I don't hope to hear from them . . . . I informed the Board that the Presbytery is to meet here and asked them . . . if one of the secretaries could come to New Mexico at that time. But of course I do not expect a reply."[22] Complaints like this one registered by Shields did force the board to alter its methods of

[21] Ibid., p. 112.
[22] Letter quoted in Alvin K. Bailey, "The Strategy of Sheldon Jackson in Opening the West for National Missions, 1860–1880" (Ph.D. diss., Yale University, 1948), p. 177.

supervising fieldwork. Recognizing that supervising all fieldwork from New York was cumbersome and inefficient, the board established a level of intermediate supervisors in its attempts to upgrade its services.

Unfortunately, small reforms in administrative procedures could not renew seminary students' interest in mission work. Not only was a missionary expected to work in isolated areas with little supervision from the board, but, as Darley's and Shields's accounts suggest, even the promised funds often failed to materialize or arrived too late. Although church literature continued to promote the importance of aggressive home mission activities, the combined social factors of the depression and the disillusionment of young men with home mission work called into question the church's ability to support its appeal. These conditions threatened to undermine the larger political mission of the enterprise; without an aggressive campaign to promote Protestantism, advocates believed there could be no expansion of democracy.

Hard-pressed to meet the spiritual demands of a rapidly expanding nation, the Presbyterian Church, like other Protestant denominations, was not immune to the effects of larger social and economic changes. The church faced a crisis: How was it to meet the spiritual needs of Presbyterians who were moving west into areas where there was no church? How could it best accommodate members who pressed for church missions to European immigrants in the cities as well as the "exceptional peoples" such as Hispanics, Mormons, Indians, and Eskimos who were in need of "Christian" guidance? In addition, how was it to meet these demands when the depressions of the 1870s and the 1890s cut into the coffers of the home mission effort and fewer young men were entering the home mission field? An answer to these questions would be found by expanding Protestant women's missionary work and, within the Presbyterian Church, the formation of the Woman's Executive Committee of Home Missions.

As the situation worsened, some home missionaries simply ignored or circumvented what they believed were the outmoded methods and rules of the board. Among the most prominent of these unorthodox ministers and missionaries was the Reverend Sheldon Jackson.[23] Entering the mission field upon his graduation from Princeton Seminary in 1858, Jackson spent the early years of his career in Minnesota and Wisconsin

---

[23] For biographical information see ibid.; Robert Laird Stewart, *Sheldon Jackson* (New York: Fleming H. Revell, 1908).

organizing parishes among the Choctaw Indians and white settlers in the region. By the 1870s Jackson had moved on to evangelize in the mountain West. His mission domain included what are today western Iowa, Nebraska, Idaho, Wyoming, Utah, Colorado, New Mexico, and Arizona. Jackson lobbied the Presbyterian Church to adopt an aggressive policy of expansion. He envisioned a mission enterprise that followed the railroads, building churches and schools, and would serve both the Anglo-Protestants moving west and those populations already residing in the West.[24] Often his actions did not have the sanction of the board. Criticized for his aggressive approach, he argued that "God blesses aggressiveness—that when we have gone forward so vigorously that the lukewarm call us rash, we have found the greatest fruit . . . we need to cultivate an aggressive spirit."[25]

Jackson found that women's mission groups supported his unorthodox methods. With money from a network of independent women's mission societies he circumvented the Board of Home Missions's rules.[26] Eager to expand mission activities among the "Spanish-speaking," he ignored, for instance, a rule which mandated that the board limit its work to the English-speaking settlers in the West.[27] Several of the missionaries under Jackson's supervision in New Mexico had already established schools with aid provided by independent women's missionary societies.[28] Using his own newspaper, the *Rocky Mountain Presby-*

[24] In exchange for Jackson's support, the railroad companies reduced their rates or provided free transportation for his travels (Stewart, *Sheldon Jackson,* p. 133; see also Bailey, "Strategy of Sheldon Jackson," p. 8).

[25] Quoted in Bailey, "Strategy of Sheldon Jackson," p. 223.

[26] Jackson was not especially interested in women's rights, but he recognized that teaching was an effective mission activity and understood the fund-raising potential of the auxiliary mission groups established by women. See Elizabeth H. Verdesi, *In but Still Out: Women in the Church,* (Philadelphia: Westminster Press, 1976), p. 51. See also Stewart, *Sheldon Jackson,* pp. 257–80.

[27] When he requested aid to open mission schools among non-English-speakers in the West, the board refused, restating its position that it would support only schools that catered to Anglo-Protestants. The Reverend Kendall wrote, "We cannot pay for . . . any work among the nationalities, till have first cared for our own . . . we wish to sustain Home Missions in New Mexico as elsewhere mainly for the incoming flood of our own people." The Spanish-speaking population was to be regarded as under the purview of the Foreign Board of Missions (Henry Kendall to Sheldon Jackson, July 18, 1870, quoted in Bailey, "Strategy of Sheldon Jackson," p. 211). On the board's refusal to support Jackson, see Stewart, *Sheldon Jackson,* pp. 257–58.

[28] In 1867 the Union Missionary Society (also known as the Santa Fe Association) promised to raise money for schools opened in New Mexico and Arizona. In 1868 these efforts were expanded into the New Mexico, Arizona, and Colorado Missionary Association, and in 1871

Sheldon Jackson (Menaul Historical Library of the Southwest)

terian, to organize support among the general Presbyterian population, he challenged the board to support these schools.[29] "The blessing has come," he wrote. "In answer to the prayers of the church an opening has been made; and a few here and there are seeking the light of that purer faith which has caused the civilization of those brave old Hollanders of the Middle States, the iron-willed Puritans of the Northeast, the sturdy sons of Scotland and north of Ireland, and the glorious Huguenot of the South to advance and take possession of the continent while Spanish Catholic civilization stood still."[30]

---

the Ladies Union Missionary School Association was started to support work at Laguna, New Mexico. For a discussion of the proliferation of small, independent women's mission societies committed to supporting Jackson's efforts see Stewart, *Sheldon Jackson*, pp. 259–61. Jackson's strategy was to establish churches and schools and then do fund-raising; see Bailey, "Strategy of Sheldon Jackson," p. 253.

[29] Through the *Rocky Mountain Presbyterian*, Jackson was able to circumvent the Board of Home Missions and increase communication between missionaries working in the West and supporters in the East (Stewart, *Sheldon Jackson*, p. 137).

[30] Sheldon Jackson, "A Missionary Tour through New Mexico," *Rocky Mountain Presbyterian* 4 (November 1875): 2.

The issues raised by maverick home missionaries like Sheldon Jackson, especially their demand that the home mission field be expanded and schools started among the "exceptional peoples," coincided with and further fueled Presbyterian women's demands for a bigger role in home mission work. Women had supported home mission activities well before the mid-1870s, but it was during this period that women's mission activities and societies were reorganized and the already existing network rationalized. By March 1876, women were pressing the church to determine "at once" the role of women.[31] One woman, writing in Jackson's *Rocky Mountain Presbyterian*, argued that there was "higher" work for women besides "organizing and carrying on sewing circles." Her complaints expressed dissatisfaction with the trifling nature of these activities. They lacked a connection to the larger purpose of the movement, limiting women's ability to deliver an evangelical message; they "do little toward purifying and elevating the churches, little towards Christianizing this broad land where all the nations are sending their children." She challenged women to give as much, or more, energy to home mission efforts and to stop looking overseas for work they could do at home. "How much easier and better to teach the heathen who come to us," she argued, "than to send half around the globe to teach those who are hedged in by the laws and usages, and guarded by the teachers of their own country." A woman could exercise a more direct and lasting influence working with home missions.[32]

The needs of these two groups, the maverick missionaries who represented the frustrations of male missionaries already in the field and who sought greater independence from the board, and women demanding a place within the organization, should not have coincided. They came together because each group alone was limited in its ability to make policy, advance new ideas, or implement and support those policies. Presbyterian women who sought to expand women's role in mission work found it to be to their advantage to work informally with dissident home missionaries like Jackson, even as they looked to the church to organize a separate women's mission organization. Jackson and other male home missionaries who had worked in the field were in a position to know what was needed, to say where Anglo-Protestants could have the most impact, and what mission activities to pursue. Even though

---

[31] For an overview of how these demands were pressed between 1872 and 1877 see Stewart, *Sheldon Jackson*, p. 266.

[32] "Woman in the Church," *Rocky Mountain Presbyterian* 5 (March 1876): 2.

women's work in support of missions began with what they asserted were the "smallest items"—fitting up boxes of clothing, supplementing the salaries of ministers in the field, and corresponding with those workers—their volunteer service and meager financial resources were much appreciated by struggling male missionaries. In this symbiotic relationship, in which women were hungry for reasons why they should continue and expand their work, the men's experiences in the field lent credibility and legitimacy to the women's modest efforts.

† † †

The prototype for the Presbyterian WEC was the Auburn Santa Fe Association. In 1867, Amanda MacFarland had written home to friends in Auburn, New York, describing the lack of educational resources in Santa Fe, New Mexico. She reiterated the concerns her husband, Presbyterian minister David MacFarland, had expressed in his pamphlet *A Plea for New Mexico*, in which he asserted that two-thirds of the population in the territory were "in utter ignorance of the simplest attainments of an intellectual education." The few schools that did exist in the territory were controlled by Catholics, and he feared that Anglo-American settlers would be converted. He stressed the need for Protestant schools, arguing that efforts be undertaken by the Presbyterian Church to convert the Hispano population. To this end, he asked that a "Christian Lady" be sent to teach the Mexican population.[33] MacFarland spoke to the general membership of the Presbyterian Church, but it was Amanda MacFarland's private appeal to family and friends that led to the formation of the Auburn Santa Fe Association, which in 1868 became the New Mexico, Arizona, and Colorado Missionary Association. Amanda MacFarland's plea encouraged the women of the missionary society to raise the money required to hire Charity Ann Gaston, the first Presbyterian mission teacher in New Mexico.[34]

The Auburn Santa Fe Association and its offspring acted as independent auxiliaries to the Presbyterian Board of Domestic and Foreign Missions of the Old School of the Presbyterian Church. After the reunification of the Old and New Schools of the church, the Ladies' Board of

[33] David MacFarland, *A Plea for New Mexico* (N.p., 1867), New York Public Library.

[34] For a discussion of Amanda MacFarland's efforts see Lois Boyd and R. Douglas Brackenridge, *Presbyterian Women in America: Two Centuries of a Quest for Status* (Westport, Conn.: Greenwood Press, 1983), chap. 2.

Missions was organized. This organization grew rapidly. In 1870, it had 45 auxiliaries in New York, Pennsylvania, and Ohio and raised $1,200. By 1883, after the formation of the Woman's Executive Committee of Home Missions, when the Ladies' Board formally became the Woman's Board of Foreign Missions and the last of its domestic work had been transferred to the Woman's Executive Committee, it represented 19 Presbyterial societies and 497 local societies and had, in thirteen years, raised $296,317.57 to support 25 missionaries, 18 schools in the United States, 32 foreign missionaries, 38 native teachers and evangelists, and 30 schools in eight foreign fields.[35]

The same social and economic forces that gave rise to the criticism of the male-dominated Board of Home Missions helped give birth to the Woman's Executive Committee of Home Missions. The Ladies' Board of Missions served a polyglot of interests, and the more glamorous foreign mission field got the majority of the money raised. Increasingly women interested primarily in the home missions felt that national interests were being subordinated to foreign interests. They argued that there were enough resources to support both a foreign and a home mission organization and that the need for the mission at home was as great as that overseas.[36]

Why were the women so optimistic when the male home mission board saw falling revenues? Perhaps taking a chapter from Sheldon Jackson, the women pursued an aggressive fund-raising campaign. Apart from publishing his own newspaper, Jackson's fund-raising strategy included establishing personal connections (his missionaries were required to write lengthy reports to supporters of their work), making personal appearances, and seeking direct cash contributions (he encouraged missionaries to solicit from private individuals). The women would employ all these strategies.[37] Women were encouraged to organize into local mission societies to study the mission enterprise and to donate time, services, and any pennies they had left over from household budgets or salaries. The WEC also tapped an entrepreneurial spirit among middle-class women who had no other legitimate outlet besides organizing for social reform. Active on behalf of home missions were women like Jane

---

[35] Ibid., p. 30.
[36] For a discussion of the difficulties in sorting out home mission activities from foreign missions see ibid., pp. 24–30.
[37] See Bailey, "Strategy of Sheldon Jackson," p. 336.

Hoge, who raised large amounts of money.[38] In a time when "concentration" and "monopoly" were rapidly becoming key words in the business world, women used strategies that might have seemed antithetical to the practices of the day. In fund-raising they pursued a strategy of decentralization, depending on a network of treasurers in local societies to make personal appeals.[39] Their demands that the church define more clearly the role of women's mission organizations, in fact create a parent body to supervise the operations of these smaller groups, however, suggest that these women were aware of the need for more central control. That women were successful in raising sums of money which increased each year while the men found that they could not count on similar patterns among male members only enhanced women's demands for a greater role in the mission enterprise.

The General Assembly of the Presbyterian Church was slow to respond to demands that it officially recognize women's contributions by establishing a separate women's mission organization. In 1872, 1873, and 1874 the General Assembly simply urged women to come to the aid of the Board of Home Missions by increasing their contributions. The women who raised this money were not satisfied to turn control of the funds over to the male-dominated mission organizations. Rather than have the money spent augmenting the salaries of male home missionaries who served as itinerant preachers, women demanded that women teachers be hired. In the early 1870s, however, no mention was made by the General Assembly of mission schools, women teachers for such schools, or women's support for them. Not until 1875 did the General Assembly recommend organization of a group devoted to women's work for home missions. In 1876 the General Assembly instructed synods to appoint committees of women to work under the Board of Home Missions.[40] In

---

[38] Jane Hoge also raised money during the Civil War for the Sanitary Commission. As Lori Ginzberg points out, women active in the Sanitary Commission quickly proved their "business aptitude" in organizing aid societies and raising money (*Women and the Work of Benevolence*, pp. 54–161). She suggests that we think of the women who shaped postwar benevolence as (quoting Grace Dodge's biographer Abbie Graham) " 'merchant'[s] who sought to invest in the 'invisible commodities of the spirit, of which her generation stood in need.' " See Ginzberg's discussion of Grace Dodge, p. 200.

[39] Woman's Executive Committee on Home Missions, "How to Organize a Missionary Society," RG 105, Box 1, Folder 8, Department of History and Records Management Services, Presbyterian Church U.S.A., Philadelphia (hereafter PHS); "Monthly Topic—The Treasury," *Home Mission Monthly* 4 (October 1890): 271.

[40] "Historical Sketch of Woman's Executive Committee," *Presbyterian Home Missionary* 11 (September 1883): 210.

1877 the General Assembly authorized the Board of Home Missions to take charge of school work, acknowledging Jackson's unauthorized formation of schools.[41] The assembly left it to the Home Board to oversee the work of the schools, arguing that they "should not be left uncontrolled." School work could be undertaken, but only if it could be supported by the monies raised by the Ladies' Board. In 1878, Jackson called for the creation of a national Woman's Board of Missions. The result was the appointment of the Woman's Executive Committee.

Women's work within the church was granted more autonomy in 1880, when the Woman's Missionary Society of Allegheny requested that women's work be more clearly defined, that "larger liberty be allowed these societies, by granting them the privilege of doing additional church work, rather than performing the part of auxiliaries in church work already provided." The General Assembly resolved that women could undertake "special enterprises" but in "subordination to the authorities of the church." If special missions were selected, they must be approved by the assembly or the board under whose jurisdiction they fell. The assembly also resolved that these local societies could have more leeway in appropriating the funds they raised and that the funds "contributed by these missionary societies, shall be forwarded to the objects or missions selected, through the Financial Agents of the Presbyteries of the Church."[42] This decision gave women at the local level more power to choose the objects of charity without interference from their local minister.

Slowly, by working within the institution and gradually reforming home mission policies, Presbyterian women gained a larger role in the church. Rather than take over work already performed by men and challenge male home missionaries directly, the WEC called for the expansion of the church's educational efforts among groups it identified as "exceptional peoples." With the support of male missionaries such as Sheldon Jackson, they urged that the Board of Home Missions embrace education as a significant tool in the evangelization process. The assembly recommended that the "Board be allowed to sustain such schools by payment of the teachers needed; such teachers to be recommended by the Presbyteries in which they are, and commissioned by the Board." Acknowledging the role women were to play in raising money for the

---

[41] Boyd and Brackenridge, *Presbyterian Women in America*, p. 24.
[42] Presbyterian Church in the U.S.A., *Minutes of the General Assembly*, 1880, p. 195.

schools, the assembly reported that "it is expected that the funds for such schools will be raised by the ladies mainly."[43]

By establishing this policy the men in the Church drew a line between the duties and work of men and women. This distinction between the ministerial functions provided by male preachers and other services redefined mission work. Before the Civil War and before women entered the mission field in large numbers, male missionaries had combined both ministerial and service functions, serving as both the town preacher and the schoolteacher.[44] Dividing the functions and distributing them between men and women proved a workable compromise to all involved. Male home missionaries were able to devote their energies to preaching, the more prestigious aspect of the profession, while women gained entree into church work as teachers.[45]

† † †

Although not officially independent, the Woman's Executive Committee was directed by women and acted as the central organizing body for the local societies. The WEC's function was to organize and maintain contact with local societies and to control and regulate the educational work of home missions, acting as the distributing agent of money and supplies to the schools under its direction.[46] Women gained power in the church by administering the educational work. Acting on its mandate from the General Assembly, "so far as it is practical, the financial support for this school work shall be committed to the women of the church

---

[43] Hayes, *Daughters of Dorcas*, p. 64.

[44] See Timothy L. Smith, "Protestant Schooling and American Nationality, 1800–1850," *Journal of American History* 53 (March 1967): 680, 689–93; David B. Tyack, "The Kingdom of God and the Common School: Protestant Ministers and the Educational Awakening in the West," *Harvard Educational Review* 36 (Fall 1966): 447.

[45] At midcentury there was a shift in the numbers as more women entered teaching, supplanting men and rendering the profession less appealing to men. See Paul Mattingly, *The Classless Profession: American Schoolmen in the Nineteenth Century*, (New York: New York University Press, 1975). Women were able to move into teaching by asserting their greater piety, arguing that in the lives of students, especially young children, they were better qualified to nurture the moral qualities demanded by the nation. Proponents of women teachers, Catharine Beecher among them, had long looked to the expansion of the mission movement as a way to enhance women's opportunities in this profession. See, for example, Kathryn Sklar, *Catharine Beecher: A Study in American Domesticity* (New York: Norton, 1973), pp. 168–83; Polly Kaufman, *Women Teachers on the Frontier* (New Haven: Yale University Press, 1984).

[46] Mrs. Calvin B. Walker, ed., *Woman's Board of Missions: A Historical Sketch* (Philadelphia: Presbyterian Church in the U.S.A., 1902), p. 6.

as their special trust, out of whose contributions, without drawing upon our regular Home Missionary Fund, shall be taken what, in our judgment, may be needed for this work."[47] As quickly as the money could be raised the WEC opened mission schools. In 1880 there was enough money to support only 25 teachers, but by 1902 the committee was able to employ 490 teachers.

The Woman's Executive Committee continued to expand the educational functions of the organization, concentrating funds and energies on the work over which they had the greatest control and that of least interest to men. They always reported deficits; no money would be available to funnel back into the main treasury of the Board of Home Missions. In 1885, for example, the WEC noted, with regret, that "thus far the Woman's Executive Committee has not been able to contribute anything towards the general funds of the Board. However, when the suggestion was made that they should support the missionaries who are laboring in connection with their schools, it was favorably received, and they decided to do so as soon as the receipts could justify it."[48] The WEC did support a few men, but as teachers or boarding school principals. In New Mexico it paid the salaries of native Hispanos hired to teach as well as several husband and wife mission teams. The WEC, however, preferred to employ single or widowed women.

Making a place for women in the mission movement was a tedious and time-consuming process. The women who oversaw this process, who composed the first board of directors and the advisory committee of the Woman's Executive Committee of Home Missions had risen to prominence in a variety of overlapping circles of benevolent and charitable activities.[49] These women fused evangelical and patriotic zeal. Collectively, their voluntary activities covered a wide range of issues. They had worked with the U.S. Sanitary Commission during the Civil War and supported temperance, as well as doing mission work. Some had helped establish orphan asylums, homes for the friendless, and societies

[47] Presbyterian Church in the U.S.A., Board of Home Missions, *Annual Report*, 1878, p. 5.

[48] Presbyterian Church in the U.S.A., Board of Home Missions, *Annual Report*, 1885, p. 31.

[49] The women on the original WEC Advisory Board were Julia McNair Wright, Mrs. S. F. Scovel, Mrs. A. H. Hoge, Mrs. M. Newkirk, Mrs. J. F. Kendall, Mrs. D. M. Miller, Mrs. J. H. Montgomery, Mrs. Osborne, Mrs. O. E. Huntington, and Mrs. G. D. Harrington. On the original board of directors were Mrs. Ashbel Green (president), Mrs. J. L. Graham (vice president), Mrs. J. B. Dunn (vice president), Mrs. O. E. Boyd (treasurer), Mrs. R. T. Haines (corresponding secretary), Mrs. A. R. Walsh (corresponding secretary), and Mrs. J. D. Bedle (corresponding secretary). See *Home Mission Monthly* 1 (January 1887): 55.

to help newsboys and worked to expand educational opportunities generally. As a group they had considerable experience in organizing for benevolent causes. Jane Hoge, in particular, had earned a reputation as a good organizer. Mary Livermore remembered her as "[excelling] in conducting a public meeting . . . [she] was a very forceful and attractive public speaker."[50] Their combined experience in building organizations also showed that they could galvanize support for reform activities.

Among the most prominent women to lend their support to the Presbyterian effort were social reformer Jane Hoge and writer Julia McNair Wright. Before the Civil War, Hoge had served as secretary to the Pittsburgh Orphan Asylum. When she moved to Chicago she helped organize the Chicago Home for the Friendless. At the outbreak of the Civil War she devoted herself to aiding the U.S. Sanitary Commission, helping to organize the Chicago branch. She organized a Sanitary Fair that raised $70,000 in two weeks and established a reputation as a successful fundraiser. She then accepted the presidency of the Women's Education Association of Evanston, which helped to raise money for the Evanston College for Ladies. Throughout this period, she was active in the Presbyterian Board of Foreign Missions in the Northwest. Among her friends she counted Dorothea Dix, Mary Livermore, and Frances Willard. The first reflected her association with the Sanitary Commission, while the latter two suggested her support for temperance and women's suffrage.[51]

Julia McNair Wright was an author and publicist of evangelical causes; she was also active in the National Temperance Society. She is best known for a popular homemaking guide, *The Complete Home* (1879), which sold over one hundred thousand copies. Mirroring her views on the role of women, *The Complete Home* urges women to shun idleness, pursue an education and take a lively interest in public affairs.[52] As for the other women attending the first meeting of the WEC and who served on the original board of directors and advisory committee, we know more about their husbands.

The collective biography of the women suggests that their families

[50] Quoted in Wayne C. Temple, "Jane B. Hoge," in *Notable American Women, 1607–1950: A Biographical Dictionary*, ed. Edward T. James and Janet W. James, 3 vols. (Cambridge, Mass.: Harvard University Press, 1971), 2: 199–201; Kathleen D. McCarthy also notes Hoge's forceful personality, in *Noblesse Oblige: Charity and Cultural Philanthropy in Chicago, 1849–1929* (Chicago: University of Chicago Press, 1982), p. 21.

[51] Temple, "Jane B. Hoge."

[52] Julia McNair Wright, *The Complete Home: An Encyclopedia of Domestic Life and Affairs* (New York: Charles Drew, 1879).

were immersed in church life. Hoge's husband, Abraham, was an elder, and Jane Newkirk's husband, Matthew, served for twelve years as the treasurer of the General Assembly. They also exhibited a concern with education generally; Wright's husband was a professor of metaphysics and mathematics at Westminster and Wilson colleges. Matthew Newkirk was a trustee of Princeton University and had served as president of the Female Medical College in Philadelphia. Caroline Scovel's husband, Sylvester, was an ordained minister and president of the University of Wooster in Ohio.[53]

The composition of the Woman's Executive Committee illustrates the extent to which church work in the latter part of the nineteenth century remained a family affair. In her study of the earliest missionary families in Hawaii, Patricia Grimshaw illustrates how deeply involved the wives of missionaries were in the day-to-day work of the missions. Indeed, many considered their husbands' successes to be largely the result of their efforts. With years of experience behind them, they chafed when the mission organizations ignored their ideas, silenced them by refusing to allow them to speak at meetings, or simply excluded them.[54] The explosion of women's mission organizations following the Civil War and the presence of ministers' wives on the organizing committees suggests that the female family members of male church workers were finally demanding recognition for years of voluntary service. No longer content to work in the shadow of their husbands or to confine their endeavors to the domestic sphere, these women brought their experience to bear in shaping the form their own work would take.

The Woman's Executive Committee of Home Missions pressed to be recognized as an official part of the church, and yet its members worked as a subgroup of the Board of Home Missions. This structure, a separate women's organization, was familiar to women who had for years worked in benevolent organizations dominated by women. The WEC did not appear to challenge the work being performed by male home missionaries or the roles given to men and women in determining and conducting church affairs. The structure presumed a partnership between men and women. Each would do separate work toward their

---

[53] For information on Julia McNair Wright, Matthew Newkirk, Sylvester Scovel, and William Wright, see *Who Was Who in America* (Chicago: Marquis Who's Who, 1967), vol. 1, and Historical Volume.

[54] Grimshaw, *Paths of Glory*, p. 194.

common goal of a more Protestant and democratic America.[55] The relationship between the WEC and the Board of Home Missions was modeled on a conception of the family laboring as a unit, each member's task integral to production and reproduction. Yet at the same time, the WEC's very existence showed how dissatisfied women had become with the role of silent partner in the patriarchal household.[56]

The reward for the efforts of those who organized and ran the WEC was to have created work for women which was sanctioned by a mainstream and national institution; they made a small opening in an institution that welcomed their membership and money but closed its governing ranks to them. Over time, many of the women who led the WEC used it most effectively as a springboard into larger political and social affairs, but they were less effective in expanding opportunities for women within the church. They demanded a larger and more activist role within the church itself, but, denied a liturgical role, they offered instead organizational and administrative skills to aid the faltering home mission movement.[57] The male-dominated Board of Home Missions preferred to think that the WEC would provide a way to fill the board's coffers. The separate women's organization came to serve a useful purpose; it allowed women to maintain control over the money they raised and to enlarge the work that employed women. By pursuing this strategy, the directors of the WEC were able to increase the number of women employed in mission work and the opportunities available to them.

[55] In this case separatism was only a strategy, not an ideological statement. See Estelle Freedman, "Separatism as Strategy: Female Institution Building and American Feminism, 1870–1930," *Feminist Studies* 5 (Fall 1979): 512–29.

[56] The model for this relationship harkened back to the ethos Mary Ryan has argued guided antebellum benevolent work. As Ryan suggests, the "women's welfare system was but one element in a complex and gerrymandered women's sphere, part of a whole social geography of gender that meshed with its male complement to ensure the production and reproduction of urban society." But she also reminds us that this gender system was full of tension; men and women worked at different tasks so as to make the "family" appear as one, which laid the seeds of transformation as women grew discontent with their limited role. See Ryan, *Cradle of the Middle Class*, pp. 217–19.

[57] At the same time that the church grew more supportive of women's mission activities it continued to deny them a larger liturgical role. The church did not allow women to stand for election as deaconess until 1915 and did not support full ordination until 1956. See R. Douglas Brackenridge and Lois Boyd, "United Presbyterian Policy on Women and the Church—an Historical Review," *Journal of Presbyterian History* 59 (Fall 1981): 383–407; R. Douglas Brackenridge, "Equality for Women: A Case Study in Presbyterian Policy, 1926–1930," *Journal of Presbyterian History* 58 (Summer 1980): 142–65; Janet H. Penfield, "Women in the Presbyterian Church—An Historical Overview," *Journal of Presbyterian History* 52 (Summer 1977): 107–24.

"A Woman's Club of National Interest"

† † †

The organization of the Presbyterian Church's Woman's Executive Committee of Home Missions is but one example of how Protestant women expanded their role in the mission enterprise. The phenomenal growth in the numbers of women drawn to the movement suggests that millions of Anglo-American Protestant women continued to believe that evangelical principles had a place in reform movements. With its roots in the social reform movements of the earlier period, the mission movement attracted a cross section of women who had been active in benevolent and evangelical causes.[58] The WEC presented itself as "Woman's Club of National Interest," securing its position among a growing network of secular and religious women's clubs. The latter part of the nineteenth century, proclaimed Mrs. Joseph Cook in an article in the *Home Mission Monthly*, was the time of women's clubs. Few women, she noted, were satisfied "with only one such organization" and generally belonged to several. The previous twenty-five years, she pointed out, had seen the "banding together of women." Spurred by their experience in equipping regiments, administering soldiers' hospitals, and serving with the Sanitary Commission, this generation of women's club leaders had been trained during the Civil War. "Women had to learn to cooperate with each other in work," wrote Mrs. Cook, "and soon after the war closed, certain prominent organizations of women came into existence."[59]

The case of the Woman's Executive Committee suggests that their experiences during the Civil War encouraged women to think nationally and to expand the scope of their reform work to encompass more than local projects. Their successes within the Sanitary and Christian commissions proved their fund-raising abilities and showed them the power inherent in organizing at the national level, but the war also left women activists divided as to the direction that benevolence should take. Before the war, most benevolent women stressed a shared social experience and

[58] Using Nancy Hewitt's categories of perfectionist, benevolent, and ultraist to distinguish between women activists, the majority of those attracted to the mission movement would have come from the first and second of these categories. See Hewitt, *Women's Activism and Social Change*, pp. 38–68, and pp. 216–58 for her delineation of the differences and connections between these different groups of antebellum social reformers.

[59] Mrs. Joseph Cook, "A Woman's Club of National Interest," *Home Mission Monthly* 10 (January 1896): 51.

the primacy of moral suasion as the best way to fight social ills. Afterward, this philosophy began to change.

As many women became active in groups that included both men and women, they advocated a professional standard over moral suasion, and, as Lori Ginzberg has argued, women "also aspired increasingly to male models for social change."[60] The women's home mission enterprise presents a more complicated case. It drew on the sense of shared social experience among women and used moral suasion even as it exhibited a growing commitment to professionalism in the field. Its popularity suggests that the majority of middle-class Protestant women were not ready wholly to accept the more secular and integrated social reform movement that had emerged in the aftermath of the war, but women missionaries in the field, those with "front-line" experience, began to move in that direction.[61] The women active in home mission work said little about women's rights. Though the extent of their commitment to women's rights is not clear, they were acutely aware of their limited role within the church. Like the WCTU, the WEC did, over time, challenge the traditional and narrow domestic role prescribed for middle-class women, but unlike the temperance movement the WEC never called for women's suffrage as a central tenet of its agenda. Women missionaries transcended traditional gender roles, but this was not the primary intention of the mission enterprise. In penetrating these male-dominated institutions and in forcing the different denominations to recognize the importance of "woman's work" on their behalf, the principal challenge of the women who built the mission movement was not to explore alternate gender roles or to fight for women's rights, but to participate as citizens in forming and building a national culture.

Presbyterian women established a separate women's organization to prove that they could make important contributions to missions and that they could effectively evangelize for God and country beyond the confines of their homes. The gender ideology to which they subscribed did not allow them, however, directly to challenge their subordinate theological role. On the issue of whether women should be allowed to speak

---

[60] Ginzberg, *Women and the Work of Benevolence*, pp. 208–9.

[61] The organization and growth of the Woman's Christian Temperance Union serves as another illustration of women's attempts to combine both evangelical, or to use Hewitt's term, "perfectionist," ideals with social reform. See Epstein, *Politics of Domesticity*, pp. 115–17; Ruth Bordin, *Woman and Temperance: The Quest for Power and Liberty, 1873–1900* (Philadelphia: Temple University Press, 1981).

in church, or to "preach," historians Lois Boyd and R. Douglas Brackenridge suggest that Presbyterian women "were generally silent." "Evidence suggests," they continue, "that Presbyterian women tended to stay in a culturally defined sphere of domesticity, maternalism, and political, social and ecclesiastical subordination and were sensitive to any accusations of impropriety."[62] A. M. Pilsbury of Brooklyn, for example, in assessing the development of woman's opportunity and responsibility in 1895, argued that women could "now pursue either a public or business career without criticism." Women had even taken a more active role in the church, but the author was quick to point out that they had done so without sacrificing their "womanliness." A woman's "duty," as sketched out by Pilsbury, was defined as a combination of patriotic, religious, and maternal concerns. "Stirred by a love of country the watchword 'Our land for Christ,' means to her a personal responsibility," explained Pilsbury:

> It means to her the practical use of her abilities, and the determination to use the opportunities God has given her as stepping-stones upon which future generations shall rise to get a nearer view of heaven. How better shall she show her patriotism than by educating the future men and women of her country; how better to teach the religion of Christ than by awakening, enlightening, training the conscience of youth?[63]

A woman's highest calling, both as devout Christian and United States citizen, was as teacher, not preacher.

Yet by challenging the mission enterprise to recognize their expanding role, women were forcing the issue of their right to speak. They found themselves championing the cause of missions before mixed groups of men and women, both inside and outside of church. Once in the field, many women missionaries found that, absent a male minister, their followers called on them to preach. Brackenridge and Boyd suggest that as women expanded their participation in the more pragmatic programs of the church such as missions, questions about their theological subordination could no longer be discounted by the church hierarchy.[64]

---

[62] Boyd and Brackenridge, *Presbyterian Women in America*, pp. 92–93.

[63] A. M. Pilsbury, "Woman's Opportunity and Responsibility," *Home Mission Monthly* 9 (September 1895): 246.

[64] See Boyd and Brackenridge, *Presbyterian Women in America*, pp. 93, 97, 101, 105.

The debate about the nature and extent of women's evangelical duties would not be resolved until well into the twentieth century. Virginia Brereton and Christa Klein have suggested that women who sought to be ordained in the late nineteenth century engaged in a "futile struggle." Echoing Boyd and Brackenridge, they argue that Protestant women avoided confrontations over women's rights issues, preferring to champion the missionary cause. Although the focus of mission work was on more pragmatic issues such as the delivery of particular services, it also offered, in its network of missionary training schools, a substitute for the theological seminaries, which excluded women.[65] There is nothing to suggest that this parallel structure created by Presbyterian women challenged the mainstream theological orthodoxy of the day. Individual congregations varied in their practices, some adhering closely to Paul's prohibitions about women's right to speak, others promoting diaconal service for women and inviting women to speak from the pulpit. The leaders of the WEC offered no opinions. They did, however, reject Elizabeth Cady Stanton's attempts to reinterpret the Bible. Presbyterian women "recoiled from the radicalism" of Stanton's work, rejecting what they believed to be "crass antibiblicalism."[66]

† † †

One must be careful not to elevate issues of gender above class considerations in the telling of this story. Like other groups of benevolent women in the Civil War era, mission supporters were concerned about securing their class privileges and enacting what they believed to be their class responsibilities.[67] But gender explains what these women believed was at stake in this enterprise. By fulfilling this class objective as women, they recognized that they were realizing not only a religious ambition of

[65] Virginia L. Brereton and Christa R. Klein, "American Women in Ministry: A History of Protestant Beginning Points," in *Women of Spirit: Female Leadership in the Jewish and Christian Traditions*, ed. Rosemary Ruether and Eleanor McLaughlin (New York: Simon and Schuster, 1979), pp. 309–11.

[66] Boyd and Brackenridge, *Presbyterian Women in America*, pp. 109, 113, 117. For a discussion of the controversy generated by Stanton's work among other Protestant women see Kathi Lynn Kern, "The Woman's Bible: Gender, Religion and Ideology in the Work of Elizabeth Cady Stanton, 1854–1902" (Ph.D diss., University of Pennsylvania, 1991).

[67] See Ginzberg, *Women and the Work of Benevolence*, p. 198; similarly, Kathleen McCarthy discusses the rise of civic stewardship among the wealthy in Chicago in this period as one way by which they secured their status and power. She notes that men and women engaged in different activities but to the same end. See *Noblesse Oblige*, pp. 3–98.

their class but also their own desire, as women, to be seen as citizens. They were involved in the work of defining the nation, a Protestant nation that included, among others, non-Protestant immigrants, Indians, and Hispanos in the Southwest, as well as the women who were doing this work. Citizenship was here identified not with the vote but with an opportunity to participate in a national Protestant reform effort.

That the Woman's Executive Committee was acutely aware of the political nature of its work is illustrated by the types of women who served on the advisory committee. The members of this committee were from families that had deep roots in the church. It also represented the national character of the organization and included women who had long served the public interest and had husbands who had done so as well. As Brereton and Klein have noted about the Protestant mission enterprise as a whole, "women missionary leaders represented an emerging elite within the denominations," who, with their husbands, created an "interlocking directorate" of prosperous families. When Mary James was chosen to be president of the WEC in 1885, her husband, Darwin, was serving as a member of Congress from New York. Darwin James, a merchant and importer of indigo and spices from the Far East, exemplifies how closely interrelated were business and public service. Before being elected to Congress, he served as the park commissioner in Brooklyn. Later in his life he was appointed to the board of U.S. Indian Commissions and served as president of the New York Board of Trade and Transportation. His service to the Presbyterian Church was a direct offshoot of his interest in the Far East; he was a valued member of the Board of Foreign Missions.[68] Darwin James was clearly not one to take his public image for granted or to renege on what he considered to be his duty to the larger community, nor was his wife, Mary, shy and retiring. In this family, husband and wife were partners in maintaining their class position.

Mary James's obituary in the *Home Mission Monthly* remembered her as "the unwearied helper of her people, uniting many hearts in different parts of her land and leading all to things above." While president of the WEC from 1885 until 1908 she had commuted in the early years back and forth from her home in Washington, D.C., to New York City. She was an ardent fund-raiser, building the treasury from an annual collection of $128,000 to half a million dollars. Remaining active at

[68] *Who Was Who in America*, vol. 1 (1897–1942), p. 627.

Mary James (Department of History and Records Management Services, Presbyterian Church USA)

the local level, in the Brooklyn district that made up her husband's constituency, she served as president of Brooklyn City Missions, was a manager of an orphan asylum and an industrial school, and was active in her local foreign mission society. At the national level, she helped to spearhead the Protestant women's campaign against admitting Utah as a state, serving as an "indefatigable" lobbyist to convince members of Congress of the "evils" of the Mormon practice of polygamy. Described as a "strong character," James was remembered as made up of "opposites,— positive, resolute, sometimes stern, sometimes severe, balanced with almost infinite tenderness, gentleness, sympathy, compassion and love." James embodied qualities the WEC hoped would become the model for privileged Protestant women. They should be "approachable" and "unaffected," as well as "genuine," all characteristics attributed to Mary James.[69] As we will see in subsequent chapters, this was the ideal to be

[69] (Mrs.) Calvin B. Walker, "Mary E. James," *Home Mission Monthly* 26 (June 1912): 185–87.

followed by all women who served the mission cause, no matter what their class position. Even though the WEC leadership reflected the class hierarchy of the larger society—Katherine Bennett, who followed James as president, was the wife of a New Jersey manufacturer—the WEC presumed that the shared commitment to evangelical principles would mitigate the tensions created by the class differences among the members.

† † †

Born in a tumultuous period, the WEC functioned as though a crisis were always imminent. A tone of urgency pervades the mission literature. Organizers made clear that this was not a ladies' literary club or a group of women in pursuit of a hobby. As the woman writing in the *Rocky Mountain Presbyterian* had said, there was more to be done than simply organizing sewing circles. The purpose of the organization was to address larger issues, to bring Anglo-Protestant women into the mainstream of political debate. What these women feared, what inspired such urgency, were the myriad of "isms" that worried the constituency of the Presbyterian Church, namely "Mormonism, nihilism, communism, atheism and infidelity." But by far the greatest danger, because of the growing number of adherents, was Catholicism. In 1887 Presbyterian minister John Bain asked the women readers of the *Home Mission Monthly* whether the settlers on the American frontier would be "saved to the Kingdom of Christ or be left to the Kingdom of Satan." "Romanism," he claimed "is there, selecting choicest locations, and securing valuable properties all over this new part of our country, Romanism teaching subjection and obedience to a foreign rule."[70] To Protestants like Bain and his female readership, the political and economic well-being of the country was at stake.

Bain's comment illustrates the complex economic and political fears generated by the growing numbers of Catholic immigrants in the nineteenth century—first Irish and German and later Italian and Polish—which increased the size and influence of the Catholic Church in the United States. By 1860, the two million Catholics living in this country constituted the largest religious denomination. The large number of im-

[70] Reverend J. W. Bain, "Woman's Power in Saving the West," *Home Mission Monthly* 1 (April 1887): 126.

migrant followers made the Catholic Church even more vulnerable to Protestant attack when anti-Catholic rioters took to the streets in eastern cities and formed organizations, such as the Know-Nothings, intended to check the growth of Catholic influence. Anti-Catholic sentiment took a variety of forms over the course of the century. Catholicism was associated with authoritarianism and feudalism in the 1840s and by the 1880s was connected to radicalism.[71] These fears served as the major impetus for the Protestant mission movement. Not only did they give rise to the many denominational mission organizations, but they also served to mask the differences among Protestant denominations, all of which appeared to be unified in their opposition to Catholicism.

Protestants argued that Catholicism was not just an alien religious tradition but was fundamentally incompatible with American political traditions. Josiah Strong was one of the most vocal critics of the Catholic Church and perhaps the most popular spokesperson for the Protestant home mission movement in the years women gained a greater foothold in it. His widely read *Our Country* argued in favor of a highly politicized Protestant home mission effort. Strong feared for the spiritual foundation of American nationalism. In his view, Catholicism represented a foreign power, an imperialistic hand reaching into the heart of America, threatening to subvert certain "fundamental principles and institutions" that protected the individual's right to free speech and action.[72]

Religion could not be divorced from politics; Strong argued that the Catholic Church was essentially a foreign power operating on U.S. soil, under the authority of Rome and the sovereignty of the pope. Outlining the differences between the United States and the Roman Catholic Church, he argued that the fundamental principles of the United States were popular sovereignty and its supreme law was the Constitution. Particularly upsetting was the power of the pope as supreme sovereign and the canon law of the Church of Rome binding all followers. The dilemma faced by Catholics, believed Strong, was whether they owed their "highest allegiance" to the United States or to the pope. He quoted the revised Statutes of the United States, noting that "the alien seeking citizenship must take an oath to renounce forever all allegiance and

---

[71] Robert T. Handy, *A History of the Churches in the United States and Canada* (New York: Oxford University Press, 1977), pp. 214, 217–19. See also John Higham, *Strangers in the Land: Patterns of American Nativism, 1860–1925* (New York: Atheneum, 1981), pp. 5–6, 55–58.

[72] Josiah Strong, *Our Country* (New York: Baker and Taylor, 1885).

fidelity to any foreign prince, potentate, state or sovereignty, in particular that to which he has been subject," to suggest that there could be no room for compromise or accommodation.[73]

Protestantism was consistent with the Constitution and the laws of the country, whereas Catholic theology could only promote treason. As a practical example, Strong discussed how theology informed the content of a Catholic education, arguing in favor of a public school system that would resist the evils of parochial education. The goal of a public school, he argued, was to teach knowledge and discipline, arouse a spirit of inquiry, inculcate self-control, and "secure intelligent obedience to rightful authority." Parochial education did the opposite. It aimed to lead rather than train, to produce submission, and to repress a spirit of inquiry, and it promoted the belief that one is controlled by superiors. In a parochial school the child was taught "unquestioning obedience to arbitrary authority." Strong saw an even greater danger in the development of a system of parochial schools. They would separate Catholic children from other American (and Protestant) children and impede the assimilating and Americanizing power exercised by the public school. By withholding children from public schools and promoting a system of parochial schools the Catholic Church was fostering difference, undermining national unity, and confirming Strong's suspicions that "Romanism is un-American and represents an alien civilization."[74]

Strong's analysis was not new, but his book was a compelling argument in favor of maintaining the course of action Protestants had been pursuing.[75] Public education had become a "potent patriotic symbol" in their struggle against Catholicism, and school building marked the Protestant commitment to democracy.[76] Catholics' objection to public schools, as well as their attempts to win state aid for parochial schools, further fueled Protestant sentiments.[77] Indeed, they were concerned that Anglo-Protestant settlers on the frontier were not establishing education-

---

[73] Ibid., p. 68.

[74] Ibid., p. 97.

[75] Indeed, these arguments had been present throughout much of the century. Lyman Beecher, in his *Plea for the West* (1832), and Horace Bushnell's sermon "Barbarism the First Danger" (1847) set the tone for later anti-Catholic tracts like Strong's. For an overview of the early anti-Catholic efforts on the part of Protestant clergy see Ray Allen Billington, *The Protestant Crusade, 1800–1860: A Study of the Origins of American Nativism* (Chicago: Quadrangle Books, 1964).

[76] Higham, *Strangers in the Land*, p. 60; Smith, "Protestant Schooling," pp. 679–80.

[77] Higham, *Strangers in the Land*, pp. 28, 59; Handy, *History of the Churches*, p. 283.

al systems to counter the parochial system that had prompted Protestant home missionaries to enlarge the ministerial functions of the movement to incorporate educational needs.[78]

To support their appeals for the establishment of Protestant educational institutions they argued that these schools would teach the principles of American citizenship. Mission advocates worried that if the only educational alternative was a Catholic mission school the "infidel people in the Mississippi Valley might succumb to Rome's advance agents," in the long run allowing the pope to "extend his political domination into the realms of the Republic." Supporters of an expanded Protestant effort suggested that Catholic education would undermine the democratic ideals intrinsic to American national ideology. As one man expressed it: "Let them have the privilege of possessing the seats of education in the West, and of molding the leading minds of millions that are to inhabit them, and we may give up all our efforts to produce in the West what Puritanism has produced here."[79]

Strong's analysis was simply another expression of what certain Presbyterians had been arguing for many years.[80] Its members urged the church to build and support schools in communities where there were no public schools. After all, if Protestantism was synonymous with the free institutions and fundamental principles of the United States Constitution, who best could initiate a school system but the Protestant denominations. Strong did not specifically advocate direct links between Protestant denominations and the operation of public schools, but Presbyterian home missionaries like Sheldon Jackson and their female supporters did not hesitate to do so.

As this debate took shape, the focus of home mission activities began to shift away from the earlier preoccupation with protecting Anglo-American settlers on the frontier to the immigrant and non-Anglo residents of the United States. Concern about Catholic conversion of Protestant settlers remained, but the movement also adopted a more aggressive strategy to convert Catholics. This change in strategy meant that increas-

[78] Ray A. Billington, "Anti-Catholic Propaganda and the Home Missionary Movement, 1800–1860," *Mississippi Valley Historical Review* 22 (1935–36): 361–84; Colin Goodykoontz, *Home Missions on the American Frontier, with Particular Reference to the American Home Missionary Society* (1939; reprint, New York: Octagon Books, 1971), pp. 362–71.

[79] Billington, "Anti-Catholic Propaganda," p. 362, quotation on p. 379.

[80] Sydney Ahlstrom argues that Strong's message and actions typified the way social concern was mobilized within the Protestant churches (*A Religious History of the American People* [New Haven: Yale University Press, 1972], p. 798).

ingly the home mission movement actively addressed the "problem" posed by the immigrants or the "exceptional populations" such as Indians, Mexicans, Mormons, and Eskimos. By the latter part of the nineteenth century, the most dynamic part of the home mission movement, that which was the fastest growing and attracted the greatest attention, concerned itself with assimilation and Americanization. At issue in this discussion was whether all these groups could be "American" and, more important, how they could be made "American."

Home missionaries such as Sheldon Jackson suggested that the Hispanic Catholics living in New Mexico be made a test case. Introducing the readers of the *Rocky Mountain Presbyterian* to New Mexico, Jackson called the territory the "center of a Mexican population of nearly 100,000, having all the rights of American citizens, and yet unassimilated, foreign, and in some measure hostile to the genius of our American institutions."[81] Jackson reminded his readers that New Mexico was pressing petitions in Congress to become a state, "as such exerting an influence." This influence had to be positive, and he argued it would be so only if there was an "early and persistent introduction of the leaven of Protestantism." Such an inroad could be made through schools. If the territorial government would not support the building of schools, then certainly the Presbyterian Church should provide this essential service.

There was no disagreement that home mission activity should expand as the country grew, but many questioned how the church would reach out to convert immigrants and "strangers" as well as provide new services such as schools when resources and personnel were limited. The women of the Woman's Executive Committee of Home Missions eagerly offered their skills and resources, placing Anglo-Protestant women directly at the center of this debate by offering women as teachers in future schools of Americanization. Expand the mission effort and allow women to participate, they argued. Increase women's work "a thousand-fold." Create "Protestant seminaries," urged Mary Holmes, "the South needs them, Arkansas needs Christian teachers, all the West needs them." "Indeed," she demanded, "where is the nook, the corner, the valley, the mountains where a Christian Lady may not be sent to bear to the homes of the people the word of life?"[82] The women argued that they might not

---

[81] Jackson, "Missionary Tour through New Mexico," p. 2.

[82] Mary E. Holmes, "Woman's Home Mission Board," *Rocky Mountain Presbyterian* 4 (September 1875): 2. Holmes's call for a larger role for women marked the first lengthy discussion calling for a women's mission effort supporting women missionaries rather than

be allowed to preach, but certainly the church could not deny that they could use their skills as teachers in a vital religious and political effort.

The male-dominated church accepted women's work hesitantly and with reluctance. The leaders preferred to think that women's work "opened" the way for ministers, but they had discovered that the strategy of "planting churches" to lessen the influence of the Catholic Church in New Mexico had proved ineffective. Henry Gordon explained that this method had failed because it had aroused "not only the hostility of the priest but of the people as well." A school, however, was a different matter: "Plant a school in the same community, put at its head a loving, motherly woman, and with her gentleness, her neighborly ways, her modern methods of teaching, she will receive a cordial welcome from the people. The priests may threaten excommunication, but the teachers will win and lay solid, deep foundations for the Church."[83] Indeed, the education and rudimentary health services provided by women missionaries did prove to be more popular than the preaching of their male counterparts.

† † †

By joining the missionary field Protestant women became involved in a crusade, but they knew better what they were fighting against than what they sought to build. Ultimately, women home missionaries did "lay deep foundations" but not for the church. What they did create, over the years, was a social service organization that took much of its direction from the pragmatic needs of its clients—those very Catholics whom Strong had warned about. As we will see, the WEC (later the Woman's Board of Home Missions), became a springboard by which Presbyterian women lobbied for government intervention on a variety of legislative issues concerning social policy. Beginning in the 1880s, for instance, the WEC petitioned Congress to deny Utah statehood until the practice of polygamy had been outlawed. They demanded investigations into charges of corruption at the Bureau of Indian Affairs. When the Pima Indians faced starvation, the WEC called on Congress to give

---

simply supplementing the supplies of male missionaries or easing the burdens of their wives and children.

[83] Henry E. Gordon, "Monthly Topic—The Roman Catholics," *Home Mission Monthly* 5 (April 1891): 129.

money for food. They also supported government investigations into land fraud that deprived Indians in Arizona and Alaskans of their homelands. In the years that followed they used the mission journal, the *Home Mission Monthly*, to rally support for the passage of a variety of laws, among them bills that ensured a permanent water supply for Pima and Papago Indians in Arizona, curtailed child labor, and called for an end to lynching.[84] Over time, the balance in the union they envisioned between church and state shifted; the politics they fashioned as a result of their work served to promote a larger role for the state than for the church.

[84] See Verdesi, *In but Still Out*, pp. 59–60; Mrs. F. H. Pierson, "Annual Report of the Secretary," *Home Mission Monthly* 15 (July 1901): 202; "Resolutions Adopted," *Home Mission Monthly* 22 (July 1908): 221; "Editorial Notes," *Home Mission Monthly* 37 (December 1922): 133.

CHAPTER TWO

A Question of Loyalty and a Contest of Faiths: The Meeting between Anglo and Hispano Cultures

In 1910 longtime mission teacher Alice Blake explained to her Protestant supporters that "the religious, moral and social conditions of the fifteenth century have crystallized along the streams of New Mexico and the entire continent to the south of us."[1] She described Hispanos as people "who have been trained in habits of thought that have not changed an iota, and who have never dreamed that there was any other manner of life," thereby confirming an Anglo misconception that Hispanos had remained unchanged, and had had no history until their land was annexed by the United States. Anglo settlers, she among them, had brought the peoples of the territory to the "portals of the twentieth century." Although Blake proved to be among the less self-righteous of the Anglo-Protestant chroniclers of Hispano culture, admitting that the transition had been disruptive and that Hispanos had seen much of their culture "swept from before their eyes," "enveloped by this new order," and "told that they must become a part of it, or be crushed by it," she shared with other Anglos the conviction that this was largely part of the inevitable course of American history. The "history" of the Hispano Southwest, marked by progress and modernity, had begun when Anglo-American Protestants arrived.

Long before the territory was annexed by the United States, Spanish

---

[1] Alice Blake, "A Fifteenth Century Survival," *Home Mission Monthly* 24 (July 1910): 204.

conquest and colonization had given rise to certain patterns of landholding, to family structure, and to forms of spirituality and faith that shaped the people's lives. United States conquest would introduce new forces and new economic, political, and social patterns. The Protestant women missionaries, like the larger Protestant culture from which they came, refused to see themselves as part of the legacy of conquest; they were unwilling to admit that they were simply one more in a series of migrations, that they were conquering what their Hispano neighbors' ancestors had conquered before them.[2] Protestant missionaries believed their efforts in New Mexico to be another test of the larger mission of the United States—the divinely ordained mission that was democracy. The question was how best to implement the larger political mission. The Presbyterians found one answer in the network of mission schools they established in northern New Mexico and southern Colorado. This effort, however, was contested by a Catholic hierarchy that challenged the Protestant assertion that their agents could more legitimately inspire the spiritual changes necessary for "Americanization." Caught in this contest of faiths were Hispanos, who had to contend with a reorganized Catholic Church, loss of lands and political autonomy, as well as a proliferation of new social institutions, all of which affected their lives and challenged the resiliency of their culture.

† † †

Following the Spanish conquest of the territory, settlers had come to claim land along the Rio Grande River from Albuquerque to Taos in the northern half of the territory, spreading into the Sangre de Cristo Valley along smaller rivers and streams. The Spanish government had provided three basic forms of land grants, the most common of which was the community land grant, given to a group of families for agricultural settlement. Under the conditions of this grant the land had no market value and was not for commercial exchange; each grantee received enough to sustain himself and his family. There were no land titles proving individual possession, and boundaries were not clearly defined.

---

[2] For a more general discussion of this "legacy of conquest" in the American West and an illustration of the "new western history," which deemphasizes the idea of the "frontier" and instead examines the West as a place undergoing constant conquest and change, see Patricia Limerick, *The Legacy of Conquest: The Unbroken Past of the American West* (New York: Norton, 1987).

The land on which the community was built was not divisible. Each member or family received a portion that would be divided by each successive generation. The community was held together by common water rights (a necessity in the arid and desert land conditions), each member's share of which was determined by the amount of land he could cultivate. Bonds were also created by shared use of the *ejido*, common lands for grazing livestock and cutting timber.[3]

By the middle of the nineteenth century, this area, which is today northern New Mexico and southern Colorado, was dotted by small communities whose lands yielded enough to feed community members. Possession was determined by settlement, not title, and boundaries were not clearly defined. Coöperation among community members was encouraged not simply by the system of land grants or by the harsh environment, which forced people to share resources, but by a complex, multilayered social structure that had developed as a result. Village cohesion was solidified through this method of land distribution, by an extended patriarchal family, and by a network of Catholic religious organizations whose members were known as Penitentes.[4]

Kinship networks were built around patriarchal families, in which authority was based on sex and age with reciprocal patterns of mutual assistance. Patriarchal authority was extended beyond a nuclear family unit by a *compadrazgo* (or godfather) system which assured that adult males would assume obligations to children other than their own. The *compadrazgo* system unified an entire village "into a functioning system of religious and economic cooperation and responsibility." The most favored and sought-after godfather was most likely to be the village

---

[3] Two other forms of land grants were made. Proprietary grants had been made to prominent individuals who established a village, built a church, hired a priest, and guaranteed to protect settlers from Indian attacks. The proprietor received payment in-kind from settlers in the form of agricultural produce, and he, in return, controlled local commerce. The least common land grant was the *sitio*, given to an individual for livestock grazing. These land grants were mainly established east of the Rocky Mountains and south of Albuquerque in the less mountainous areas of the territory. See Roxanne Dunbar, "Land Tenure in Northern New Mexico: An Historical Perspective" (Ph.D diss., University of California at Los Angeles, 1974); Clark S. Knowlton, "Changing Spanish-American Villages in Northern New Mexico," *Sociology and Social Research* 53 (1969): 457–59; Victor Westphall, *Mercedes Reales: Hispanic Land Grants of the Upper Rio Grande Region* (Albuquerque: University of New Mexico Press, 1983), pp. 35–37. For a general discussion of the early Hispanic settlers in the region see Frances L. Swadesh, *Los Primeros Pobladores: Hispanic Americans of the Ute Frontier* (Notre Dame: University of Notre Dame Press, 1974).

[4] Swadesh, *Los Primeros Pobladores*, p. 158.

patron, a merchant, a head of a powerful village family, or a political leader. His was not an imposed patronage but rested on the consensus of community members. Expected to assist village families, settle disputes, and provide leadership, he was also likely to be the *hermano mayor* (principal brother) of the local Penitente *morada* (meeting house).[5]

Though they were generally subordinated within the patriarchal ethos that structured village life, Hispanas distinguished themselves by their expertise as *parteras* (midwives) and *curanderas* (healers).[6] Spanish law had provided for shared property rights within marriage and equal inheritance between sons and daughters; thus women inherited and controlled land. What power and influence accrued to Hispanas from their roles as healers and property owners had to be reconciled with a social code imposed by the Spanish in which marriage and a woman's sexuality were carefully controlled so as to maintain social boundaries dividing the nobility, landed and landless peasants, and Indian slaves. A man's honor was determined in part by a woman's virtue, which ideally was protected by sheltering and secluding her.[7] As Ramón Gutiérrez suggests, this ideal would have been difficult for the small landholders of these remote villages to maintain. "The peasantry," he notes, "undoubtedly had to reconcile gender prescriptions with the exigencies of production and reproduction. The required participation of all able-bodied household members at planting and harvest meant that there were periods when contraints on females of this class were less rigorously enforced."[8]

Lending cohesion to the community structure, reinforcing the patri-

---

[5] Knowlton, "Changing Spanish-American Villages," pp. 460–62; George Foster, "Cofradía and Compadrazgo in Spain and Spanish America," *Southwestern Journal of Anthropology* 9 (1953): 7–10.

[6] Sarah Deutsch, *No Separate Refuge: Culture, Class, and Gender on an Anglo-Hispanic Frontier in the American Southwest, 1880–1940* (New York: Oxford University Press, 1987), pp. 41–62.

[7] On the status of Hispano women see Janet Lecompte, "The Independent Women of Hispanic New Mexico, 1821–1846," in *New Mexico Women: Intercultural Perspectives*, ed. Joan Jensen and Darlis Miller (Albuquerque: University of New Mexico Press, 1986), pp. 78, 80; Deena J. González, "The Widowed Women of Santa Fe: Assessments on the Lives of an Unmarried Population, 1850–1880," in *Unequal Sisters: A Multicultural Reader in U.S. Women's History*, ed. Ellen C. DuBois and Vicki Ruiz (New York: Routledge, Chapman & Hall, 1990), pp. 34–50; Ramón A. Gutiérrez, *When Jesus Came, the Corn Mothers Went Away: Marriage, Sexuality, and Power in New Mexico, 1500–1846* (Stanford: Stanford University Press, 1991), p. 235.

[8] Gutiérrez, *When Jesus Came*, p. 215.

archal ethos and kinship networks, and connecting these small villages to a larger political and social tradition was the Cofradía de Nuestro Padre Jesus Nazareno (Confraternity of our Father, Jesus of Nazarene), whose members were known as Penitentes. Organized by Franciscan missionaries in the eighteenth century to oversee the religious and ritual needs of Spanish settlers to the territory, the Penitentes were intended to substitute for the inadequate numbers of priests in the territory. Subsequently, they took on a variety of social functions in addition to their spiritual role.[9] They performed religious rites when priests were unavailable to give sacraments to the dying and they led prayer services, but they also acted as a relief organization, concerning themselves, for instance, with the problems of the sick. They provided material aid by digging graves, helping with plowing and other tasks, and collecting funds for needy families.[10]

All brotherhoods had essentially the same hierarchy even though there was local autonomy and the social services they provided depended on the needs of a particular community. Each group had a *hermano mayor*, *coadjutor*, who washed the members after their disciplines (penances), *mandatario*, who informed of meetings and collected dues, *celador*, group disciplinarian, *enfermero* who looked after sick members and their families, *maestro de novios*, who taught the novitiates, *secretario*, who maintained record books, *picador*, who prepared the novices for their penances, *regador*, who read the prayers and rituals, and *pitero*, who played the flute at services.[11] Membership was open to the men of

<hr>

[9] The dates on the organization of the Penitentes vary. Reginald Fisher argues Penitental customs have been described in New Mexico as early as 1630 ("Notes on the Relation of the Franciscans to the Penitentes," *El Palacio* 48 [1941]: 264). Juan Hernandez, "Cactus Whips and Wooden Crosses," *Journal of American Folklore* 76 (1963): 217, notes that Penitente rituals were first reported in 1594. Ralph Emerson Twitchell, *Leading Facts of New Mexico History* (Cedar Rapids, Ia.: Torch Press, 1917), vol. 5, Appendix B, pp. 480–88, dates the Penitentes from the eighteenth century.

[10] Marta Weigle, *Brothers of Light, Brothers of Blood: The Penitentes of the Southwest* (Albuquerque: University of New Mexico Press, 1976), pp. 151–52; Swadesh, *Los Primeros Pobladores*, p. 74; Dorothy Woodward, "The Penitentes of New Mexico" (Ph.D diss., Yale University, 1935), p. 2. For discussion of the meaning and function of the Cofradía in Spanish America see Foster, "Cofradía and Compadrazgo," pp: 12–13. Maurilio E. Vigil, "Ethnic Organizations among the Mexican-Americans of New Mexico: A Political Perspective" (Ph.D diss., University of New Mexico, 1974), pp. 65–70, notes the political importance of Penitente groups and calls them a form of mutual aid society which constituted the first phase of Mexican-American organization effort from annexation to 1920.

[11] On the structure of the Penitente brotherhood see Knowlton, "Changing Spanish-American Villages," pp. 460–62, and Weigle, *Brothers of Light*, p. 140.

the village, who were initiated as teenagers, generally sponsored by another member of their family, either a father or an uncle. Each member took an oath committing himself to the fraternity. He agreed to comply with the constitution and rules, imitate Christ's example, and observe the Ten Commandments. He also swore his willing adherence to the corporation and agreed to conduct himself according to its regulations and to repent his misdeeds when necessary. Brotherhoods were "organized to serve community needs and enact spiritually beneficial rituals." If there was an example they were to follow that would connect them to a larger tradition, it was to "imitate the life and suffering and death of Jesus."[12] Women were not admitted to the membership of the Penitente *morada*; instead they served as auxiliaries. During Lenten processions, for example, they followed behind chanting. They also prepared food for the festivities.[13]

The Penitente groups played a major role in the community, particularly after Mexican independence in 1821, when the Franciscan priests lost their financial support from the Spanish crown and were forced to withdraw from the territory. Few priests remained so that the responsibility for maintaining Catholic religious practices fell to these local Penitente groups.[14] Lacking the formal and imposed authority of the Franciscan priests, the Penitente brotherhoods emerged in the thirty years before American annexation as a powerful community organization, taking on a central role in governing remote New Mexican villages. They acted as the church and as a benevolent organization, and their leadership mirrored the political hierarchy in the community. For people in these villages, religious, social, and political behavior was synonymous. Officially, the inhabitants of these villages were Mexican citi-

---

[12] On the requirements for membership see Weigle, *Brothers of Light*, pp. 140–52; Woodward, "Penitentes," p. 222. Weigle argues that the membership was drawn from among the ranchers, tenant sheep tenders and laborers, not from the wealthier or the elite of the territory.

[13] Hernandez, "Cactus Whips and Wooden Crosses," p. 219; Harold N. Ottoway, "The Penitente Moradas of the Taos, New Mexico, Area" (Ph.D diss., University of Oklahoma, 1975), pp. 127–28, outlines women's duties as cooking and cleaning. He argues that they used the organization primarily for the burial insurance programs and to nurse and care for the sick. Deutsch agrees that in Penitente rituals women were auxiliaries but argues that these rituals should not be seen as the sum total of women's religious experiences. She argues that religion was the "property" of both sexes. Men may have dominated the Penitente rituals, but women dominated the devotions to Mary which took place in May. See *No Separate Refuge*, pp. 50–51.

[14] Ottoway, "Penitente Morada," p. 11. Fisher notes that Franciscans had completely withdrawn by the 1840s ("Notes on the Relation of the Franciscans to the Penitentes," p. 263).

zens and Roman Catholics, but both the Mexican government and the church hierarchy were distantly removed. The most significant institution in the lives of Hispanos in this region was the local Penitente brotherhood.

Penitentes concerned themselves with a myriad of community activities throughout the year, but they were especially important in organizing the celebrations at feast days and during Holy Week. Hispano adherents understood these rituals to reflect community solidarity and the depth of their religious faith. Penitentes planned and executed the passion play, which reenacted the crucifixion of Christ and *las tinieblas*, or the "darkness," that followed the crucifixion. The details of the rituals varied from village to village, drawing on the experiences of the families and individuals within each village, but Holy Week observances generally included penitental processions in which followers would bear the cross or practice self-flagellation. Stations of the Cross were set out in each community, and villagers would move through them bearing standards and holy images. On Good Friday, Penitentes would drag a death cart in a penitental procession and simulate a crucifixion, raising a cross on which a brother would be bound for a short period of time while prayers and songs were offered. The climax of these celebrations came when brothers, along with the community, gathered at the *morada* and simulated an earthquake by extinguishing all lights, clapping hands and rattling chains to create a tremendous noise. The noise was alternated with prayer and members calling out the names of loved ones, and light would gradually be returned to the *morada*.[15]

Anthropologists who have studied the Penitentes have suggested that these rituals reaffirmed "basic interpersonal ties which [made] continued existence both possible and significant."[16] To the Hispano man who scored his back or walked in the procession whipping himself, or the woman who followed the procession singing, the event confirmed the importance of community. In reenacting the last days of Christ's life, his crucifixion, and later rebirth, Penitentes relived a period of crisis in

[15] Marta Weigle and Thomas R. Lyons, "Brothers and Neighbors: The Celebration of Community in Penitente Villages," in *Celebration: Studies in Festivity and Ritual*, ed. Victor Turner (Washington, D.C.: Smithsonian Institution Press, 1982), pp. 231–51. See pp. 241–46 for a description of Holy Week celebrations.

[16] Weigle and Lyons, "Brothers and Neighbors," p. 246; Thomas Steele, "The Spanish Passion Play in New Mexico and Colorado," *New Mexico Historical Review* 3 (July 1978): 256.

human history. That they could experience the crisis of crucifixion yet share the rewards of redemption reaffirmed the solidity of the local community. In describing *las tinieblas*, Marta Weigle has argued that it is the "dramatic highpoint in the village year. Families and neighbors literally huddle together in the din-filled, disorienting darkness—in the midst of chaos. At the same time, they symbolically take a stand in the face of this disintegration and are, in a sense, 'heartened.' In calling out the names of their beloved departed, they vividly recall the human history and foundations of their community."[17] Anthropologists have suggested that these rituals reinforced corporate community structure and the insularity of these mountain villages, but they also served to connect small villages, seemingly remote and isolated, to a historical tradition larger than one community. The rituals also connected the residents of these small villages, by connecting with a historical event of such importance as the crucifixion of Jesus, to a social dynamic larger than their own village.[18]

Both the independence of Mexico and the subsequent annexation of Mexico's northern territories by the United States impinged on the social fabric of these small villages. In the years when New Mexico was still part of Mexico, the geographic distance from the central authority of the Mexican government and the Catholic Church benefited as well as alienated New Mexicans. On one hand, groups such as the Penitentes were autonomous and had greater significance in the people's daily lives, but on the other hand the distance led to a political alienation that eased the process of transferring the territory from Mexican to American jurisdiction.

In the early part of the nineteenth century New Mexicans were caught between the ideals and problems of Mexico, the newly independent nation to the south, and the expansionist desires of the United States. Many Hispano New Mexicans greeted Mexican independence from Spain in 1821 with skepticism.[19] Their ambivalence grew when New

---

[17] Weigle and Lyons, "Brothers and Neighbors," pp. 246–47.

[18] Ottoway, "Penitente Moradas," p. 16, suggests that the solidarity affirmed by the brotherhoods also made it possible for members to save much of their culture and to "delay their own integration with the more aggressive outside world." See also John Van Ness, "Hispanic Organization in Northern New Mexico: Corporate Community Structure in Historical and Comparative Perspective," in *The Survival of Spanish-American Villages*, ed. Paul Kutsche (Colorado Springs: Colorado College Studies, 1979), pp. 40–41.

[19] Randi J. Walker, "Protestantism in the Sangre de Cristos: Factors in the Growth and Decline of the Hispanic Protestant Churches in Northern New Mexico and Southern Colorado,

Mexico was not made a state but rather a territory of Mexico. Angered, they demanded greater political freedom. Increasingly, as the territory's economic links with the United States grew, New Mexico's southern trading routes with Mexico were replaced by northern ones. Disrupted by frequent Indian raids and subject to harsh environmental conditions, the southern trading routes could not compete with the more lucrative American markets.[20] Additionally, greater numbers of Euro-American immigrants were moving into the territory.[21] In the 1840s Mexico opened new lands to private development. Land grants were given to Euro-Americans in partnership with Mexicans. As Mexico failed to populate its frontier, increasing numbers of Euro-Americans settled the land, and the Mexican government found itself hard-pressed to control foreign investment in land grants.[22]

For most inhabitants agricultural production remained at the subsistence level, but the demand for wool made sheep raising New Mexico's primary industry. As exports of wool increased, a simultaneous demand arose in the territory for goods manufactured in the United States, which were of better quality and available at lower prices. The Mexican government did not have the strength, politically or economically, to counterbalance American economic pull. As David Weber has argued, American investment "gave impetus to the economic growth of northernmost Mexico, and at the same time pulled that region into the American commercial orbit and away from its own weak metropolis."[23]

After the expulsion of the Franciscans, the Penitente brotherhoods maintained an ambivalent relationship with the Catholic hierarchy. Bishop José Antonio Laureano de Zubiría, bishop of Durango, had visited New Mexico in 1833, 1845, and 1850 and each time had sought to

---

1850–1920" (Ph.D diss., Claremont Graduate School, 1983), p. 43. For a discussion of the reforms imposed by the Spanish which led to Mexican independence and their impact on the northern territories see Thomas D. Hall, *Social Change in the Southwest, 1350–1880* (Lawrence: University Press of Kansas, 1989), pp. 134–66.

[20] David Weber, *The Mexican Frontier, 1821–1846: The American Southwest under Mexico* (Albuquerque: University of New Mexico Press, 1982), pp. 15–42, 83–105.

[21] Ibid., pp. 90–195. In the 1820s and 1830s, when desirable land was scarce in New Mexico, only small numbers of immigrants were attracted. These were primarily French-Canadian trappers, who assimilated to Hispano culture, learning Spanish and marrying into Hispano families.

[22] Dunbar notes that between 1840 and 1847, twenty-three grants were made to local and foreign entrepreneurs ("Land Tenure," p. 183); see Westphall, *Mercedes Reales*, p. 26.

[23] Weber, *Mexican Frontier*, pp. 129, 144–46, 157.

undercut the influence of the brotherhoods.[24] In a pastoral letter in 1833 he stated his opposition to the Penitente groups, calling them a possible threat to the church. He opposed the use of the church building for informal lay religious activities and ordered that penances be performed at home instead.[25] In response to Zubiría's order, the performance of Penitente rituals moved outside the church, into a separate structure called a *morada*. Zubiría did not object to self-discipline but rather to mortification; he sought to end excessive penances and unsupervised meetings.[26] Durango, though, was a thousand miles from northern New Mexico, which made Zubiría's pronouncements all but unenforceable. Additionally, he had little support from the few remaining parish priests, whose status and position in their community depended on maintaining connections with a social structure of which the Penitente brotherhood was an integral part.

New Mexican Penitentes faced another challenge from the Catholic hierarchy when the territory was annexed by the United States. In 1850, Pope Pius IX established New Mexico as a Vicarite Apostolic, attaching it to the Archdiocese of St. Louis. In 1853 the Diocese of Santa Fe was formed, and in 1875 it was elevated to an archdiocese. In 1850 a French priest, Friar Jean Baptiste Lamy, arrived to assume control over the newly established Vicarite Apostolic. He brought with him a number of French priests and in succeeding years recruited European priests to fill vacant positions in New Mexico.[27] Shortly after his arrival, Lamy set about reconstructing the formal church hierarchy, which had fallen into disrepair following Mexican independence. At his arrival Lamy found only ten priests, churches in ruin, and no schools. By 1865 he had recruited thirty-seven priests, built forty-five churches, repaired eighteen to twenty others, and recruited the Sisters of Loretto to maintain schools.[28]

[24] Weigle, *Brothers of Light*, p. 24.

[25] Fray Angelico Chavez, "The Penitentes of New Mexico," *New Mexico Historical Review* 29 (1954): 111.

[26] Weigle, *Brothers of Light*, p. 24. Also Paul Horgan, *Lamy of Santa Fe: His Life and Times* (New York: Farrar, Strauss and Giroux, 1975), p. 149. Weigle argues that Zubiría's action was an attempt to suppress penances completely, while Horgan asserts that Zubiría simply did not want penances performed in the church.

[27] J. B. Salpointe, *Soldiers of the Cross* (1898; reprint, Albuquerque: Calvin Horn, 1967), p. 209.

[28] Louis H. Warner, *Archbishop Lamy: An Epochmaker* (Santa Fe, N.M.: Santa Fe, N.M. Publishing Corporation, 1936), p. 327.

If New Mexican Hispanos, and Penitentes in particular, understood the American military occupation as a threat to their political institutions, Lamy's appointment signaled the invasion of the formal church hierarchy and attempts to reform basic social institutions. Lamy moved to reinstate discipline and order to a church run by what he believed to be "scandalous native clergy." He attributed the church's shortcomings to the failure of the clergy to observe strict discipline. He condemned local clergy for allowing social customs he considered sinful and degraded. In a pastoral letter that went into effect in January 1853, Lamy condemned divorce, dancing, and gambling. Divorce was no longer to be condoned. Dancing, he wrote, was "conducive to evil . . . occasions of sin . . . and provided opportunity for illicit affinities and love that was reprehensible and sinful . . . [it was] a recreation closer to paganism." Finally, gambling was, in his view, "absolutely and essentially evil and reprehensible."[29] Lamy's attempts to reorganize the Catholic Church, to centralize and bring a new order to it, had a more powerful impact on Hispano New Mexicans in the small villages of northern New Mexico. This reorganization of the church and its attempts to control Penitente activities would touch the most basic Hispano social institution in New Mexico.[30] In the words of his biographer, Paul Horgan, Lamy represented yet another non-Mexican power that Hispano New Mexicans "must however unwillingly accommodate to . . . and to the disciplines which soon enough began to come clear also."[31]

The effect of these changes on the lives of Hispano New Mexicans is not easy to assess. Much of the population was illiterate, and written sources are not readily available.[32] One can, however, begin to get a sense of how they might have responded from the actions and words of a popular representative, the priest at Taos, Father Antonio José Martínez. Much of what is known about Martínez comes from the stories told from one generation to the next. Among Hispanos he has attained mythological dimensions and stands as a folk hero. It is said that in 1833,

---

[29] Horgan, *Lamy of Santa Fe*, pp. 170–72.

[30] Chavez argues that Lamy did not believe the Penitentes fit in the modern church and would generate bad publicity for New Mexico ("Penitentes of New Mexico," p. 99).

[31] Horgan, *Lamy of Santa Fe*, p. 127.

[32] The high rate of illiteracy was another argument used by the U.S. Congress for denying New Mexican petitions for statehood after the territory had been annexed. A governor's report to the secretary of the interior in the 1880s noted that 42,000 people in the territory could not read or write in a population of approximately 120,000. See Howard B. Lamar, *The Far Southwest, 1846–1912: A Territorial History* (New York: Norton, 1970), p. 169.

Martínez had been made *comisario interino* (temporary director) of the Penitentes.[33] Martínez, who was among the few priests remaining in the territory after Mexican independence, emerged as one of the most influential intellectual and political leaders of New Mexicans. Because he was simultaneously damned and claimed as one of their own by both the Anglo-Protestant governing elite and the post-1850 Catholic hierarchy, Padre Martínez's life illustrates the tensions felt by Hispano New Mexicans and their attempts to accommodate a new government while retaining their unique cultural heritage.[34]

Born in 1793 in northern New Mexico, Martínez was the eldest son of an influential landowning family who became a priest in 1822, after marrying, having a family, and being widowed.[35] He served as curate at Tome and Abiquiu before being appointed to the curacy at Taos in 1826. Martínez was a student and advocate of the Enlightenment ideals that fueled the democratic revolutions of his era. He struggled with the church hierarchy, and his protests to Bishop Zubiría made him popular with his followers in New Mexico. Martínez objected to the collection of tithes by the church. Because of the imposition of tithes and the additional fees charged by priests, poor families could not bury family members

[33] Fray Angelico Chavez, *But Time and Chance* (Santa Fe, N.M.: Sunstone Press, 1981), p. 45.

[34] Martínez is a controversial historical figure and has been portrayed as both hero and villain. Lamar, in *The Far Southwest*, argues that Martínez was the leader of the anti-American faction that organized an unsuccessful rebellion against American troops stationed in Santa Fe in 1847. Others argue that the evidence does not clearly support this contention. Horgan reports this same information, suggesting that it was a "rumor," and writes that Martínez gave refuge to people fleeing the violence (*Lamy of Santa Fe*, p. 130). Recent revisionist history has reclaimed Martínez as a native Chicano leader (see Weigle, *Brothers of Light*, for example). Lamar describes Martínez's support for statehood as motivated by political and economic self-interest. He sought statehood as one way of achieving "home rule," thereby maintaining Hispano hegemony in the territory and undermining the growing economic power of Anglo-American interests. This coupled with his support for indigenous social institutions and his confrontations with the Catholic Church have won him his reputation as an early Chicano activist. My reading of the literature suggests that Lamar is probably right to assert that many of Martínez's political actions were motivated by self-interest, but he also emerges as an articulate and passionate spokesman for the interests of his fellow Hispano New Mexicans during this time of turmoil.

[35] Biographical information on Martínez is limited but includes Pedro Sanchez, *Memorias sobre la vida del Presbitero Don Antonio José Martínez* (Santa Fe, N.M.: Compania Impresora del Nuevo Mexico, 1903); Chavez, *But Time and Chance*; Chavez, "Penitentes of New Mexico"; Horgan, *Lamy of Santa Fe*; Henry Wagner, "New Mexico's Spanish Press," *New Mexico Historical Review* 12 (January 1937): 1–40; Cecil V. Romero, trans., "Apología of Antonio José Martínez, 1838," *New Mexico Historical Review* 3 (1928): 327–46.

properly or have children baptized and declined to be married officially. His protests proved successful, and in 1833 tithes were removed. He also convinced the Federal Mexican Congress to remove civil enforcement of arbitrary tithes.

Martínez proved to be a liberal priest. In the 1830s he wrote a book on religious toleration and advocated that the church adopt a more aggressive policy toward education. He taught school and prepared several young men for the seminary. He served for six years in the Territorial Assembly under Mexican rule and for three years under American rule. His power and popularity were reinforced when he became the owner of one of the few printing presses in the territory. It has been claimed that Martínez did not support United States annexation, but in 1847 he signed a petition in favor of annexation.[36]

Martínez's signature on the petition favoring U.S. annexation was not simply the action of a shrewd and pragmatic politician accepting the inevitable but also evidence of the ambivalence many Hispano New Mexicans felt about Mexican rule. Surrounded by people angered by the incompetence of government-appointed governors and administrators, he recognized that his neighbors had little faith in the central government. In his role as curate, Martínez faced additional problems: the New Mexican Catholic Church was unable to recruit priests to frontier outposts, and land reform drained wealth from the church. People objected to paying tithes. Much of the money collected flowed south to Mexico, draining "hard cash from circulation on the frontier, further deepening resentment," according to Weber. The church was unable to fill its historical role of fortifying and securing the northern frontier. In Mexico, "in the nation's core, where the church stood as a powerful defender of tradition and the status quo, the weakness of the secular church on the nation's periphery left frontier society more tolerant and receptive to change."[37]

"Time and chance happenth to them all," Martínez had written, recognizing, perhaps, that U.S. annexation was inevitable.[38] In 1848 he

---

[36] Sanchez, *Memorias sobre la vida*, p. 42.

[37] Weber, *Mexican Frontier*, p. 81.

[38] This quotation comes from a chapter of Ecclesiastes quoted by Martínez in his Apología of 1838: "I returned, and saw under the sun, that the race is not to the swift, nor the battle to the strong, neither yet bread to the wise, nor yet riches to men of understanding, nor yet favor to men of skill; but time and chance happenth to them all" (Romero, trans., "Apología," p. 327).

seized a moment, a "chance," to make a place for New Mexican Hispanos in the process of annexation when he presided over a convention in Santa Fe which adopted a statement to Congress asking for a territorial government. At this convention fourteen New Mexicans (four Anglo-American, ten Hispano) gathered to ask for the formation of a civil government.[39] When a territorial legislature was finally elected, meeting for the first time on June 1, 1851, its membership was predominantly Hispano. Of the senators elected, eleven were Hispano and only two were Anglo-American. In the lower house, there were nineteen Hispanos and six Anglo-Americans.[40] Martínez was elected as a senator from Taos County. He was not the only priest. Also elected were José Francisco Leyba, Vicar General Juan Felipe Ortiz, and José Manuel Gallegos. The election of Martínez and other native priests illustrates that little distinction was made between religious and political life. Although the church, as an organized and centralized authority, may have been weak in northern New Mexico, certain individual priests played important political roles. Martínez's prominence came not simply from his being a priest but because in that role he was rooted in Hispano New Mexican social institutions and traditions. The eldest son of a wealthy family, Martínez was not just a priest but a *patron*, a godfather to many Taos children, a man who supervised the education of village children. While the church hierarchy warred with the Penitentes, Martínez embraced them and sought their support.

Faced with the choice of an indefinite United States military occupation or the formation of a civil government, New Mexicans such as Martínez chose the latter. Military government precluded any possibility of a Hispano presence in the governing process. Civil government, though largely appointed by the president, did allow for elected bodies such as the territorial senate and lower house. Although it was a form of accommodation, a recognition of U.S. authority, home rule would allow for the election of priests like Martínez and extend the New Mexican tradition of combining religion and politics into the American electoral process. To Anglo-American observers, who could not see that the election of priests such as Martínez was an outgrowth of local traditions, this act was a sign of the "influence of the Roman Catholic

---

[39] Benjamin M. Read, *Illustrated History of New Mexico* (Santa Fe, N.M.: New Mexico Printing Co., 1912), p. 454.

[40] Count based on a list of delegates elected to the New Mexico legislature (ibid., p. 464).

church . . . brought into the contest at the polls."[41] Thus for Anglo-Americans who preferred to think of the election results as yet another sign of Catholic expansionism rather than as an expression of local political tradition, this was an occasion for concern.

† † †

Historically, Anglo-Americans themselves had had an ambivalent relationship with that part of the continent which is the Southwest. For many the Mexican-American War was a reminder of growing sectional conflicts within the United States; the annexation of new territories fueled debates concerning slavery and peonage as well as the political balance among the states.[42] To others, annexation was a reflection of the United States's "manifest destiny," proof positive of America's ability to extend the "temple of freedom" across the continent.[43] Yet others, preoccupied with "race mixing," voiced their reluctance at admitting to the American nation people of a different race.[44] Soon after New Mexico had been annexed, Colonel E. V. Sumner, a leader of the United States troops occupying the territory, recommended that the troops be withdrawn and the territory abandoned. Reflecting on the character of Hispano New Mexicans, he argued that the territory could only be a financial burden to the United States government. "There can never be the slightest return for all this outlay," he wrote, referring to the public money expended in the annexation efforts. Calling the Hispano population "worthless and idle," Sumner believed that civil government could never be maintained without the aid of the military. He questioned the honesty and industry of Hispanos, admitting that there were some gentlemen but that the lower classes were generally "depraved," citing, for example, the "commerce between the sexes." The people of New Mexico, concluded Sumner, were "thoroughly debased and totally incapable

[41] From the House of Representatives debate regarding the contested election of priest José Manuel Gallegos, May 23, 1856, U.S. Serial Set, H. Mis. Doc. 114(34–1) 867.

[42] Frederick Merk, *Manifest Destiny and Mission in American History* (New York: Vintage Books, 1963), pp. 164–79.

[43] Ibid., pp. 24–60; see also Albert K. Weinberg, *Manifest Destiny: A Study of Nationalist Experience in American History* (Baltimore: Johns Hopkins Press, 1935), and Russell S. Saxton, "Ethnocentrism in the Historical Literature of Territorial New Mexico" (Ph.D diss., University of New Mexico, 1980), p. 1.

[44] Merk, *Manifest Destiny and Mission*, pp. 157–63.

of self-government, and there is no latent quality about them that can ever make them respectable."[45]

Addressing the House of Representatives in January 1853, the territorial delegate from New Mexico, Richard Wrightman, called Sumner's report an "atrocious libel." Defending the character and morals of the Hispano population, he decried plans to abandon the territory. Wrightman's primary concern was to stop Secretary of War Charles Conrad's recommendation that the Hispano inhabitants of the New Mexico territory be bought out, thereby inducing, in the words of the secretary, the "inhabitants to abandon a country which seems hardly fit for the inhabitation of civilized man." This logic was "folly," claimed Wrightman, and he criticized the secretary for "recommending the depopulation of the best line for a railroad to connect the Mississippi with the Pacific." To abandon New Mexico would be, he argued, to "prevent the natural, healthy growth of this young nation."[46]

Wrightman's and Sumner's arguments reflected the spectrum of debate concerning territorial expansion. But once expansion was accepted as inevitable—as part of the American "mission"—the issue that would most preoccupy Anglo-Americans was that of the joining of two cultures presumed to be incompatible. In this meeting with Hispanos, Anglo-Americans were guided by two sets of preconceptions. They feared the presence of the "evil priest" and disparaged the people and their living habits, yet they also held romantic notions about the geography of the territory. Like the Spanish *conquistadores*, they too dreamed of cities paved with gold and treasures.[47] Anglo-American impressions were molded by the accounts of travelers to New Mexico who found it to be a strange land. One visitor, describing his trip into the region in 1853, noted as its "distinguishing features" the "arid elevated plains, lofty and barren mountains, and narrow valleys along the watercourses." This was a part of the country, he wrote, "little known to the people of the United States. . . . Its very position precludes an intimate intercourse

[45] *Congressional Globe*, 32d Cong., 2d sess. (January 10, 1853), Appendix 104. Sumner's report was quoted in full by Richard Wrightman in a speech to Congress. See Robert W. Larson, *New Mexico's Quest for Statehood, 1846–1912* (Albuquerque: University of New Mexico Press, 1968), for a discussion of the early debates concerning the territory's political status.

[46] *Congressional Globe*, 32d Cong., 2d sess. (January 10, 1853), Appendix 104.

[47] Susan Reyner Kenneson, "Through the Looking-Glass: A History of Anglo-American Attitudes towards the Spanish-Americans and Indians of New Mexico" (Ph.D diss., Yale University, 1978), p. 32.

with other sections of the Union and the inhabitants, with the manners and customs of their Moorish and Castilian ancestors, are both new and strange to our people."[48]

Marked by its mountain ranges, canyon valleys, and mesas, this land stood in stark contrast to what Anglo-Americans understood to be fertile and virgin soil.[49] Overwhelmed by a geography of contrasts, startled by the extremes of weather, with no treasure to be easily secured and land that defied whatever rules of farming they knew, Anglo-Americans quickly judged the culture that had arisen from the soils as "arid." In describing the Hispanos who had settled on this land, Anglos traveling through New Mexico focused on a variety of cultural activities which they believed signaled moral laxness and made Hispano New Mexicans at once suspect.

There was no precedent in the United States for the annexation of Mexico's northernmost territories in 1848. As historian Howard Lamar has argued, it fit none of the assumptions set forth in the Ordinance of 1787.[50] Annexation of New Mexico presented Anglo-Americans with the dilemma of "settling" a territory with a large population of white settlers and Indians.[51] The most obvious motivations were those represented by Sumner and Wrightman, the desire to prove military superiority and to secure economic advantage, but the conquering Anglos were divided as to how best to proceed with settlement. Some believed that Anglos should cooperate with Hispanos, learn Spanish, and share political power. Others, echoing fears of moral corruption, believed that Hispanos were incapable of governing themselves.[52]

[48] W. W. H. Davis, *El Gringo: New Mexico and Her People* (1856; reprint, Lincoln: University of Nebraska Press, 1982), pp. 57–58.

[49] For a discussion of how Anglo-Americans judged the fertility of land see Henry Nash Smith, *Virgin Land: The American West as Symbol and Myth* (Cambridge, Mass.: Harvard University Press, 1978), p. 175.

[50] Howard R. Lamar, "Political Patterns in New Mexico and Utah Territories, 1850–1900," *Utah Historical Quarterly* 28 (1960): 364.

[51] Population figures for non-Indians in New Mexico in the latter part of the nineteenth century are as follows: 1850, 61,547; 1860, 93,516; 1870, 91,874; 1880, 119,565; 1890, 160,282; 1900, 195,310; 1910, 327,301; 1914, 383,551. The figures are from census studies as reported in Jay Stowall, *The Near Side of the Mexican Question* (New York: George H. Duran, 1921), p. 55. Until the twentieth century the census made no distinction between Anglo and Hispanic settlers, counting both groups as white. The dramatic increase in the 1880 figure is owing to the completion of the railroad and probably indicates an increase in Anglo settlers in the territory. The increase between 1900 and 1910 reflects continuing Anglo immigration to the area but also Mexican immigration because of political problems in Mexico.

[52] Lamar, "Political Patterns," p. 367.

If asked what they knew about Hispano New Mexicans in the latter part of the nineteenth century, Anglo-Americans would very likely have said that the population was largely Spanish-speaking and Catholic. Pressed for more details, they would probably have commented on the Penitentes and their "weird" rituals of "strange . . . idol worshipping." This attitude was the result of popular accounts of the territory, missionary reports, and journalistic accounts, as well as numerous novels, all of which highlighted Penitente rituals.[53] Beginning in the 1850s in the accounts of traders and merchants and reaching well into the twentieth century, every passing writer seemed to feel required to report and comment on the activities of the Penitentes. Mary Austin made the Penitentes a centerpiece in her collection of essays on folk customs of the Southwest, and even Willa Cather could not resist the dramatic qualities of their rituals. In *Death Comes for the Archbishop*, Cather's main character, Father Latour (modeled after Catholic missionary Father Lamy), the representative of the new European order, must face Padre Martínez, who warns Latour that, should he "abolish the bloody rites of the Penitentes," he will die an early death.[54] When compared to missionary reports describing Penitentes, Austin's and Cather's descriptions are suffused in a romanticism that presaged the rise of New Mexico's reputation in this century as a museum to the "richness" of America's geographical and cultural history.[55] The romantic image became more pronounced in the 1920s, when Anglo settlement in the state had in-

[53] Marta Weigle, "The Penitente Brotherhood in Southwestern Fiction: Notes on Folklife and Literature," in *The American Self: Myth, Ideology, and Popular Culture*, ed. Sam Girgus (Albuquerque: University of New Mexico Press, 1981), pp. 221–30. For the observation of an itinerant Protestant preacher see Alex M. Darley, *The Passionists of the Southwest or the Holy Brotherhood: A Revelation of the "Penitentes"* (1893; reprint, Glorieta, N.M.: Rio Grande Press, 1968), p. 59. For the comments of a journalist, first published in 1893, see the popular travelogue by Charles F. Lummis, *Land of Poco Tiempo* (Albuquerque: University of New Mexico Press, 1966), pp. 77–108. The rituals of the Penitentes are vividly and luridly described.

[54] Mary Austin, *Land of Journey's Ending* (London: George Allen & Unwin, 1924); Willa Cather, *Death Comes for the Archbishop* (New York: Vintage Books, 1971), p. 148.

[55] The preface to the Works Progress Administration's *New Mexico: A Guide to the Colorful State* (New York: Hastings House, 1940), claims that "no state is richer in historical incident." The land and the people—the "many points of view as a mixture [that is the Indian, Spanish, and Anglo-American] of these can supply"—are the basis on which the tourist industry is to be built (p. vii). This image persists; in 1987 one guidebook described Santa Fe's inhabitants, "Spanish, Anglo, Indian, and Black," as "[demonstrating] the stolidity mixed with whimsy that characterizes the region." See *Fodor's New Mexico: Santa Fe, Taos and Albuquerque* (New York: Fodor's Travel Publications, 1987), p. 48.

creased significantly.[56] While Anglos remained in the minority, invoking the presence of the Penitentes simply reaffirmed Hispano difference, calling into question the desirability of extending citizenship rights to an alien people.

The debate concerning New Mexico's assimilation was immediately cast in moral terms; before Hispano New Mexicans could be extended political rights, their moral standards would have to be transformed. Both Protestants and Catholics vowed to step into the moral breach that Anglo travelers and visitors to the territory had identified. Through their respective mission activities each group promised to Americanize the population, to prepare Hispanos for citizenship. Each group was to play a central role in reshaping the social consciousness of New Mexicans. There was an argument not only about which church, Catholic or Protestant, should take the lead in remaking Hispano culture but also about which mechanisms should be used to introduce new moral standards and undermine the old. The Hispano challenge to religious intervention also provided a new dimension to the process of Americanization that Anglo settlers had not originally envisioned—it raised the specter of pluralism. The intricate interplay between the Catholic Church, Protestants, and Hispano New Mexicans yielded no clear-cut winner, but it did reveal the complexity and resilience of a local culture that surprised all concerned and forced a reevaluation of the original mission.

Bishop Lamy, one of the first of the moral reformers to stake a claim in New Mexico, occupied an uneasy position in New Mexican society. He was a Catholic and presumably shared certain religious beliefs with Hispanos in the territory. Yet there were differences that proved to be handicaps in overcoming obstacles and gaining the wholehearted support of the people in the territory. One was language; Lamy was French and learned Spanish after he arrived in the territory. Even though Anglo-Protestants chose not to recognize it, Lamy, too, was embarking on a mission of Americanization. Lamy had spent much of his priesthood working in the United States. He understood his appointment to the

---

[56] Austin's and Cather's books were both published in the 1920s. In 1940 the Hispanic population in New Mexico was said to be 49.6 percent of the total non-Indian population. See E. B. Fincher, *Spanish-Americans as a Political Factor in New Mexico, 1912–1950* (1954; reprint, New York: Arno Press, 1974), p. 9. George Sanchez estimated that in 1931, 50 percent of the school census was Spanish-speaking and argued that this indicated that 50 percent of the population in New Mexico was Spanish-speaking even though census figures were much lower ("The Education of Bilinguals in a State School System" [Ph.D. diss., University of California at Berkeley, 1934], p. 13).

Santa Fe Vicarite Apostolic as essentially a mission to reform the New Mexican church, to remove it from the rubric of the Durango, or Mexican, authority and bring it into the American church.[57]

The concerns of Anglo-Protestants and Catholics overlapped in other areas. Friar Lamy did not support the highly political role played by some of the New Mexican native priests. And even though it was perceived as an antagonistic moral influence by Protestants, the Catholic Church, as led by Lamy, did not dispute the Anglo-Protestants' criticisms of the moral state of Hispano New Mexicans. Rather, Lamy reinforced the impressions of moral degeneracy. Writing to dispute charges brought by the native priests against Lamy, his aide, Father Joseph Machebeuf, claimed that New Mexicans were "generally deprived of all schooling and are little accustomed to governing themselves according to the laws of the United States . . . the immense majority do not know how to read." He described the legislative assembly as "composed of ignorant men, most of them corrupt, dishonest, who hold the people in fear of them. . . . These people are mostly related to each other by different degrees of affinity and the corruption of this society illustrates their prejudice towards a foreign bishop who is obliged to reform their morals."[58]

Neither was Lamy comfortable with the symbolism of the indigenously inspired Penitente traditions. He emphasized the symbols of the Trinity, inculcated devotion to the Virgin Mary, established the practice of the rosary, and enrolled Catholic New Mexicans in the Scapular.[59] Although he hoped to train native priests in the long run, in his early days he recruited Italian and French priests.[60] In his advocacy of a resurrected Catholic hierarchy, he did little to incorporate local prac-

---

[57] Horgan, *Lamy of Santa Fe*, pp. 169–210; Frances Campbell, "Missiology in New Mexico, 1850–1900: The Success and Failure of Catholic Education," in *Religion and Society in the American West*, ed. Carl Guarneri and David Alvarez (Lanham, Md.: University Press of America, 1987), pp. 62–63. Lamar, in *The Far Southwest*, argues that Lamy did not intend to undermine Spanish-American culture or to Americanize or secularize New Mexico but rather sought a "restoration of the church in the life and society of New Mexico" (p. 102). But he does concede that Lamy's programs "had far-reaching and sometimes unexpected consequences" (p. 103), creating splits within the church that had political repercussions.

[58] Quoted in Horgan, *Lamy of Santa Fe*, p. 228.

[59] James H. Defouri, *Historical Sketch of the Catholic Church in New Mexico* (San Francisco: McCormick Brothers, 1887), pp. 119–21. These practices were introduced to the people by the Jesuit missionaries recruited by Lamy.

[60] Salpointe, *Soldiers of the Cross*, p. 209.

tices, and he wished to undermine or, at the very least, limit expressions of local culture.

From the outset, Lamy condemned behavior he believed to be immoral such as dancing and gambling, and he also attacked fundamental social organizations such as the Penitentes. He wished to end their rituals, which he believed to be regressive and backward. In his view, the Penitentes were not an indigenous group but rather a remnant of the Third Order of Franciscans. Attempting to assert control over the Penitentes, he tried to impose the rule of the Third Order. In these rules, which he enunciated in 1853, he proclaimed that the Penitente brotherhoods had to be regulated by a local priest. He specified the responsibilities of the leaders and defined membership procedures in ways that undercut the autonomy of the groups and demanded that they recognize his authority. To enforce these regulations, Lamy instituted practices of verification before administering sacraments.[61] He hoped thus to force Penitentes to give up their membership in the brotherhoods.[62] Lamy was not wholly successful. He met with resistance from Penitente members and also from community priests, who continued to give the sacraments without demanding verification.[63] Under this pressure from the church, the Penitentes became less public in their rituals, but the groups did not disappear. Indeed, church disapproval forced the organization to emphasize its political role and to downplay the religious aspects.[64]

The Catholic Church and the Penitentes did not reach a formal accommodation until well into the twentieth century.[65] The hierarchy's assault in the latter part of the nineteenth century probably served to curb some of the excessive ritualistic practices such as self-flagellation, but as New Mexico grew the Penitentes took on larger political and social functions. Just as Lamy objected to priests who ran for political office, he was increasingly concerned about the political role of the Penitentes. When the groups began to incorporate in 1861 as benevolent societies, the Penitentes took a step toward separating themselves from the adminis-

---

[61] Swadesh, *Los Primeros Pobladores*, pp. 75–76.

[62] Weigle, *Brothers of Light*, pp. 54–57.

[63] Swadesh, *Los Primeros Pobladores*, p. 76.

[64] Salpointe followed Lamy as bishop and was especially critical of the politicization of the Penitentes (*Soldiers of the Cross*, p. 167). On the Penitentes' political role see Weigle, *Brothers of Light*, p. 60; Woodward, "Penitentes," pp. 265–66.

[65] Weigle, *Brothers of Light*, pp. 101, 121, 136–38; Ottoway, "Penitente Moradas," pp. 198–201.

trative church.[66] When they incorporated, the Penitente brotherhoods began to make legal distinctions between their religious and sociopolitical functions. They remained committed to the religious beliefs of the Catholic Church, but neither the Catholic Church nor the Protestants who followed recognized the mutual aid and community functions of the brotherhood.[67]

The members of the brotherhoods recognized their foundations as religious, but the people had begun to think of the social functions of the group as more secular in nature. Anthropologist Marta Weigle has argued that in the latter part of the nineteenth century, Penitentes learned to make a distinction between "true" Catholicism, the traditional Hispano practices, and the "administrative" church, as represented by Lamy. The existence of an administrative church and the subsequent arrival of Protestant missionaries who provided educational services available to all members of the community regardless of religious affiliation were, to people in these small communities, examples that religious beliefs could be separated from the functions or the services rendered by religious organizations. Over a period of years, this recognition that a separation could be made between the beliefs and services of a social organization or institution allowed the Penitentes to diversify their activities. They could maintain their religious rituals but take on social and political functions that were not strictly religious in origin. Making these distinctions also allowed members of these small villages to accept services from different social institutions outside of the community, from Protestant churches as well as the Catholic Church.[68]

† † †

When the Presbyterian church began its mission efforts in New Mexico, it concentrated its work in the northern half of the territory where the largest numbers of people lived and where the Penitentes were most active. Presbyterian missionaries followed the Catholic Church, capitalizing on the wounds created by Lamy's reorganization efforts. The earliest missionaries established churches and schools in Las Vegas, an

---

[66] Swadesh, *Los Primeros Pobladores*, p. 75; Paul Kutsche and Dennis Gallegos, "Community Functions of the Cofradía de Nuestro Padre Jesus Nazareno," in *The Survival of Spanish-American Villages*, ed. Kutsche, p. 91; Woodward, "Penitentes," p. 262.

[67] Weigle, *Brothers of Light*, pp. 61, 75.

[68] Ibid., pp. 75–76.

active trade center and also the center of Penitente activities east of the Sangre de Cristo Mountains, and on the other side of the mountains in Taos, the home of Lamy's foe Father Martínez and another area of Penitente activity.[69]

In Taos, Martínez's disputes with Lamy played an integral role in the establishment of the first Presbyterian church. Father Martínez's death at his home in Taos in 1867 did not end the schism but left many of Taos' residents with a bitter distaste for church politics. Lamy had suspended Martínez for obstructing the work of a priest sent to replace him. The new priest was not a native Hispano, and he regarded the favorite son Martínez with disdain, treating him and other residents as "mere colonials."[70] In defiance, Martínez continued to conduct services, not in church but in his home, as an independent pastor. He drew away a sizable part of the regular Catholic congregation from the new priest. Lamy responded by excommunicating Martínez.[71]

Lamy's action did not stop Martínez. He continued to conduct his illicit church even after excommunication, but his death left his followers in a spiritual vacuum and at odds with the Catholic hierarchy. It was from among this core of dissident Catholics that Presbyterians organized their first church and school in Taos. When Presbyterian missionary Rev. James Roberts arrived in 1872, he was welcomed by Vincente Romero, a relative of Father Martínez. Along with José Domingo Mondragon, another early convert, Romero helped Roberts bring together a small congregation of Hispano New Mexicans who converted to Presbyterianism. Mondragon had been a *hermano mayor* of the Penitentes in the Taos area. After his election to the territorial legislature in 1856, he had met a Baptist minister in Santa Fe who had introduced him to the Protestant New Testament. Both Mondragon and Romero became native Presbyterian evangelists, and Romero later taught in the mission day school in El Prado de Taos.[72] The schism between Martínez and Lamy

---

[69] Hernandez, "Cactus Whips and Wooden Crosses," p. 217, establishes the geographical stronghold of Penitentes to include Rio Arriba, east from Raton, south through Mora and Las Vegas, across through the Santa Fe region, up on the west through Cuba and Dulce and north across into southern Colorado around the counties of Archuleta, Conejo, Costilla, Las Animas, Alamora, and Saguache.

[70] Horgan, *Lamy of Santa Fe*, p. 231.

[71] Ibid., pp. 240–45; Defouri, *Historical Sketch*, p. 125. For an overview of the conflict between Lamy and Martínez see Ray John de Aragon, *Padre Martínez and Bishop Lamy* (Las Vegas, N.M: Pan-American Publishing Company, 1978).

[72] Ruth K. Barber and Edith Agnew, *Sowers Went Forth: The Story of Presbyterian Missions*

and Penitente alienation from the Catholic Church aided Roberts's efforts in the Taos area. Other Presbyterian missionaries would benefit from these tensions, and the conversion of Penitentes, particularly, was soon looked upon as a measure of the church's success in Americanizing Hispanos.

The Presbyterian missionaries' success in Taos was not readily duplicated in other towns. Less than 10 percent of the Hispano Catholic population in New Mexico converted to Protestantism.[73] Unable to attract and baptize large numbers of Catholics, Presbyterians turned their attention to establishing schools, which they quickly found proved to be more popular. The Elizabethtown, New Mexico, newspaper, the *Press, Railway and Telegraph*, noted in 1873 that the recently opened mission school in Taos "is prospering and promises to be of great assistance to the children of poor parents in Taos precinct until the public school system in that county is put in operation."[74] From Las Vegas, Rev. John Annin wrote that his school had been built with the aid of Catholics and Jews as well as Protestants. The land, he reported, was "given by the citizens of the place, and Roman Catholics and Jews united with others in raising money with which to make the purchase. This is a pleasant feature of the case."[75]

The mission school in Las Vegas was opened in 1870 with four pupils; by 1872, seventy-four pupils were attending regularly. Tuition was free, and supplies were provided by the teachers, Rebecca and Laura Annin, Rev. Annin's daughters. Asserting that the "greater part of the scholars are Mexicans and members of Catholic families in or near Las Vegas," Annin described the school as having a "religious element in it." The school day started with Bible readings and recitation of the Lord's Prayer in Spanish.[76] The daily reading exercise was from the New Testament, and each day closed with a benediction. Citing the increasing numbers of students, Annin wrote to Presbyterian supporters in the East, "It will

---

in New Mexico and Southern Colorado (Albuquerque: Menaul Historical Library of the Southwest, 1981), pp. 24–25.

[73] Weigle, *Brothers of Light*, p. 75.

[74] Quoted in the *Rocky Mountain Presbyterian* 2 (November 1873): 3.

[75] "The Work at Las Vegas," *Rocky Mountain Presbyterian* 2 (November 1873): 2.

[76] Lessons were supposed to be conducted entirely in English. Many mission teachers found this unfeasible because many students spoke little or no English when they entered the schools. Instead, those teachers who spoke Spanish adopted bilingual methods, starting new students in Spanish and gradually introducing English. Religious materials that had been translated into Spanish, particularly the Bible and prayerbooks, were used in the schools.

thus be clearly seen that the school is growing, and the growth of the school in this place, of a school under Protestant control, is, as it seems to your correspondent something to be thankful for, and something which gives hope for the future."[77]

† † †

Ironically, in 1850 Father Lamy had opposed, not United States rule but Hispanos like Martínez, those who sought accommodation while attempting to retain the social structure essential to their definition of culture. Both the Catholic mission of Lamy and the Protestant mission efforts that followed were intended to make this Hispano population "American." The difference, and later source of antagonism, lay in how an "American" was defined and who would do the defining. Lamy wanted to institute a new social order, to banish divorce, control dancing and gambling, promote a central governing authority, and introduce a system of taxation within the church which would redistribute funds to poorer churches. None of these directives were necessarily antithetical to being American. In fact, Protestant missionaries also supported curbs on dancing and gambling and called for elevation of moral standards. What they objected to was sharing political power with the Catholic Church. Educators of good citizens were to be judged not just by the objectives toward which they claimed to be working but by the nature of their institutional affiliations. Even though Protestant and Catholic goals for New Mexico were similar, the Americanization of New Mexico was characterized as a struggle between Protestant and Catholic. For the objects of the struggle, Hispano New Mexicans, it was not entirely clear that either of these institutions represented their interests, and their loyalties were constantly challenged and tested.

Education, specifically schooling, became the battleground on which Protestants and Catholics fought for the making of good citizens. The Catholic Church and the Presbyterians who followed them recognized that missionary efforts should begin with education. There was little semblance of an educational system in New Mexico at its annexation. Prominent individuals such as Father Martínez ran private academies in their homes, but public education was nonexistent. In 1863 the territorial legislature created a Board of Education and the office of terri-

---

[77] "The Work at Las Vegas," *Rocky Mountain Presbyterian* 2 (November 1873): 2.

torial superintendent in the face of growing criticism concerning the high level of illiteracy and because one of the reasons for denying petitions for statehood was the lack of a common school system. This initial legislation yielded few positive results.[78]

In the years that followed, other attempts were made to create a unified state school system. Justices of the peace in each county were authorized to conduct school matters such as hiring teachers. In 1872 the legislature called for a system of elected county boards of supervisors and school directors. This system was soon undermined by charges of corruption. Justices were accused of hiring family members or political cronies to teach regardless of their qualifications. Not until 1889 did the legislature declare "that anyone who cannot read and write sufficiently to keep his own records in Spanish and English shall not be employed as a teacher."[79]

The underlying dilemma for advocates of education in New Mexico was how best to support a school system. In 1855 and 1856 the legislature tried to extract a tax of one dollar from property owners. Large landowners successfully evaded the tax, leaving the small property holders to shoulder a burden they could not afford. In 1872 and 1876 the legislature tried again, imposing fines on those who participated in activities central to Hispano village life. Fines were to be collected from those who buried their dead on Sundays, or participated in Sunday sports such as cockfighting, or married "close relatives." All these fines were to go into the county school fund.[80] Not surprisingly, these measures were not popular with Hispano New Mexicans. In predominantly Hispano villages, where the very people responsible for overseeing this legislation participated in any number of these activities, the law went unenforced and school coffers remained empty.

Unfettered by accusations of corruption or favoritism, parochial schools fared better in the early period of New Mexico's territorial

[78] Tom Wiley, *Politics and Purse Strings in New Mexico's Public Schools* (Albuquerque: University of New Mexico Press, 1968), p. 32. See also Alvin R. Sunseri, *Seeds of Discord: New Mexico in the Aftermath of the American Conquest, 1846–1861* (Chicago: Nelson-Hall, 1979), pp. 242–50; Jane Atkins, "Who Will Educate: The Schooling Question in Territorial New Mexico, 1846–1911" (Ph.D. diss., University of New Mexico, 1982); Dianna Everett, "The Public School Debate in New Mexico, 1850–1891," *Arizona and the West* 26 (Summer 1984): 107–34.

[79] Wiley, *Politics and Purse Strings*, p. 30.

[80] Ibid., p. 32; Sunseri, *New Mexico in the Aftermath*, p. 247; Everett, "Public School Debate," pp. 109–10.

history. Father Lamy hoped to offset what he thought was an appalling lack of concern about education among the people. In this way he anticipated Presbyterian Rev. MacFarland's lament about the status of education in New Mexico. Early Catholic missionaries agreed with Anglo-American Protestant critics of Hispano culture when they proclaimed that all efforts made by the Franciscans under Spanish rule had been overturned during Mexican rule: "Churches and schoolhouses were in a crumbling state, and ignorance reigned in the land. It is sad to relate all this, but it is the truth."[81]

Stressing the importance of building schools, Lamy's aide Machebeuf wrote in 1852 on the issue of educating New Mexicans: "As the source of evil here is the profound ignorance of people, the first remedy must be the instruction of youth of both sexes, but especially for the young girls. The means of forming them to virtue and good example, which is rare in New Mexico, is the establishment of religious houses conducted by persons devoted to their calling and filled with the spirit of self-sacrifice. To this end the Bishop has already opened a school for boys in our house, and he has knocked at many doors in the United States in order to secure sisters for the girls."[82]

Lamy recruited the Sisters of Loretto to conduct a school for girls in Santa Fe in 1853. In the 1860s the Catholic Church expanded educational efforts by opening St. Michael's College for Boys (run by the Christian Brothers) in Santa Fe and schools for girls in Mora, Las Vegas, and Las Cruces (run by the Sisters of Loretto).[83] Looking back in the 1880s over twenty-five years of Catholic missionary work in New Mexico, Father James H. Defouri wrote that by pursuing reforms in the field of education, Lamy had been able to remove "immorality from the family" and allow "morality, virtue and religion . . . to flourish in the desert of past passions."[84]

Ironically, Defouri's claims came just as the Presbyterian Church began to send women missionaries into New Mexico to combat the "immorality" which Protestants believed was not abating but growing far

[81] Defouri, *Historical Sketch*, p. 49.

[82] Louis Avant, "The History of Catholic Education in New Mexico since the American Occupation" (Master's thesis, University of New Mexico, 1940), p. 9.

[83] Ibid., pp. 17–33; William Ritch, ed., *The New Mexico Blue Book, 1882* (reprint, Albuquerque: University of New Mexico Press, 1968), pp. 23–45, provides a chronology of resources of New Mexico, in which he notes the opening of parochial schools before 1882.

[84] Defouri, *Historical Sketch*, p. 142.

worse. Like the Presbyterians who followed him in New Mexico, Lamy understood his actions to complement the developing civil government. He and his priests did not see the role of the Catholic Church as antagonistic or anti-American. Instead, they were providing services not provided by the civil government and creating institutions not thought at the time to be within the purview of government. Defouri wrote that New Mexico had "felt many beneficent influences, both of the spiritual and civil kind. . . . When Congress was organizing it as a territory, Rome was organizing it as a Diocese. The civil Government formed counties, districts, etc . . . the Church formed parishes, colleges, hospitals, schools, etc." Defouri went on to claim that New Mexico would not have been organized as a political entity or have made any progress at all without the aid of the Catholic Church.[85]

Historians of education have noted that the common school became a symbol of nationalism in the nineteenth century.[86] As Carl Kaestle has argued, state-regulated common schools were established to "integrate and assimilate a diverse population into the nation's political, economic and cultural institutions," emerging as the "principal agent of cognitive and moral teaching and as an important instrument of public policy."[87] Furthermore, they were to be agents of control, the vehicle for "incorporation," whether it be to teach democratic values or to assimilate new groups of people.[88] Early advocates of common schools envisioned a nation built on "an integrated economy, more centralized public education, improved communication, and a common moral and political culture based on Anglo-American Protestantism, republicanism and capitalism."[89] They had no quarrel with a curriculum that combined both secular and religious instruction and encouraged the participation of clergyman—assuming, of course, they were Protestant.[90] In New Mexico, however, American conquest was preceded by a school tradition that was Catholic, and Lamy stepped into the educational

---

[85] Ibid.

[86] Lloyd P. Jorgenson, *The State and the Non-Public School, 1825–1925* (Columbia: University of Missouri Press, 1987), p. 1; Carl Kaestle, *Pillars of the Republic: Common Schools and American Society, 1780–1860* (New York: Hill and Wang, 1983).

[87] Kaestle, *Pillars of the Republic*, p. x.

[88] Paula Fass, *Outside In: Minorities and the Transformation of American Education* (New York: Oxford University Press, 1989), p. 230.

[89] Kaestle, *Pillars of the Republic*, p. 77.

[90] Jorgenson, *The State*, pp. 37, 54.

breach to build and maintain the first system of schools following American occupation. He intended to seize an opportunity for the Catholic Church to establish the educational precedent, to determine the shape of common schooling, essentially to construct the foundation for a public school system. What ensued was a forty-year struggle between Catholics who sought to assert their control over New Mexico public schools and Anglo-Protestants who fought Catholic sectarianism. Between 1870 and 1890 the number of public schools expanded from 5 to 678. The passage of territorial legislation in 1891 which led to the formation of a statewide system of common schools, overseen by the office of the territorial superintendent of public instruction, spurred tremendous growth in the number of public schools. Between 1891 and 1900, the number of schools and pupils doubled.[91]

In opening mission schools, Presbyterians exploited not only divisions within the Catholic Church but also an ongoing controversy concerning the public school system or, more accurately, the lack thereof. Specifically, they opened schools in areas where public education was lacking and in areas where the Catholic parochial schools served only a small segment of the population. Just as the Catholic hierarchy envisioned that its schools would set the precedent for common schools, so too did the Presbyterians. They fully expected that their mission schools would serve as a model for the development of a common school system in the territory. The expansion of the Presbyterian network of schools worried the Catholic clergy. Using the newspapers and circulars they produced to combat each other's influence, Catholic priests and Presbyterian ministers exchanged charges. The Presbyterians asserted that the priests were corrupt. They stymied "independent personal thinking" and the "cause of popular enlightenment and elevation."[92] For its part, the Catholic hierarchy remained critical of the Protestant emphasis on individual interpretation of the Bible and accused Protestants of changing theological doctrine to suit their needs. Charges were leveled at both Protestant ministers and mission teachers. The church was especially critical of

---

[91] Everett, "Public School Debate," p. 134.

[92] This idea that priests were representative of an older, less enlightened era was a common theme in Protestant literature of the period and may be found especially in the *Revista Evangélica* and *La Aurora*, Presbyterian Spanish-language circulars prepared in New Mexico by prominent ministers. See, for example, *Revista Evangélica*, July 1877, Information File, Menaul Historical Library of the Southwest, Albuquerque.

Hispanos who converted, whom they called "deserters" and "disloyal."[93] Referring to Penitentes who left to join Presbyterian churches, the *Revista Católica* argued that the Catholic Church should be glad to get rid of such rebels.[94] As Hispano Catholics began to send their children to Presbyterian schools in larger and larger numbers, the Catholic hierarchy responded by threatening to excommunicate the families.[95]

It is not clear what impact this debate between the Catholic hierarchy and Anglo-Protestants had on the Hispanos living in small villages in the northern part of the territory, nor can we be sure where their loyalties lay. Her findings that attendance figures were high no matter who ran the school led Jane Atkins to speculate that the disagreement between Catholic and Protestant leaders was not shared by most people in New Mexico.[96] Indeed, the evidence suggests that Hispanos took a practical approach to education, using the services of different groups, depending on what was available. Even members of the Catholic hierarchy recognized that their attempts to curb the numbers of Catholic children attending Protestant schools were fruitless because they could not provide the services that their followers desired. In 1909 Father John Baptist Pivital, of the Archdiocese of Santa Fe, described the dilemma of Catholic parents wishing to educate their children. He pointed out that the Protestants had been quick to establish schools, which they supported with mission funds. They presented the schools to the Hispano population as "nonsectarian." "Try and persuade a Mexican not to send his children to such a school and to deprive him of the only available opportunity of giving his children an education," Pivital said, to explain why Catholic opposition to Presbyterian schools was largely ineffective, "and he will answer: 'For the love of God, Bishop, what shall I do? Why do you not give us schools as the Protestants do?'"[97]

---

[93] Catholic views were aired in the *Revista Católica*, first published in 1875. See, for example, "'La Revista' y los protestantes," *Revista Católica*, December 10, 1899, p. 594.

[94] Weigle, *Brothers of Light*, p. 72. Many of the Penitentes who did leave were *hermano mayores* or leaders of local Penitente groups.

[95] There are numerous reports of people threatened with excommunication or excommunicated. Marta Weigle quotes Mary Austin relating a story about one *hermano mayor* of Truchas who had been forced to leave the brotherhood because the priest had two counts against him. "He was a Penitente and he had his children in the local Presbyterian mission school. He compromised with the priest; he gave up being a Penitente 'as he thought it more important to keep his children in a good school.'" (*Brothers of Light*, p. 104).

[96] Atkins, "Who Will Educate," p. 418.

[97] Quoted in Walker, "Protestantism in the Sangre de Cristos," p. 64.

While Catholics and Protestants exchanged charges, the majority of Hispano New Mexicans had other, more pressing concerns than to engage in debates over the moral standards, or lack thereof, of their communities. Between 1880 and 1910 New Mexico villages lost almost all commonly held grazing lands. Two million acres of private lands, 1.7 million acres of communal lands, and 1.8 million acres of timber lands were taken by the state and federal governments without compensation. The land was taken by various means. In the 1870s money taxes were imposed on land, posing a hardship for farmers who had little or no cash income and forcing them to sell to land speculators. Many Hispanos did not even have the chance to sell. Uninformed or misinformed about new laws, they failed to pay taxes, and their land was repossessed by the state, which then sold the land to speculators who, in turn, evicted the original owners. In addition, stream channels were eroded because of overgrazing and timber cutting, reducing the water supply available for farming.[98] Those farmers who managed to retain their land could not expand their holdings. As cattle raising expanded, farmers found themselves locked in. Subsistence farmers lost 80 percent of their land in the late nineteenth century. Stripped of their former means of production, Hispano New Mexicans turned from agriculture to wage labor.[99] Growing numbers of New Mexico's villagers would leave home for extended periods, migrating seasonally in search of wage labor.[100]

† † †

In the conquest of the borderlands, of which New Mexico is one part, both Catholics and Protestants had presented themselves as the spiritual agents of the new government. The Catholic Church's effort was larger and seemingly more faithful to the Hispano culture. In the matter of Penitente practices, the Catholic Church simply sought control, whereas Protestant missionaries argued that they be outlawed. In its schools, the

[98] Knowlton, "Changing Spanish-American Villages," p. 463, nn. 14, 15, 16; John Burma, *Spanish-Speaking Groups in the United States* (Durham, N.C.: Duke University Press, 1954), p. 15.

[99] For a description of the process by which subsistence farmers became wage laborers see Dunbar, "Land Tenure," pp. 201–44. See also Carolyn Zeleny, *Relations between the Spanish-Americans and Anglo-Americans in New Mexico: A Study of Conflict and Accommodation in a Dual-Ethnic Situation* (New York: Arno Press, 1974), p. 153.

[100] Deutsch, *No Separate Refuge*, discusses the various ways Hispanos found to adapt to these economic changes.

Catholic Church made Spanish the primary language, while Presbyterian missionaries insisted on English. The Catholic Church could temper the conquest and soften the blows to Hispano culture, but in these early years the church did not consistently stand with the people. Rather, the intention of the church, as Defouri had claimed, was to serve as the spiritual arm of the new civil government. Having vilified the Catholic Church as un-American, Anglo-Protestants could not allow this claim to stand.

As Catholics and Protestants made New Mexico into a battleground on which to test church-state relations, Hispanos in the territory engaged this debate in an economic and political context in which they were, quite literally, losing ground. Paradoxically, both Catholic and Protestant institutions brought with them pejorative definitions of the Hispano people and culture of the region, but they also provided the respite that some local Hispanos required so that they could exert some power and control over the process of "Americanization." In towns where both the Catholic and Presbyterian churches were present they competed for the loyalty of local residents. While both Catholic and Protestant missionaries hoped to assimilate Hispano culture, to temper, if not eliminate, behavior they found distasteful, the struggle between Catholics and Protestants over the religious content of the new moral code widened the spectrum of choices available to Hispano New Mexicans.

For the Protestant missionary who moved into the territory after annexation, the most basic definition of an American was that citizens should read, write, and speak English. Beyond this it was hoped that the Hispano Catholics of New Mexico would exhibit a patriotic sensibility in economic, political, and social matters. It is difficult to define the nature of this patriotism because it was most often defined in negative terms—what one should not be like. The Protestant literature suggests that this patriotism was Christian and anti-Catholic in nature and principle. Ultimately neither the literature nor the rhetoric and not even the words capture how soft these definitions were and how often they were modified. The contradictions inherent in everyday life simply did not allow for the creation or retention of strict rules for patriotism.

As the Presbyterian mission effort widened, from one school in 1867 to some fifty schools by 1900, one mission teacher after another reported increases in enrollment as well as an enthusiastic response to the education provided. Others reported that the people seemed eager to avail themselves of mission services. Mission women were right when they reported that they were successful—people were clamoring to learn English and seemed interested in improving sanitary conditions. Others even fashioned their homes on the models presented by mission workers. Still, Hispanos were not converting; most chose to remain Catholic. In the fifty years after annexation, this cultural interplay between Anglo-Protestant and Hispano Catholic culture was repeated in many small villages in New Mexico. Depending on a variety of social, economic, and political variables that changed depending on circumstances, locations, and people, the making of Americans was an inconsistent process at best. By 1900, it would have been impossible, as Colonel Sumner had suggested in 1847, to abandon the territory. One could not just close off, or ignore, that which was alien or different. But what if attempts had been made to change the people, to convert them, all to little avail? These were issues and questions raised year after year in Protestant periodicals such as the *Home Mission Monthly*. The answer came from the mission women assigned to teach in these villages. Somewhat hesitantly, they began to suggest that toleration of difference might be one answer.

CHAPTER THREE

"Understanding the Way": Becoming a Missionary

The women who created and administered the WEC had in mind an organization that would wield considerable influence in national affairs and spread the glories of a "free" and "Christian" nation in places like New Mexico, inhabited by people they considered "foreign." In 1880 the WEC employed 25 teachers and raised $11,467 to support their activities; by 1899 the number of teachers had increased to 347 and the organization raised $330,000 to maintain mission schools across the nation and in Cuba and Puerto Rico.[1] Forty-eight were employed in New Mexico, responsible for 25 schools which reported a total enrollment of 1,446 students.[2] The women's mission enterprise continued to expand, suffering only temporary setbacks when the nation was plunged into depression in the 1890s.[3]

---

[1] "Summary of Two Decades," *Home Mission Monthly* 14 (May 1900): 149.

[2] *Home Mission Monthly* 14 (July 1900): 201.

[3] After showing steady increases in both the numbers of teachers employed and monies raised from 1879 to 1890, WEC records show that the numbers employed decreased by 21 from 1890 to 1891, with a very small increase of $1,000 in donations. The organization recovered in 1892, showing a one-year increase of $25,790 in contributions. The 21 employees who had been cut were rehired, but revenues declined again in 1893–94 by $37,483 and the number of teachers was once again cut. The organization recovered again in 1895, only to suffer declines in 1896. The high point in the 1890s came in 1892–93, when the organization raised $373,142 and employed 379 teachers. For a list of the numbers employed and monies raised see "Summary of Two Decades," p. 149.

Their success, however, was largely dependent on the actions and work of the individual women missionaries they employed. Unlike the more prominent women who sat on the board, Jane Hoge or Julia Wright McNair, or even the leaders of the organization, Mary James and her successor, Katherine Jones Bennett, the individual women who entered the mission field had more humble motivations and aspirations. Their choice of mission work reflected their deep religious devotion and a search for a structure that would allow them to unite spiritual with practical needs. Most of them desired to do "useful" work or work that served some larger purpose. They were guided by what they read in the mission literature and heard from returning missionaries—religious and sentimental appeals to women to contribute their labor in the cause of the nation and other women. When they arrived in New Mexico they knew little about the history of the land or of the people. What they knew best was that they had been promised rewards that had little to do with earthly and practical needs.

The very success of the enterprise, its ability to raise large sums of money, to open new schools in new fields, and to hire additional teachers each year, highlights its more practical side. The women who entered the movement found that they had to balance the ideals, the promised spiritual rewards, with the realities of the work. It was the paradox of women's work in the late nineteenth century—that performed by middle-class Anglo-American women—that, if need be, they should work without seeming to. The mission leaders capitalized on this paradox to recruit women. Their intention may have been to expand women's opportunities by pushing slightly at the limits of roles determined by the ideology of domesticity, but the administrative requirements, as well as the Hispano response to mission teachers, led women to challenge those limits. Once in the field, at their mission schools, individual missionaries came to understand how fleeting the spiritual rewards were and how difficult it was to convert Hispanos, and they focused instead on their work as teachers, highlighting the more secular skills they had brought to the job.

† † †

When Mariette Wood of Trenton, New York, applied for a position with the Woman's Executive Committee in 1881, mission work was one of several jobs she was pursuing. At the time of her application Wood was twenty-nine years old and had taught kindergarten in Rome, New York, for eight years.[4] Wood was one of the 230 women the Woman's Executive Committee of Home Missions assigned to New Mexico before 1920.[5] All were single women, though sixteen had been widowed.[6] Wood was one of seven missionaries who hailed from New York State. The largest group came from Pennsylvania, while the majority of the women assigned to New Mexico were from the states that had constituted the Old Northwest—Ohio, Indiana, Michigan, and Wisconsin—and those along the Mississippi River Valley—Minnesota, Illinois, Iowa, and Missouri.[7]

Very few came from large cities; most had grown up in small towns, which had been largely rural but were in the process of being indus-

[4] Biographical information for Mariette Wood is drawn from a series of letters she exchanged with Faith Haines, corresponding secretary of the WEC. See Wood to Haines, August 18, 1881, RG 105, Box 2, Folder 7, PHS.

[5] This is an approximate figure because the haphazard record-keeping procedures used by the WEC do not allow for a more exact count. The names of the 230 missionary women were compiled from a reading of the *Home Mission Monthly* and the lists of teachers published in the Appendix to the *Annual Report* of the Home Missions Board of the Presbyterian Church. In the *Annual Report*, teachers were listed by station within a particular field. Of these 230, the Department of History and Records Management Services, Presbyterian Church (U.S.A.), Philadelphia (hereafter PHS) has biographical, or H5, files for 80 women, 15 who began mission work before 1890, 12 between 1890 and 1900, 29 between 1900 and 1910, 17 between 1910 and 1920, and 7 who were assigned to this field after 1920. The numbers assigned dwindled after 1920, but I have included those who were in charge of the stations that remained open, such as Edith Agnew. For a basis of comparison with other home missionaries see, for instance, Ronald Butchart, "Recruits to the 'Army of Civilization': Gender, Race, Class and the Freedmen's Teachers, 1861–1875," *Journal of Education* 172 (1990): 76–87. Butchart has compiled a data base of over 5,000 missionaries who worked with the freedmen following the Civil War. Other, more qualitative studies, include Polly W. Kaufman, *Women Teachers on the Frontier* (New Haven: Yale University Press, 1984); Jacqueline Jones, "Women Who Were More Than Men: Sex and Status in Freedmen's Training," *History of Education Quarterly* 19 (Spring 1979): 47–59; Jones, *Soldiers of Light and Love: Northern Teachers and Georgia Blacks, 1865–1873* (Chapel Hill: University of North Carolina Press, 1980); John P. McDowell, *The Social Gospel in the South: The Woman's Home Mission Movement in the Methodist Episcopal Church, South, 1886–1939* (Baton Rouge: Louisiana State University Press, 1982); and Peggy Pascoe, *Relations of Rescue: The Search for Female Moral Authority in the American West, 1874–1939* (New York: Oxford University Press, 1990).

[6] Women who had been widowed were indicated by the inclusion of the designation "(Mrs.)" by their names in the *Annual Report*.

[7] I was able to determine a home state for 86 missionaries. The largest number, 18, were from Pennsylvania, 11 hailed from Ohio, and 7 each from New York, Illinois, and Minnesota. Five listed their home state as Missouri. Colorado, Iowa, and Kansas each produced 4. Indiana, Michigan, and Wisconsin each claimed 3. Others listed included Arkansas (1), Washington, D.C. (1), Massachusetts (2), Nebraska (1), North Dakota (1), New Jersey (1), New Mexico (1), Tennessee (1), and West Virginia (1).

trialized in the latter part of the nineteenth century. From eastern Pennsylvania, from Kennett Square and Germantown, came Annie Speakman and Mary Yeats; home for Eva Rupert and Harriet Elliot was Bloomsburg and Williamsport, in central Pennsylvania; and from western Pennsylvania came the Craig sisters, Elizabeth and Lucy, who claimed Pittsburgh and Homestead as their hometowns. Joining them from western Pennsylvania were Grace Russell and Annetta Bell from Clarion County and Meadville. By the late nineteenth century, most of these towns had developed a manufacturing base. Williamsport was a lumbering center, while the backbone of the economy in Bloomsburg was silk weaving and carpet manufacturing. In Homestead, steel plants would dominate the local economy; Meadville would become home to the "slide fastener" or zipper. Kennett Square was described as a "prosperous appearing community of red brick and stone houses on narrow winding streets." Its major industry was a mushroom cannery, and it had become the "major shipping center for fresh mushrooms."[8]

Just as their "sisters" in Pennsylvania had watched as manufacturing took the place of agriculture, so did the other young missionaries who came from farther west, from Ohio, Indiana, Illinois, and up into the Great Lakes region of Wisconsin, Michigan, and Minnesota. Jennie Herron grew up in Munising, Michigan, where the lumber industry was the mainstay of the economy. In 1904, the year Laura Soule moved to New Mexico, the first automobile factory in her hometown of Flint opened. Previously the town's economy had been built on lumbering and carriage building. By 1870, Minneapolis, home to Angeline Badger and Hannah MacLennan, was the leading producer of flour in the nation. Both Minneapolis and St. Peter, homes to Anna Krohn, were important market centers for outlying farms.[9]

Abbie Sawyer came from Galesburg, Illinois, which had been settled by Presbyterians a generation before her birth in 1864. Alarmed by the dearth of religious and educational institutions in the West, Presbyterian minister George Gale had, in 1835, led his followers to western Illinois, where he dreamed of building a manual labor college that would, in turn, support a village of farmers. By the 1860s, Galesburg was well

---

[8] For information about these towns see *Pennsylvania: A Guide to the Keystone State*, compiled by the Federal Writers' Program (New York: Oxford University Press, 1940).

[9] *Michigan: A Guide to the Wolverine State*, compiled by the Federal Writers' Program (New York: Oxford University Press, 1941), pp. 562, 248; *Smithsonian Guide to Historic America: The Great Lakes States* (New York: Stewart, Tasri & Chang, 1988).

established, serving as the home of Knox College, as well as a railroad hub and as a supply center for surrounding farms. From further west came Alice Blake, born near Okoboji, Iowa, an area known for its rich farmlands but also as the site of an Indian uprising in the late 1850s. Clover Mahan listed Lyon, in the dairy farming region of Iowa, near the Mississippi River, as her home.[10]

At the outset of the enterprise, in the 1870s and 1880s, the application process to become a missionary was informal, suggesting that this network was extensive, flexible, and fluid. Along with appeals made in the *Home Mission Monthly*, new teachers were often recommended by their ministers or other women already in the field or were found from among families who had several members already serving as missionaries. Applications were not made in any systematic fashion. Recruitment was by word-of-mouth. Often mission teachers requested that special friends or relatives be appointed to assist them. For example, soon after her arrival in Albuquerque, Salome Verbeck asked the Woman's Executive Committee if a place could be found for her old friend Harriet Phillips. Verbeck suggested that she could even find a church willing to pledge Phillips's salary. Soon thereafter, Phillips arrived in Albuquerque to work as matron at the school.[11]

Other mission teachers in New Mexico had relatives already serving the home mission movement.[12] Sisters joined sisters, and widowed mothers came to work with their daughters.[13] Three female relatives of male home missionary James M. Shields were employed as mission teachers. Shields himself married mission teacher Belle Leech in 1879.[14] Marriage between missionaries was not uncommon in this early period. Jessie Lime married E. M. Fenton; each of them also contributed sisters

---

[10] *Illinois: A Descriptive and Historical Guide*, compiled by the Federal Writers' Project (Chicago: A. C. McClung, 1946), pp. 550–52; *Iowa: A Guide to the Hawkeye State*, compiled by the Federal Writers' Project (New York: Hastings House, 1938), pp. 408, 469.

[11] Salome Verbeck to Faith Haines, November 27, 1880, RG 51, Box 1, Folder 16, PHS.

[12] Of the total number of women who served in New Mexico, forty-eight claimed other family members in the mission field. Most worked with another family member in New Mexico, generally a sister or mother.

[13] Missionary teams of sisters included Elizabeth and Lucy Craig; Alice, Bertha, and Cordelia Hyson; Rebecca and Mary Rowland; and Prudence and Jennie Clark. Mother-daughter teams included Leva and Annie Granger, S. E. and Lizzie Carpenter, and Mrs. J. P. Hills and Delia.

[14] The three missionary teachers with the name Shields were Floretta, Lora, and M (no full name given).

to the home field.[15] Widow J. W. Sharon began work as a Bible reader in Santa Fe, accompanied by her young son Willie, and in 1879 she married missionary J. D. Perkins. Charity Ann Gaston, the first mission teacher to New Mexico, married the Reverend John Menaul in the early 1870s.

The core of the home mission movement in the years before 1900, composed primarily of workers connected by family or marriage, was expanded by bringing in unrelated single women. In their late twenties, with few prospects for marriage, these spinsters were asserting autonomy, searching for work independent of family, challenging traditional ideas that they should remain at home to care for elderly parents.[16] They were pious women, their sincerity attested to by the ministers who recommended them. They knew very little about the work itself, and as they prepared their applications they seemed less concerned with the conditions of the work than with the spiritual benefits it provided.

In his letter of recommendation, Mariette Wood's minister explained that in her case mission work was an afterthought, a choice she had come to recently. She had had, he explained "comparatively slight experience in visiting the poor and sick," and her church work consisted of heading the Primary Department of the Sabbath school. Her decision to apply for a mission position had apparently been made with some hesitation. Wood's mother, a widow, objected to her daughter traveling any distance from home. Wood herself preferred foreign mission work. At her sister's intervention, Wood's mother agreed that her daughter might join the home mission movement. Her sisters agreed to assume the care and support of the widowed Mrs. Wood, leaving Mariette free from financial responsibility for her mother and able to pursue opportunities independent of family.[17]

Wood's training as a kindergarten teacher made her a particularly appealing candidate. As the enterprise grew older and larger, family connections would not suffice. The Woman's Executive Committee preferred women who had specialized teaching skills or who had acquired some higher education. Of the twenty-eight women who appear to have attended college, seventeen attended a Presbyterian college. The most popular institution among this group of missionaries was Park College, in Parkville, Missouri. Founded in 1875 as a coeducational institution,

---

[15] Mary Lime and Carrie Fenton.

[16] For the seventy-three women for whom we know the age at application, the average age was thirty-one years.

[17] Reverend Taylor to Faith Haines, June 23, 1881, RG 105, Box 1, Folder 7, PHS.

Park College educated ten of the mission teachers who were assigned to New Mexico, from Mary Higgins and Jennie Kipp, who traveled to New Mexico in 1881, to Edith Agnew, who, in 1929, was one of the last women teachers assigned there.

Park College was intended to train leaders for the church, and its mission and structure are indicative of the economic position of many of the women who chose home missions. The founders of Park believed that the "best leadership of the church and state might come from those men and women who lacked financial resources." This philosophy served as the basis for the cooperative plan the college instituted. No student was refused admission because of inability to pay the tuition. Instead, students helped to run the college, and their days were divided between physical labor and course work.[18] As a part of the Protestant effort to Christianize the West, Park College aimed to train young men and women of the West and Southwest. These people, the founders of the college believed, would be better able to spread the Gospel among the peoples of the West. This group, more than those from the East, would be "inured to hardship, acquainted, and in sympathy with the people among whom they are to live and labor."[19] By 1890 the college had graduated four hundred students, and 50 percent of its graduates had become missionaries.[20]

Although it is impossible to determine what qualities drew students to Park, whether it was the cooperative work plan or its reputation for training missionaries, the college's social philosophy may have appealed to many of these young women. A 1907 history of the college stated that Park sought to promote an education intended to "advance a genuine brotherhood among men." By the time that Irene Bernheim, Henriette Caskey, Alexia Duncan, Emilie Gillespie, and Alice Reid attended Park in the early 1900s, the college had a larger goal than simply training "moneyless" students to spread the Gospel. The "solution" to the country's "social and industrial problems" was to be found in its graduates. "Practical sympathy can alone bridge the chasm between labor and

[18] For more information on Park College see Lucinda Templin, "Some Defects and Merits in the Education of Women in Missouri" (Ph.D. diss., University of Missouri, 1926), pp. 123–34.

[19] See the Park College charter of 1879, RG 32, Box 22, Folder 3, PHS.

[20] Templin, "Some Defects and Merits," p. 123. See also *Presbyterian Colleges* (New York: College Board of the Presbyterian Church in the U.S.A., 1913). In 1913, the college claimed 795 graduates, 181 of whom worked as ministers; 53 women were listed as missionaries, with an additional 161 listed as teachers. It is not clear whether those listed as teachers were working within the mission movement.

capital," intoned the leaders of Park College, "practical sympathy once established and by wholesome training maintained will do far more than bridge—it will abolish the chasm; it will institute in our society the true community of life."[21]

Other missionaries sought this emphasis on social harmony, sympathy, and friendship in their education as well. Charlotte Richardson graduated from high school but never attended college. She did seek out preparatory training before applying for mission work by enrolling at the Schauffer Missionary Training School in New York. Schauffer was described as an interdenominational and interracial training school for Christian service among the needy. Organized to train young women to work among immigrants, it was intended to introduce American young women to their "foreign born sisters." "Familiar intercourse" between Americans and foreigners would benefit both groups, but for the Americans this meeting would enlarge "their outlook, conquer prejudices, create respect, and deepen and broaden their sympathies." "Friendships," argued the founders of Schauffer, "mould society. The Christian friend is the salt of the earth and the light of the world."[22]

Not all the women who joined the enterprise had an explicitly Christian education. Instead, they had attended normal school, seeking a more practical education.[23] Bessie Hunt and Anna Melton had both attended National Normal, while Carrie Rigg and Abbie Sawyer had taken teacher training at Illinois Normal. Founded in 1857, Illinois Normal quickly came to be considered one of the best of the normal schools in the country. The course of study was designed to take three years, but was of different lengths depending on what grades and subjects a student wanted to pursue. Students desiring to teach the elementary grades generally attended for one year. At Illinois the favored pedagogy was one called Herbartianism, which preached what was called a "doctrine of

[21] See "The Story of Larger Things," unpublished history of Park College, 1907, RG 32, Box 22, Folder 5, PHS.

[22] Henry Tenney, *The Schauffer Missionary Training School*, (1912), NYPL.

[23] For the forty-eight women whose educational background is known, eleven noted having attended a normal school. These all appear to have been public institutions, Oswego and Ogdensburg Normal in New York, Pittsburgh Normal in Pennsylvania, National Normal in Ohio, Northern Normal in Michigan, Illinois Normal in Illinois, and Kirksville Normal in Missouri. Some missionaries also attended the summer sessions held at Colorado Normal or (later) State in Greeley, Colorado, while stationed in New Mexico.

interest." Teachers, the faculty stressed, should organize their curriculum less around textbooks than the children's special interests.[24]

Although normal schools specifically prepared women to teach, the flexibility of the courses offered may also have made them particularly attractive to the future missionaries, many of whom may not have had the wherewithal to attend college. Normal schools provided in-service training, allowing a woman to gain experience while she gained an education. In addition, she could teach during the year and attend summer sessions at the nearest normal school, again combining work and education.[25] Anna Melton, in her application for mission work, distinguished between the two normal schools she had attended, asserting that at Western Normal in Bushnell, Illinois, she had taken a "classical" course that had included both Latin and Greek, while at National Normal in Lebanon, Ohio, she had taken a "scientific" course that covered the pedagogy of teaching.[26] While colleges emphasized the more traditional "classical" course, the normal schools proved more flexible in meeting the needs of a group of women who were constantly weighing their desire for more education with their need for financial security.

† † †

In their search for useful work, the women drawn to the mission movement evidenced confusion about work itself. As Daniel Rodgers has suggested, middle-class women "faced a paradoxical set of expectations. They were to work but . . . not seem to work."[27] The dilemma for these women, who needed to earn an income, was how to do so yet

[24] For a brief overview of the history of normal schools, including a discussion of Illinois Normal, see Charles A. Harper, *A Century of Public Teacher Education* (Trenton: National Education Association of the United States, 1939), pp. 83–127.

[25] The summer term at the Colorado State College of Education, the normal school founded in 1894 and the school attended by some of the missionaries assigned to New Mexico during their summer breaks, offered a six-week summer term that proved extremely popular. Most of those who attended this course were female (80 percent), the average age was twenty-one, and most had taught an average of thirty-five months. The summer session was intended to allow students to complete a normal course and to do advanced work. See William Fred Hartman, "The History of Colorado State College of Education—The Normal School Period—1890–1911" (Ph.D diss., Colorado State College of Education, 1951), pp. 150–57.

[26] See application, Anna Melton Biographical File, H5, PHS.

[27] Daniel T. Rodgers, *The Work Ethic in Industrial America, 1850–1920* (Chicago: University of Chicago Press, 1978), p. 208.

remain "gentlewomen." The process of choosing work could be arbitrary because women were limited by the various forces that exercised influence in their lives. Mariette Wood, for example, did not apply to the WEC with the express purpose of doing missionary work in New Mexico. In fact, in describing her choice of mission work, the minister wrote that Wood's "sympathies had been specially moved toward the Africans." Nor did Wood fall into the work for lack of other choices. As she waited to hear back from the WEC, she was also being considered for a job at a local kindergarten.

Indeed, Wood seems to have taken a passive role in the process. Her application was the result of a lengthy negotiation in which Wood sought to balance her own needs with those of her mother and her minister. A sister suggested that her mother's objections could be overcome if she chose work close to home, and Wood had rejected a suggestion by the Reverend Taylor that she go to Alaska. It was the area that most interested him, he admitted, but Wood did not know "herself as in comparison with such work." She had accepted the guidance of the minister in choosing mission work, at the same time respecting her mother's desire that she work closer to home. Home mission work seemed an ideal compromise: Wood would be performing work that would serve a larger cause and gain some measure of independence from her family without compromising her respectability.[28]

If Wood had some sense of the larger opportunities inherent in mission work, it was not based on her knowledge of the "rules and customs of the mission," of which she knew little. Rather, it may have come from the teachings of her minister and the mission literature she had read, which emphasized that mission work offered women such as Wood a new way to gain self-respect, although it was self-respect earned through self-sacrifice. Writing in the *Home Mission Monthly*, poet Lillian Blanche Fearing posed the spiritual problem facing working women: "Alas? What have I done? What have I done?" Seeking to locate the source of

---

[28] In his letter to Faith Haines, the Reverend Taylor outlined the family problems Wood faced in making this decision. See letter of June 23, 1881, RG 105, Box 1, Folder 7, PHS. In her book on women in rural New York, Paula Baker has argued that mission work held a special appeal to women in small towns and villages because it "guaranteed praise and fascinating stories" and "greater satisfaction than working with local people." She also suggests that rural women preferred to support missionaries, to address social problems elsewhere before they turned their attention to local problems. See Baker, *The Moral Frameworks of Public Life: Gender, Politics, and the State in Rural New York, 1870–1930* (New York: Oxford University Press, 1991), pp. 64, 80.

the spiritual malaise she felt, Fearing surveyed her life's work and concluded that she was not an idle woman ("No idle hands into my bosom creep"). Yet her life seemed lacking in accomplishment and spiritual contentment ("So, viewless, melt my days, and from me run"). She had enjoyed many fine experiences ("I have not missed the fragrance of the flowers / or scorned the music of flowing rills"). Still, she felt a loss. Turning to God, she looked for a divine sign that would illumine her life's worth. She was waiting for a "light of mighty triumphs won."[29]

Mariette Wood's patience and sense of self-sacrifice were tested from the outset. Her application accepted, Wood waited to hear about her station assignment. She found herself waiting and waiting. Worried that she would soon have to earn some money, Wood wrote Faith Haines, the corresponding secretary, an urgent note: "I am quite anxious to know very soon, whether or not you have a place for me in the mission fields. I would wait patiently for the matter to be decided were it not that I must engage myself in other work if I am not needed as a missionary."[30] Wood confided that she was being considered for a position as a kindergarten teacher and would have to respond to that offer soon. Time was of the essence, she insisted, and asked Haines to respond quickly. Three weeks later, Wood wrote to the Woman's Executive Committee again, saying that "if the matter is *wholly decided*" she was prepared to leave for New Mexico immediately. Only after she had received her assignment did Wood inquire about money, even though her letters to Faith Haines imply that she was worried about her finances. She was embarrassed that she did not have more money and worried that it might in some way alter her status when she hesitantly stated, "There is one matter of which perhaps mention should have been made earlier and that is the state of my finances." She wrote that she had not "thought very much about the finances," and she also acknowledged that she knew little about the "roles and customs of the mission."[31] Her request for information about the practicalities of mission life came as an afterthought.

What are we to make of Wood's afterthoughts? It is unclear from the correspondence which job provided better opportunities—teaching kindergarten or working as a missionary. Salary seems not have been the prime consideration or Wood would have inquired about it earlier in her

---

[29] Lillian Fearing, "What Have I Done," *Home Mission Monthly* 1 (June 1887): 169.
[30] Mariette Wood to Faith Haines, August 9, 1881, RG 105, Box 1, Folder 7, PHS.
[31] Mariette Wood to Faith Haines, August 29, 1881, ibid.

correspondence with the Woman's Executive Committee. The kind of work required by each position was not dissimilar. In both jobs she would teach. Independence may have been a more important consideration. The kindergarten job was closer to home, whereas going to New Mexico would take her far from her family. Wood's actions, however, were far from defiant. Reconciling herself to her mother's doubts about foreign mission work, Wood had compromised by choosing home mission work. Perhaps piety or her religious commitments influenced Wood's choice. About her desire to do mission work, her minister said, "She means it: Her heart is in it: She is a mild, gentle person, of few words, but is a choice spirit."[32]

In her poem in the *Home Mission Monthly* Lillian Fearing had warned that even in mission work, in the service of God, a woman could feel dissatisfaction. If she expected earthly rewards she was sure to be disappointed. Nor was it enough to forsake the promise of material rewards to pursue reform work; women must be prepared to feel disillusioned. She urged women to be "still," to "restrain thy lips from woe." The "fruits" of this "mighty" work would come only after death. Life itself, she argued, is "but a flower." For her service, a woman would receive her reward in heaven. Her life would take shape, become visible to others only after her death ("Death is life's mourning"). This point is proved by the fact that volunteers in the cause of home missions were generally recognized in the mission literature only after their deaths; we learn their biographies only in their obituaries.

The mission literature was not atypical; popular literature echoed these sentiments. In all the debate concerning women's work, that which may have represented most faithfully the sentiments and desires of the middle-class women who found their way to the mission movement was Louisa May Alcott's novel *Work*.[33] In this novel, the principal character, Christie Devon, leaves home at age twenty to take a job, seeking certain material and spiritual rewards, as well as independence. In the succeeding years she progresses through the series of respectable but emotionally taxing jobs available to Anglo-Protestant women in the mid-nineteenth

[32] Reverend John Taylor to Faith Haines, June 23, 1881, ibid.

[33] Louisa May Alcott, *Work: A Story of Experience* (1873; reprint, New York: Schocken Books, 1977). Patricia Hill surveys other examples of popular literature which she argues contributed to the romance of missions, helping to prepare young women for this kind of work (*The World Their Household: The American Woman's Foreign Mission Movement and Cultural Transformation, 1870–1920* [Ann Arbor: University of Michigan Press, 1985], pp. 8–22).

century. As a servant she encounters the petty tyranny of a vain and selfish mistress. She becomes an accomplished actress even though her success causes jealousy among other members of the company. Her career on the stage ends when she suffers a serious and debilitating accident. As a governess Christie fends off unwanted romantic advances from her employer's brother. Hired to serve as a companion to an emotionally disturbed young woman, Christie must sit by helplessly as the woman's condition worsens and she finally commits suicide. She moves on to work as a seamstress. In this job she befriends another seamstress, grows to value her companionship, but later finds that she must choose between her work and her friendship when her friend is fired for past indiscretions. Without work, Christie finds herself penniless, lonely, without friends or hope.

Unlike Horatio Alger's rags-to-riches Dick Hunter, the hero of the popular primer for young boys in this era, *Ragged Dick*, Alcott's Christie Devon learns that she cannot expect material rewards from a life of respectable work. In fact, a woman's respectability is tested at every turn, if not by an employer, then by the conditions of work that leave single or independent women living on the margins of poverty. Christie can forgive her fellow seamstress's former life as a prostitute because she too has lived on that margin. The central question posed by Alcott in the first half of her story is, How, given the reality of the unrewarding nature of women's work, are women to make work a worthwhile endeavor?

Alone at a pier one night, Christie tries to end her life, and herein begins her conversion. She wakes to find that she has been saved by a group of evangelical social reformers who nurse her back to physical and emotional health. Within this milieu of Christian evangelism, Christie discovers work that is both meaningful and useful. What distinguishes this work from the other jobs she has held is that her employers, those who shape the work, recognize and reinforce social connections, placing a premium on social contact and visiting. The mechanics are no different: reform work requires the wide range of domestic skills she has acquired in her past experience. She employs the nursing skills gained as a governess and companion. Her experience as a servant and seamstress make her invaluable household help. Her acting has developed her voice. But this work does not lead to the end of a pier. Rather, she takes to the platform making public speeches in support of social reform.

As a reformer, Christie uses her skills in the service of others. They are not ends in and of themselves. Using the skills she has acquired, she learns that to be a productive worker she must value the social relations over the mechanics or the daily routine of the work. Women must look not for financial or material but for spiritual rewards. In fact, material rewards are dangerous; they lead to a life of idleness. At a reunion with several other women who have toiled with her in past jobs, Christie asserts that her own liberty, as well as women's in general, is predicated on "learning that the greatest of God's gifts to us is the privilege of sharing his great work." In Alcott's book, service in the name of God is the purest form of work. Placed in this perspective, the routine of daily tasks, the petty tyrannies and bad temperaments exhibited by others, and the lack of material reward cease to be burdens. Instead, they ennoble women. Christie and other women performing similar work are not alone. Evangelical Christian work has brought together a "loving league of sisters." Together, "young and old, black and white, rich and poor," they will work for a harmonious social order.[34]

Sentimental literature like Alcott's presented a charmed picture of reform work. In reality, no pretense was made about the difficulty of the work. The *Home Mission Monthly* stated that "mission work is not preaching grand sermons, or witnessing marvelous baptisms; it is patient Christlike life, day by day, far from external help, far from those we love; a quiet sowing of tiny seeds, which may take long years to show above the ground, combined with a steady bearing of loneliness, discomfort and petty persecutions."[35] The difference between the drudgery of mission work and that of secular work was that mission work was what God himself, the highest authority, did, and he explicitly called on women to aid him. Reform work was the "master's command," the "Gospel's call."

Implicit in this language was a political message. The literature that called women to this work invoked an ideology of domesticity or a preoccupation with family, but the work was appealing not because women could recreate familial relations but because of its promise to empower them and send them beyond the family into the public world.[36] The

[34] Alcott, *Work*, pp. 442–43.

[35] "The Right Kind of Missionary Teachers," *Home Mission Monthly*, 3 (November 1888): 8.

[36] The impact of the ideology of domesticity on women's political behavior has been debated by historians of women. Most argue that this ideology separated women from the arena of traditional politics, creating a dichotomy between men's and women's activities. Mary Ryan in *Cradle of the Middle Class: The Family in Oneida County, New York, 1780–1865* (New

appeal was not to do "woman's work" but to do everything. As a Professor Tyler wrote in the *Home Mission Monthly*: "Why prescribe the limits? Go everywhere and make all things new."[37]

How were women to interpret this literature? Warned that the work was difficult, full of drudgery, they were also made to feel that by doing this work they were engaging in a noble political and spiritual cause and promised that adversity would be rewarded. Useful work was equated with "loneliness, discomfort and petty persecution," with no material return or a tangible product. Instead, self-sacrifice was rewarded. The Reverend J. W. Bain juxtaposed women's work as missionaries with the work of educators, writers, philosophers, and scientists, arguing that "they are doing something, nay are doing much, to promote personal, social and domestic and political well being on earth, and fill life with comforts." But, he stressed, mission work was much more important: "They may adorn the temple; you are laying the foundation and building the edifice." Women missionaries were unsung heroines for their unseen work. "They may train, develop, invigorate, and delight the human interest," he continued. "You are bringing hope to human hearts, and revealing life and love, eternal happiness and glory to Immortal souls."[38]

Although intended to empower women, the image that mission and sentimental literature promoted was, paradoxically, that of a woman worker with no self-interest. The emphasis on self-sacrifice was a heightened emphasis on the self, but it was a self who worked without complaining. A woman was to have a public role, but she was to perform it without raising her voice. Women were discouraged from acting and speaking in ways that could be construed as selfish. As a reformer, as a missionary, a woman had a direct relationship to God and a personal calling to do the work. The ideal presented was that the work of Christian reform was large, the mission magnificent, the workers small but peerless, and the rewards bestowed not by humans but by God. The literature that promoted Christian reform movements presented both the

---

York: Cambridge University Press, 1981), and Barbara Epstein in *The Politics of Domesticity: Women, Evangelism, and Temperance in Nineteenth-Century America* (Middletown, Conn.: Wesleyan University Press, 1981), both suggest that nineteenth-century women self-consciously created a separate sphere for themselves, emphasizing the "private" concerns of family and social reproduction.

[37] Professor Tyler, "Young Women, Go West," *Home Mission Monthly* 1 (September 1887): 9.

[38] Reverend J. W. Bain, "Woman's Power in Saving the West," *Home Mission Monthly* 1 (September 1887): 126–27.

fictional heroines, the Christie Devons, and the real-life heroines, the Mariette Woods, with the possibility of useful, noble work unimpeded by the horrors Alcott placed in Devon's path. The relationship was a pure one—between the mission woman and her God.

One cannot underestimate the attraction that this promise of a closer relationship to God held for the women who entered mission work, drawn to Christian social service. In their applications many women referred to the religiosity of their families, to fathers who were elders in their churches, to mothers active in missionary societies, and to their own years spent in Christian Endeavor societies.[39] Some wrote that they felt they had been born to be missionaries; others were following in the footsteps of beloved family members. Violet Alden, who called herself "a woman of few words" and one not given to expressing deeper feelings, described herself as part of a family of "missionary spirit." Her brother and sister had been drawn to the mission enterprise; their deaths had left a void in Alden's life. The "two choicest lives of our family were laid down in this cause," she recalled, and she believed she could pay her deepest respects by following their lead.[40] Mission work was not just a change of jobs and scenery or a way to gain some distance from family members. Instead, for most women it offered an order and structure through which to make sense of disappointment and dissatisfaction. For those women privileged enough not to have felt disappointed or dissatisfied, mission work would serve as an antidote to boredom or ennui. Mission work made difficulty into a virtue.

Josephine Orton, who later accepted an appointment to New Mexico as a home missionary, discussed her "Christian experience" and her "motives for seeking missionary service" in her application to the Presbyterian Board of Foreign Missions in 1906. She was forty-seven when she applied to be a Presbyterian missionary and had already served in Puerto Rico with the American Missionary Association for four years. She described herself as growing up in "religious surroundings." Her grandfather had been a Baptist evangelist. As a child she had wished to be a Christian, but she "could not understand the way." Her first conversion experience came at age fourteen, when she realized that all she had to do "was to keep on taking Jesus as my pattern and guide and trust

---

[39] See, for example, Memo from Grace Russell, October 30, 1933; statement of Edith Agnew, October 25, 1933; and statement of Ruth Barber, January 1934, all in Biographical File, H5, PHS.

[40] Violet Alden Biographical File, ibid.

him for the rest." The thought of Christian service was no longer a "duty" but a "joy." After ten years of teaching in the Chicago public schools, she had begun to feel "yearnings for the mission field." These feelings began when her family moved to California, leaving her alone to board with family friends in Chicago. Soon thereafter she accepted a position with the American Missionary Association for which her minister recommended her even though she was not sure that she had been "called" to the work. Though it was difficult, she had found satisfaction in mission work, and she claimed that it gave her the pleasure that she had not found in public school teaching.[41] Orton would spend ten years in New Mexico moving among schools in Tierra Amarilla, Chimayó, and Dixon.

Like Mariette Wood, Orton had personal motivations for joining the mission enterprise. That ministers directed each of them to mission work suggests that both had sought guidance and comfort in religion at a point of crisis or self-doubt. Both embraced that aspect of the mission movement which was concerned with salvation. Mission work had "saved" them and had offered a new opportunity. This movement of women into mission work might best be described as a kind of hegira, with the mission organizations serving as a structure congenial to women in search of a new identity. Women embraced the opportunities offered by the movement, but its popularity also points to how deeply displaced or unsettled this group or generation of women may have felt. Certainly industrial capitalism and urbanization had opened opportunities not known to their mothers or grandmothers. Changing social mores might allow them to move away from family, but connection to family still served as a major stabilizing force, especially when the jobs available could not ensure a comfortable independent existence. Mission work and all the ideas attached to it allowed women to make a "journey," or "passage," from one life to another within a structure that offered some protection and was familiar. It provided both the ritual and the community necessary to enable these women to change their own lives as well as adapt to the social changes of the times.[42]

---

[41] Josephine Orton to Reverend A. W. Halsey, July 25, 1906, Biographical File, ibid.

[42] In her book about contemporary conversion experiences, *Cities on a Hill: A Journey through Contemporary American Culture* (New York: Simon and Schuster, 1986), Frances Fitzgerald makes a similar argument. She argues that the destination an individual arrives at is not as important as the passage or journey, that it is the journey itself that reveals the "possibility of communitas" (p. 405). The journey allows for dissolution of all known structures and

As Evelyn Brooks Higginbotham has argued in her work on African-American women Baptists, mission work allowed Protestant women to see themselves as "saving force" rather than as "victim." They: "rejected a model of womanhood that was fragile and passive, just as they deplored a type preoccupied with fashion, gossip, or self-indulgence. They argued that women held the key to social transformation, and thus America offered them a vast mission field in which to solicit as never before the active participation of self-disciplined, self-sacrificing workers." The appeal of the mission societies was that they promised not only a job but also rewarding work that would allow Protestant woman to express their religious commitment and spirituality.[43]

Women entered the mission movement expecting to find God at the center of the enterprise. The God depicted in the literature was kind and gentle, promising a haven to all who sought him out. Mission work was God's work, the path had been opened, and the goals predetermined. The promise of the mission movement was a renewed spiritual life; women could live, in the words of missionary Josephine Orton, "an upright and Christ-like life."[44] The ideals of the work tended to discourage individual initiative because all it asked of its workers was self-sacrifice and dedication. The experience of workers contradicted this ideal, however. One's piety was quickly challenged by practical realities. Mission work demanded tremendous initiative and creativity, and God's guidance could sometimes prove illusive. A woman's choice of mission work, her "understanding the way," meant much more in the long run than simply accepting God's word or doing work that fit the prescriptions for respectability.

In her analysis of the missionaries who established rescue homes in the

---

conventions and serves as a "beginning," or a "creative ooze from which new life-forms would emerge" (p. 408). If this formulation is applied to the experience of nineteenth-century Anglo-Protestant women, it would suggest that women embarking on the journey of being a home missionary would be more open to political "re-education."

[43] Elizabeth Brooks Higginbotham, *Righteous Discontent: The Women's Movement in the Black Baptist Church, 1880–1920* (Cambridge, Mass.: Harvard University Press, 1993), p. 122. Higginbotham argues that mission work was one example of the "feminist theology" of these women. Although they did not reject the religious doctrines of the traditional denominations, they did argue for a wider influence within the denominations; they "seized orthodox theology in defense of sexual equality." This may have been the case among African-American Baptists, but I am hesitant to make a similar claim for Anglo-American Presbyterians because I have no evidence that they discussed the issue of sexual equality until after the turn of the twentieth century.

[44] Josephine Orton to Reverend A. W. Halsey, July 25, 1906, Biographical File, H5, PHS.

West in this same period, Peggy Pascoe has argued that these women sought to influence the development of the territory and to counterbalance the excessive masculinity of the West.[45] Patricia Hill has suggested that women were attracted to the mission enterprise by the promise of adventure and escape from the mundane but also by a sense of duty born of the domestic role this society assumed women would fill.[46] In both Pascoe's and Hill's analyses, mission work promised its adherents an enlarged social role without challenging the dominant domestic ideology. Indeed, the founders of the WEC and the subsequent directors of the organization relied heavily on the ideology of domesticity as a vehicle by which to hold together the various groups composing the enterprise. In pursuing the goal of the home mission movement, which at its broadest intended to make a cohesive national culture embracing many different groups, the WEC called forth the experiences of its supporters as mothers, wives, and daughters. The importance and sanctity of the family were emphasized on every page of each piece of mission literature.

For the women's mission enterprise, the family was the symbolic ideal, albeit not an uncomplicated one. The primacy of the family was both glorified and compromised by workers at all levels at different times. An individual's family responsibilities and the demands of the national family did not always coincide. For example, Mariette Wood was attracted to the more abstract ideal of serving the national family, but to work as a missionary, she compromised her own family responsibilities. Most women missionaries remained single. Although some worked with other family members in the field, thereby partially reconstituting their original blood family, others came to think of their clients as family. There was no one definition of family or family duties and obligations, which were shared by all.

The emphasis on family was more than just an appeal to women's maternal instincts or roles as mothers. Running the organization presented the directors with certain difficulties and challenges. They were appealing to two groups of women at the same time—those who would "go to the front," and those who would be "stay-at-homes." The difference between the two groups was based largely on marital status—the expectation was that those women employed as mission workers went to

---

[45] Pascoe, *Relations of Rescue*, p. xvi.
[46] Hill, *The World Their Household*, pp. 23–60.

the "front" because they had no pressing family responsibilities. Hence a woman's place in the life cycle determined the nature of her participation. In the early days of the movement there were places for widows and older single women making career changes. The rules and requirements for employment were often relaxed or overlooked to make room for those women who had a desire to "go to the front." It was only later, after the turn of the century, when the board looked for teaching certification and experience, that the categories of "stay-at-homes" and workers became codified in practice. Initially they existed as a rhetorical device to identify the various roles necessary to the success of the enterprise. Recognizing that these two "classes" of women existed and that both were necessary to the success of mission work, the WEC went to great lengths to create an ideal that transcended the two categories and could lend ideological unity to the movement. The home mission woman—and there was only one regardless of her station and situation—was described as "thoughtful," as a "reader," as "largehearted," as "patriotic," and, of course, as a "Christian . . . above all else."[47]

The WEC hoped to reproduce social interaction similar to that expected of family life, particularly social harmony. By using the rhetoric of family, the WEC was appealing to a set of responsibilities and obligations entailed in family life. There were drawbacks to using the nuclear family as a model for a national family in that the roles of husband, wife, and children were seen as complementary. There is no discussion in the *Home Mission Monthly*, for instance, of social equality in family life or even the need for it. The reluctance to recognize and discuss inequities in the family or to admit that their own lives might not be a good model would ultimately affect the way mission workers and supporters thought of clients. As they fashioned ideas about national culture, or a national family, the social hierarchy they accepted as part of their own families was expressed in the social relationships they fostered with various groups of "exceptional peoples." New Mexican Hispanos, for instance, were thought of as "children" and female clients referred to as "backward" sisters.

The most successful tactic used by the WEC to build support for the nascent women's mission movement was to inject patriotic appeals into discussions of women's social roles. Young women were reminded that

---

[47] J. L. Hamilton, "Home Mission Women," *Home Mission Monthly* 6 (October 1892): 284.

their comfort and security, indeed their self-interest, were at stake if the goal of the mission movement were not realized. "This is our country; it is our home," advised one article, arguing that the national family was threatened by "strangers here who do not love the home they have entered." Hence the responsible daughter, the Protestant daughter, was called upon to volunteer herself in the fight to check this evil influence. Mission literature reminded her that she was strong and enthusiastic and that she had a duty to set aside her projects, to forgo "the calls, the entertainments, the reading of new books which her circle in society demands," so that she could help her "less forward sisters." Lack of experience was no excuse to refuse appeals for the home mission effort.[48]

Hence the work a missionary would perform had its roots in family activities. She would help her "less favored sisters to learn their first lessons in reading and writing, and in the art of useful living," drawing on her experience as daughter and sister.[49] The women going to "the front" were making a sacrifice, rejecting immediate material comforts for a more elusive ideal that promised ongoing national political stability. Using the family as a symbol reminded women of the qualities of life they valued. This ideal was to move Anglo-Protestant women, as a group, to action, but it was not necessarily what moved individual women to become missionaries nor was it a blueprint they followed once they entered the work.

The loving network of Christians whom Alcott had depicted as being at the center of religious missions was a significant part of the appeal of the work, but ultimately most mission women recognized that this too was an ideal. More often than not, the promise was tempered by an expanding mission bureaucracy which frustrated missionary efforts as often as it helped. Work that seemed straightforward turned out to have hidden agendas and many layers of meaning. Missionaries would become familiar with the mediating role of the Woman's Executive Committee after accepting the "call," and it would remind them that, no

---

[48] "Why Should Young Ladies Work for the Home Missions?" *Home Mission Monthly* 1 (June 1887): 169–70.

[49] Ibid., p. 170.

matter how "noble" the cause, they did not answer just to God but ultimately to their employer.

Whatever questions individual women missionaries may have had regarding their readiness to do the work or the nature of their "calling" were compounded by a mission effort in the throes of constant reorganization. Intended to promote women's activities and to give women a greater voice, the Woman's Executive Committee instead promoted an image of its workers and supporters as self-effacing. Composed of individuals who were moved by a spirit of generosity and self-sacrifice, the board of directors, which ran the day-to-day operations of the Woman's Executive Committee, as well as the thousands of women who raised money for the effort, did so on a volunteer basis. They sought to subordinate self-interest and personal gain to the larger ideal of a Christian America. To realize these goals, they employed women who could commit their full attention and time, as well as go to the places where they were needed.

In searching out interested young women, the Woman's Executive Committee warned that the home mission field was not "for an indolent, effete, unprogressive people, slumberously rocking to and fro in the well worn cradle of ancestral custom." Recruits to the mission effort were expected to be models of the "most enterprising, inventive, nervous, forceful race of earth, who more than any other people are destined to affect the world for weal or woe."[50] Mission teachers were promised duties extending beyond "secular instruction." Applicants were warned that they could be called on to perform a range of ministerial functions from teaching in the Sabbath school to holding prayer meetings. They should be prepared to visit from home to home, to provide basic medical services, and perhaps even to "pray over a grave." More generally, the Woman's Executive Committee demanded of its applicants a spirit that was described as "bright," "brave," "earnest," "patient," "persevering," and "plodding"; they must not be "easily daunted by failure at first," and, of course, they should be marked by a spirit of "self sacrifice."[51] Behind these idealistic terms, the WEC used more specific and practical criteria to screen applicants. Although the *Home Mission Monthly* optimistically advised that the "weakest need not exclude themselves" from volunteering for mission work, the pamphlet issued by

---

[50] "The Evangelization of the Great West," *Home Mission Monthly* 4 (January 1890): 55.
[51] "The Right Kind of Missionary Teachers," *Home Mission Monthly* 3 (November 1888): 8.

the Woman's Executive Committee explaining the guidelines made good health a prerequisite. It warned that a woman whose health was failing could not expect to see any improvement, especially "when embarking upon new and hard duties." "Delicate women" rarely made good teachers. Education was the second requirement—"not so much the amount as the quality." A normal school training course was desirable but not necessary. In any case, women must have a "thorough" knowledge of the "rudiments" and be able to maintain discipline. A knowledge of music and a good voice were also required.[52]

The Woman's Executive Committee sought women with "well-balanced" minds, described as bright, tactful, practical, and with a sense of "mother-wit." They should have the "power of overcoming obstacles, of rising above difficulties, of meeting objections, of being strong without being strong-minded." The Woman's Executive Committee assumed a certain level of piety among its applicants but warned: "The ardor of first love, a gushing enthusiasm, even a fiery zeal will not carry one through. There must be a *deep* love for the Redeemer, a self-sacrificing spirit, a consecration of life; there must be the chastened temper, the wisdom of meekness, the sweetness of peace and joy."[53]

The Woman's Executive Committee required four certificates of recommendation before approving a candidate: a certificate of membership in a Presbyterian church, a certificate testifying to teaching ability and experience, a statement from a physician indicating the state of the candidate's health, and one from the woman's presbytery testifying to her Christian character and suitability for mission work. Additional suggestions for screening applicants came from the field. A home missionary in Utah urged that candidates be required to have two years of teaching experience and emphasized their ability to act as disciplinarians. If a woman failed in "government" of her classroom, this missionary warned, she would lose the respect of students and parents. It was also suggested that the mission teacher not be under twenty-five or over thirty-five. A woman younger than twenty-five was considered to lack judgment and one over thirty-five was thought to be less adaptable.[54]

[52] Quoted in a draft of a handbook prepared for missionary teachers by the Woman's Executive Committee in the 1880s, "To Our Missionary Teachers" (n.d.), RG 105, Box 6, Folder 23, PHS.

[53] Ibid.

[54] "Requirements for a Mission Teacher," *Presbyterian Home Missionary* 12 (August 1883): 186.

The WEC walked a fine line. The organization did not want to seem to be exclusive; its primary goal, after all, was the expansion of a Christian nation. The directors believed that everyone could have a conversion experience; all Protestants should be missionaries. Yet the work was taxing and demanded strength. Certain requirements were necessary, and they often contradicted the subservient role the male-dominated church demanded of women. Although the church asked women to refrain from preaching, the WEC told its employees that they might need to conduct prayer services or officiate at funerals. The very act of sending single women (or women alone) into remote areas of the country, removed from the direct supervision of men, constituted one more challenge to the patriarchal authority upon which the church rested. Extending the mission movement to include single women represented yet another step in the feminization of Protestantism in the United States.

† † †

Some mission teachers spent only a few months in the field, finding the work unsuitable. The majority worked as mission teachers for a few years before marrying and starting their own families, moving on to other work, or returning to their hometowns to care for elderly and sick parents. A smaller number spent the rest of their lives as missionaries.[55] For the last group, those women who made a life and career in the mission movement, the volunteer spirit that impelled them into the work was quickly replaced by more practical concerns about funds to support themselves and their work. It was this last group who complained in letters to the Woman's Executive Committee corresponding secretaries about the inefficiency and inadequacy of administrative procedures and raised concern about the lack of support and money to do this work properly or to fulfill the job requirements. And, ultimately, it was this

[55] The survey of those assigned shows that 161 spent less than five years in New Mexico, while 30 women remained between five and ten years, 14 between ten and fifteen years, and another 24 worked in New Mexico for more than fifteen years. These numbers tell us only about the number of years women worked in New Mexico. Of the 230 women assigned to the field, 79 had worked in other home mission fields and had been transferred from field to field, suggesting that they considered this to be a career, rather than temporary work. In some cases the biographical files reveal the various fields women worked in; in other cases the only way to determine whether women worked in more than one field is to go through the lists of mission stations and the assigned missionaries, year by year, cross-referencing who worked where and when.

group who made the enterprise as much a social reform as a religious undertaking.

Any veil that had tempered an incisive and honest appraisal of the practicalities of mission work was quickly removed once missionaries were on the job. They learned that teaching was not all that was required of them. They were also to act as preachers and administrators. They would become "jack[s] of all trades." This reeducation occurred in the field as they worked with clients and negotiated with the WEC for supplies and salary. Even then, they exhibited an odd schizophrenia— they wrote with a rhetorical flourish about the ideals of the enterprise in the reports intended for public consumption in the pages of mission journals such as the *Home Mission Monthly* or in fund-raising letters to mission societies. Their letters to the administrators of the WEC, how-ever, show little concern with ideology; they are primarily concerned with administrative neglect. Mission women were not critical of the purpose of their work although some expressed concern about methods and strategies, but most limited their criticism to comments about the lack of supplies and the demanding conditions they faced. Indeed, women in the field seem to have hesitated in confronting the administra-tors with their problems as if to address such mundane issues would call their piety into question. As the home mission effort expanded and more mission stations were opened and greater numbers of teachers em-ployed, the practical side of the enterprise could not be downplayed. In the *Home Mission Monthly*, the appeals to piety and women's sense of service began to share space with requests for donations to support increased salaries or new school buildings. As secular concerns moved to the forefront, the reality of mission work was more fully revealed. By the turn of the century the Woman's Executive Committee had hired typists and clerks to help with correspondence and had established the position of school superintendent to oversee school work in a more orderly and sustained way. In the work itself piety was giving way to professional-ism; lines between volunteers and workers were more clearly delineated. The language of piety became a way to explain away the occasional lapses in professional conduct.

This differentiation between volunteers and employees had not always existed. In the 1870s and 1880s there seems to have been a fluidity between the roles of middle-class volunteers and workers. The questions raised about useful and meaningful work seem not to have been exclu-sive to one group. What distinguished the experiences of the fictional

Christie Devon, for instance, from those of women who had not worked for a wage was not her skills but the education provided by her various work experiences. Fearing's refrain, "What have I done," was a question that could have been asked by any woman, whether a housewife volunteer or a reform worker. Meant on one hand to encourage women to volunteer in the cause of missions on the home front as well as in the field, it also carried a message for women engaged in wage labor. The distinctions grew as the mission administration became increasingly concerned with the training and credentials of its employees. By the turn of the century each group contributed to the life of the organization in different ways, and a greater commitment was expected of the employee than the housewife volunteer even though the administrative end of the enterprise continued to be dominated by volunteers.

By the 1890s, when the Woman's Executive Committee changed its name to the Woman's Board of Home Missions, it boasted of systems and plans and had proved itself an effective fund-raiser, but its heavy reliance on volunteer labor at the administrative end meant that it was not a model of efficiency. For women who had turned to the mission enterprise in search of structure and to mission work to reorder their lives, the administrative confusion of the WEC could be galling. Procedures were unclear and the committee's methods haphazard from the moment women were recruited. Mariette Wood was not the only missionary to wait for an assignment. Alice Hyson's application was solicited by Faith Haines, who wrote to Hyson asking to hear from her "in case you would like to go as a missionary teacher to the Mexicans in that territory." Haines asked Hyson to let her know her age and "what teaching experience you have." Ironically, her teaching experience was apparently less important than the requirement that teachers be able to sing and play the organ. Haines added that unless Hyson had "enough experience to lead children in the Moody and Sankey hymns there is no place at present to which you could go." Despite her knowledge of Moody and Sankey hymns, Hyson was not immediately assigned. In August 1883 the Woman's Executive Committee was considering sending her to Albuquerque. By June 1884 Hyson still lacked an assignment, and Haines reported to her that "I have given up the plan for your going to Utah," proposing instead to send her to Ranchos de Taos in New Mexico. Haines warned her that there might be further changes in plans—"should there be any change do not be surprised"—adding perhaps to reassure a bewildered Hyson, "I presume it will really make no difference as any place would be new to you."[56]

Alice Hyson was eventually sent to Ranchos de Taos. She spent the next thirty years there teaching and administering a plaza school until illness forced her to retire. In those thirty years Hyson saw the WEC expand, become the Woman's Board of Home Missions, and grow into a truly national organization, drawing applicants from across the country, with stations in both rural areas and cities and client populations drawn from among many different minority groups. Missionaries were transferred from station to station; 79 of the 230 missionaries assigned to New Mexico served among two or three different groups in the course of their mission careers. Within the New Mexico field, 55 missionaries worked in more than one community. Initially, teachers were the most sought after. Later, as schooling gave way to providing medical care, nurses and doctors were prized. Not all teachers hired by the WEC worked as teachers. Like the business corporations that would become the Woman's Board's model, mission women were promoted, demoted, even fired if the organization was not satisfied with their performance, or asked to accept jobs that had little to do with teaching except that the missionary was attached to a school; women could be assigned to be community workers, Bible readers, or school matrons.

In the New Mexico field missionaries were sent either to work in a boarding school or in a plaza school. The majority of the women assigned to New Mexico served in one of the three boarding schools that were opened.[57] These schools eased the transition into a foreign culture and provided built-in companionship, but they also had the highest turnover. A core group might remain for some years, but each year there were two or three new recruits, few of whom remained more than one or two years.[58] These boarding schools were more visible than the plaza

[56] Faith Haines to Alice Hyson, August 14, 1883, June 26, 1884, RG 105, Box 2, Folder 9, PHS.

[57] Fifty-six women served in Santa Fe between the years 1867 and 1920, 42 in Albuquerque, and 24 in Las Vegas. In all three locations several attempts were made over a period of years to turn day schools into boarding schools. The boarding school in Las Vegas was short-lived, lasting only a few years in the early 1890s. In Albuquerque, the Indian school gave way in the 1890s to a boarding school for Hispano boys. After several early attempts in the 1870s, what became the Allison-James School for Girls was opened in the 1880s in Santa Fe.

[58] For example, at the Allison School for Girls in Santa Fe (renamed Allison-James in 1913) between 1898 and 1905, a small core of teachers were joined by a constant flow of women who

schools, and they received more attention and resources. They were deemed more successful in Americanizing students because larger numbers of their students ultimately converted to Protestantism. Their supposed success and high visibility among church members and leaders had other consequences. They were among the first missions run by the Woman's Board over which women employees lost control; ultimately women principals would be replaced by men.[59]

Even though an assignment to a plaza school proved more daunting, at least initially, it was in these stations that women missionaries were able to exercise the greatest influence and power. Plaza schools were one-room schools established in the remote villages of northern New Mexico and southern Colorado. They were where the missionaries with the greatest longevity in New Mexico could be found.[60] Generally a single missionary was responsible for teaching and maintaining a plaza

---

served for only a few months of the year. In 1898 the staff was composed of Matilda Allison (serving twelve months), Laura Moore (twelve months), Ellen Moore (twelve months), Lydia Hays (twelve months), Mrs. L. L. Adams (seven months), Myrta Morrow (three months), Mrs. Louise Jones (three months), and Mrs. Jean Leckie (three months). In 1899 the list included Allison, Laura and Ellen Moore, Mrs. Jones (twelve months), Emma Brown (seven months), Myrta Morrow (twelve months), Lydia Hays (twelve months), and Mrs. Adams (five months). Allison, Antoinette Brengle, Laura and Ellen Moore, Jones, Brown, Morrow, and Hays all served the full twelve months in 1900. In 1902, Allison, Brengle, the Moores, Jones, Brown, Morrow, and Leckie were joined by Kate Zimmerman and Caroline Courtney, who transferred in from mission schools in Sunderland, North Carolina and Tahlequah, Indian Territory. By 1904, there was a relatively new crew of teachers: Allison, Brengle, Brown, Morrow, and Zimmerman, joined by Bertha Leadingham, Olinda Meeker, Harriet Woodward (all serving seven and a half months), and Mary Foresman and Eva Rupert (serving four months each). By 1905, Allison had retired, and the staff was composed of Leadingham, Meeker, Woodward, Bessie Reid, Brengle, Rupert, Brown, Morrow, and Zimmerman (all serving the full twelve months). See list, "Missionary Teachers," at the end of the Board of Home Missions, Presbyterian Church in the U.S.A., *Annual Report*, 1898, 1899, 1900, 1902, 1904, and 1905.

[59] The boarding school for girls in Santa Fe, named after its founder, missionary Matilda Allison, was merged with the Menaul School for Boys in Albuquerque and all its operations moved to Albuquerque. The school had always had a female principal. When the merger took place in 1934, Ruth Barber, the principal, was made dean of girls of the Menaul School, a subordinate position under Harper Donaldson, the principal. See Ruth K. Barber and Edith Agnew, *Sowers Went Forth: The Story of Presbyterian Missions in New Mexico and Southern Colorado* (Albuquerque: Menaul Historical Library of the Southwest, 1981), p. 112.

[60] Of the twenty women in this survey who spent more than fifteen years in New Mexico, five worked in the boarding schools, two split their time between plaza and boarding schools, and the remaining thirteen worked primarily in plaza schools. Alice Blake spent forty-one years in four plaza schools, most of them in Trementina. Mollie Clements devoted thirty-six years to San Juan, Colorado, Elizabeth and Lucy Craig, forty-three and sixteen years respectively to El Prado de Taos, Alice Hyson thirty-one years to Taos. In Chimayó, Zoe Ellsworth worked for thirty-two years, and Sue Zuver spent twenty-five years in Peñasco.

school though often the board did allow for a companion—a family member, a former student, or a volunteer. Alice Hyson, for instance, called on the services of two sisters, Cordelia and Bertha Hyson, in the course of her tenure. With the plaza school as a base, the more successful missionaries expanded their duties. Free from the constant supervision of a principal or a local minister, they decided how visible they wanted their schools to be to the larger enterprise. Some women preferred to go about their work with little fanfare, remaining at the periphery, largely invisible. Sue Zuver spent twenty-five years in Peñasco, from 1885 until she retired in 1910, yet there is little correspondence between her and the board, only brief mention of her work is made in the *Home Mission Monthly*, and no biographical information is available. Others, like Alice Blake, made their schools into a public platform from which they relentlessly publicized their work and the needs of the Hispanos among whom they lived, as well as commenting on the direction of the mission enterprise.

Whatever their assignment, women new to the movement quickly discovered how difficult the work was. After being hired and guaranteed a particular wage—rarely more than $450 yearly—many of the women assigned to New Mexico were sent to live in remote communities.[61] Most received little supervision, finding that they did indeed have to rely on "mother-wit." Dutifully, they submitted quarterly reports and awaited a paycheck in return. Like their male counterparts, many of the

---

[61] In 1884, the WEC reported that it employed 133 teachers at an average annual salary of $450. This average seemed to change little over the years. In 1911, it was reported that the average salary for women working among "Mexicans" was $441 (see article "The Whole Work for 1883–84" in Sheldon Jackson Scrapbook on Woman's Home Missions, 1875–84, no. 62, PHS, and the report "Scholarships and Salaries, Re: Assignment of a Particular Pupil or Teacher to a Particular Contributer," RG 105, Box 6, Folder 23, PHS). Salary was determined by a number of factors and the average based on a full year's work. Women who worked fewer months made less. Those who served as the executives at bigger missions also earned more, though not significantly more. In 1889, the Reverend George Smith of Santa Fe wrote the Reverend Henry Kendall recommending that Matilda Allison's salary be raised above the $500 she was then receiving. "She is a marvel of executive ability, economy, and grace," he wrote, "and as head of the school ought to have a larger salary" (Smith to Kendall, December 5, 1889, RG 51, Box 1, Folder 24, PHS). Jennie Ordway, who served in Taos between 1888 and 1891, earned $500 annually. When she resigned in 1929, she had risen to be the superintendent of the Presbyterian San Juan Hospital in Puerto Rico, where in the early 1920s she was earning $900. Mary Donnelly, also a career missionary, began her career in Utah at $400, served in New Mexico from 1898 to 1902, subsequently served at missions in Tennessee, Kentucky, Cuba, and finally retired in 1938 after forty-one years. Her salary at retirement was $800. See Biographical Files, H5, for Jennie Ordway and Mary Donnelly, PHS.

women waited for months, growing anxious as their funds dwindled and they had to borrow from neighbors or other missionaries at nearby stations. Once in the field and aware of the very difficult tasks they confronted, mission women discovered how inadequate the support from the Woman's Board was.

Woman's Board correspondence indicates that mission teachers complained constantly about the conditions under which they lived and worked. The limits of their self-sacrifice were tested by overcrowded schools, having to carve a tiny space in the dining room or schoolroom for a bedroom, or having no building at all. Harriet Phillips, matron at the Indian Industrial school in Albuquerque, complained bitterly of the conditions. A veteran, she compared the conditions to her other mission stations and declared New Mexico the most difficult she had encountered. She explained that the work of school matron was not new to her, that she had supervised whole mission houses and families, but she had never "before coming here . . . [had] to go into the kitchen and with my own hands actually do the work of a servant. Early in life I was taught to keep house and direct the help, but never done the hard work I am compelled to do here."[62] Phillips did work hard. She baked between sixteen to twenty loaves of bread and prepared 110 meals a day and had to entertain a seemingly endless stream of guests, mostly other mission teachers passing through Albuquerque.

Phillips's complaints bear little resemblance to the problems encountered by newly appointed plaza teacher Delia Hills when she arrived to take up her commission in Salazar, a small town in the Jemez Mountains in northwestern New Mexico. Hills's letters to the WEC illustrate the larger and more profound problems that mission teachers faced as they struggled with the bureaucratic and administrative obstacles presented while they tried to teach school. After three months at her job, Hills had not yet received her commission or the quarterly blanks she was to complete before she could receive money. Discouraged, Hills wrote, "We are among strangers, and Spanish-speaking people at that: and I have not the money to do with." Facing an eviction from the room she was using for the school, she reported that "there is no house to be rented." She suggested that unless land was purchased and a schoolhouse built, there would be no way to continue work in Salazar. Her most pressing problem, though, was money. Confused as to who was

---

[62] Harriet Phillips to Faith Haines, March 14, 1881, RG 51, Box 1, Folder 16, PHS.

providing her support and informed by her field supervisor, the Reverend James Shields, that some eastern mission society was sponsoring her, she appealed to the Woman's Executive Committee for a long list of supplies. She had nothing and asked for everything: desks, blackboards, books, and an organ.[63]

Frustrated by the lack of response from the Woman's Executive Committee, Hills explained her dilemma:

A long time before coming to New Mexico, I wrote to Mrs. Haines, asking, "If I had to furnish out of my salary, school supplies." The answer came back to me, that I did not, and if I spent money in providing for the wants of the school, to place the amount in my Quarterly Report and the money would be refunded to me. As I understand school supplies, school supplies included everything needed in a schoolroom. Rent of building, fuel, lights for evening school, desks, blackboard, schoolbooks, slates, etc. and also a Bell; that is an essential adjunct to a schoolroom. But among the qualifications I was obliged to furnish to the Ladies Board, when they were considering the matter of commissioning me, as a missionary teacher, was the fact that I could play the Organ, but I certainly cannot play an Organ, unless I have one, and to buy one out of my salary is out of the question. I did not enumerate, all the articles needed in a schoolroom, when I wrote to Mrs. Haines; but included all under the head of school supplies: naming some of them, however. I naturally judged, that an Organ was supplied from the fact, that I was not asked, whether, I had an Organ, but whether I could play on the Organ. That question was put to me several times.[64]

Hills's preoccupation with the organ reveals the conflict between a mission teacher's expectations and the resources, or lack of them, of the Woman's Executive Committee. Much of the misunderstanding resulted from the committee's desire to hire a young woman whose personality and qualifications suited the expectations of the eastern supporters of the mission movement. Quizzed about their qualifications for leading Moody and Sankey hymns or their ability to play the organ, teacher candidates expected that these skills would play a central role in their work. Misinformed, or simply uninformed, about the conditions they

[63] Delia Hills to Faith Haines, October 24, November 17, 1884, RG 51, Box 1, Folder 17, PHS.
[64] Delia Hills to Faith Haines, November 14, 1884, ibid.

could expect in the field and not prepared to undertake a financial burden, mission teachers expressed exasperation and frustration, prompting responses like Hills's, who wrote, "I hardly think you have an idea of Salazar." Hills was unique in her statement of problems and needs in that she directly addressed the issues troubling her. Many others resorted to writing of their illnesses, as if complaining about physical health was a legitimate way to discuss job-related needs and problems they might not otherwise raise. Hills stuck closely to the presumed requirements of the job, asserting that she was supposed to "build up an attractive school." She could not do so without "something to work with."

Veteran missionaries looking for a new field or in the process of being reassigned were less patient with the Woman's Executive Committee's lack of clarity or commitment and more likely to ask questions. Originally commissioned to teach in Jemez Hot Springs, New Mexico, Salome Verbeck was surprised to learn that she was to open a school. "Is there no school at all yet at Hot Springs," she asked. "Is there some kind of building for a school?"[65] She had heard nothing about the location or the work she was to perform. Asking about the climate, she said she had not been able to find the Hot Springs on a map. Her questions continued: Would she teach Mexican or Indian children? Would she be expected to teach in English? Verbeck never went to Jemez Hot Springs; she ended up as matron in the Industrial School for Indians in Albuquerque. Her questions may have proved irrelevant because assignments changed according to need and available resources. By the time Verbeck was assigned to New Mexico, however, she was experienced in the ways of the WEC. Her complaints probably served a variety of purposes; they were a way to express her dissatisfaction with the organization itself as well as a ploy to secure a different and better assignment.

The ethos of mission work required that missionaries voice their dissatisfaction without seeming confrontational or stretching the limits of respectability. Newly appointed missionaries were warned to "guard against any worldly conformity that may injure your influence for good." They were to refrain from "amusements of questionable character," which included playing cards and attending "dancing parties."[66] Severe reprimands were issued to women who flaunted these rules, and

---

[65] Salome Verbeck to Faith Haines, November 27, 1880, RG 51, Box 1, Folder 16, PHS.
[66] Faith Haines to Jennie Smith, June 27, 1884; Faith Haines to Ella Campbell, July 21, 1884, both in RG 105, Box 2, Folder 10, PHS.

occasionally commissions were rescinded. The case of Jennie Herron illustrates the board's limited tolerance for women who transgressed the code of conduct. Fired for having failed to repay a loan in timely fashion, Herron discovered that, unlike the God who inspired the work, the Woman's Board did not forgive trespasses, especially when they sullied the reputation of the enterprise. The respectability conferred by being appointed a missionary was as easily withdrawn as it was conferred.

According to the minister who recommended Jennie Herron to the Woman's Board in 1908, she had come from a family of questionable reputation but had triumphed over her background. Herron's example illustrates how broadly young women may have interpreted the enterprise's promise of "salvation." She left her job as a country schoolteacher to join the mission enterprise. Her letters of recommendation suggest that Herron was seeking to escape shadows cast over her reputation by a saloonkeeper father and a Catholic stepmother.[67] As a missionary, Herron found "respectability," or more specifically a kind of social mobility, which had eluded her at home. Herron had grown up in a boardinghouse in Munising, Michigan, where she was placed by her father after her mother's death. She "simply grew up" with "anyone who would keep her." "In spite of circumstances," noted her minister, she had in 1899 "united with this church," even though her actions were opposed by both her father and stepmother. Like other women who joined the mission movement, Herron had begun teaching when she graduated from high school. She had attended Marquette Normal School during her vacations and had taught in lumber camps and in an Indian community. She had organized and taught a Sunday school in one of the lumber settlements; she had, in the words of her minister, "carried on in the face of obstacles which would have discouraged some of the bravest of us."[68]

In the picture she provided with her application, Jennie Herron appears to be a young woman much too grand for the lumber camps of Michigan. Outfitted in a bold plaid dress, she is looks regal in her hat, fur collar, and muff. The image she fashioned for herself stands in stark contrast to that presented by most applicants, who were attired more simply and modestly, most in white blouse and collar.[69] As it turned out,

[67] Jennie (Jane) Herron Biographical File, H5, PHS.
[68] Henry Sheir to R. M Craig, April 23, 1908, ibid.
[69] Photograph of Jennie Herron, ibid.

Jennie Herron (Department of History and Records Management Services, Presbyterian Church USA)

her tastes were also too grand for mission work. Herron's first assignment was in Puerto Rico; in 1911 she was transferred to Embudo, New Mexico. On her return trip from Puerto Rico to New York she borrowed money from a fellow passenger and did not repay the loan promptly. When the person who made the loan informed the board,

Herron was told that her contract would not be renewed. The board would not tolerate indebtedness or her failure to repay her loans.[70] For Herron this was a bitter blow. In 1914, three years after her dismissal, she pleaded for a second chance and to be reinstated, writing, "I do not see why I should always be considered a failure, and I should like to show the Board that I am not a failure now."[71]

Herron proves to have been an exception. The majority of missionaries seemed to have had no problem adhering to the rules of conduct. They did not gamble, they refrained from dancing, and they did not drink. Their behavior conformed to the board's dictates. Many might have sympathized with Herron's indebtedness, even her need to take a loan. Others took loans, but they were careful to let the board know that they did so because they had not received their salaries and that they could not conduct school without supplies. Successful missionaries adeptly couched their needs in the language of mission worker or professional teacher. When Lexie Barlow borrowed money to keep her school in Antonito, Colorado open, she was quick to admonish the WEC to send her paychecks as hastily as possible so she could make her payments. "I am willing to put all my salary into the work," she wrote, "but here are my creditors staring me in the face at every corner." Asserting that but for the money she had borrowed there would be no school, Barlow reminded her superiors that "I do not care for money for myself. I only want it to use in the work."[72] Herron had implored the board not to think of her as a failure; those missionaries more facile with the language and ideology of the enterprise reminded the board that if they, as individuals, failed, then so did the mission enterprise.

Mission literature such as the *Home Mission Monthly* presented an idealistic portrait of mission work. A middle-class Protestant woman reading this journal was encouraged to reflect on her life, to measure its usefulness, and to stretch her imagination. By asking her to test her limits, the home mission enterprise offered adventure. It was not meant to be an adventure for personal gain. She was being sent forth by an organization that considered itself national in scope. She was to be an envoy, a messenger, with a particular errand. Professor Tyler's com-

---

[70] David Boyd to Jennie Herron, November 23, 1910; Herron to Boyd, November 25, 1910; Herron to Boyd, November 29, 1910; A. H. Paul to David Boyd, December 26, 1910; Jennie Herron to M. C. Allaton, April 5, 1911; Allaton to Herron, April 25, 1911, ibid.

[71] Jennie Herron to Dora Mabel Fish, March 14, 1914, ibid.

[72] Lexie Barlow to Faith Haines, October 30, 1885, RG 51, Box 1, Folder 18, PHS.

mand to "go everywhere and make all things new" and the Reverend Bain's claims that mission work was the noblest of all were passionate appeals to the idealist in all women.

Unfortunately, passion for the cause of a Christian America could not sustain a woman's dedication once in the field. More pragmatic concerns rose to the fore: without equipment how was she to do her work, without money how was she to eat and clothe herself, not to mention procure the equipment she needed? Reporting in the *Presbyterian Home Missions* from her station at the Jemez mission, Mariette Wood wrote that kindergarten material had been provided by the First Presbyterian Church in Waterville, New York, but that her "attempts to introduce the system into my school failed for lack of requisite furniture." She was convinced that "under more favorable circumstances, the most desirable results would have been effected." She went on to describe visits she had made to aid the "distressed" and to encourage conversion. They were "pursued with much pleasure and some personal profit," she concluded, but "they were unsatisfactory as regarded Christian teaching."[73]

As early as 1882, home missionaries to New Mexico, like Wood, were reporting resistance to their efforts at conversion but a great receptivity to their secular skills—like teaching kindergarten—which, they argued, could prove successful if given greater institutional support. In their queries to the board from the field we see more clearly these women's developing sense of themselves as professionals. Jacqueline Jones has argued that mission women who served among the freedmen had a "keen sense of professionalism." Most of the women in Jones's survey had some higher education, were committed both to the cause and to teaching, and tried to employ the latest pedagogical techniques, exhibiting professional self-confidence gained from their training.[74] While the women in New Mexico shared these attributes, their concern with professionalism became evident only after they began their work; it was not exhibited in the application process. Wood had said little about her experience as a kindergarten teacher in her letter of application. Nor did other applicants discuss the nature of their training. They refrained from commenting on the content of their normal school training, for instance, except to say what subjects they were able to teach.

There may have been several reasons for this hesitation to flaunt one's

---

[73] Report by Mariette Wood in *Presbyterian Home Missions* 11 (October 1882): 238.
[74] Jones, "Women Who Were More Than Men," pp. 47–48.

relevant experience. Mission work was supposed to be an expression of faith, not a career. Applicants may have felt that there was no disjunction between their work experience and faith, hence discussing and confirming one's piety was also a discussion of one's work experience. Other applicants may have felt that, as graduates of Presbyterian academies or colleges, they had no need to explain the content of their education. Others may have consciously downplayed their education and experience so as not to appear controversial. The directors of the WEC may, for instance, have welcomed women trained to teach kindergarten, but there is also evidence that in the 1880s the union of kindergarten methods and Bible education was not universally accepted. Religious educators may have readily adopted the secular pedagogy of kindergartening, but their actions provoked condemnation from conservative evangelicals who saw it as a brand of liberal Protestantism.[75] In 1881, Sarah Cooper of the San Francisco Presbytery had been charged with heresy when she attempted to introduce Froebelian methods to the teaching of the Bible. She was accused of holding "sentimental and humanitarian" views which were deemed incompatible with the orthodox creed and teaching "allegorical and mythical interpretations of the scriptures."[76] Applicants may have refrained from commenting on their qualifications for fear of being cast into either liberal or conservative camps and denied a place in the enterprise.

Finally, there is the issue of the ethic that governed women's work, the seeming confusion about how one should approach work or speak about it. Let us return to the example of Mariette Wood. At the time of her application, her choices, like those of other women who became missionaries, were few. At twenty-nine years of age, unmarried, and feeling the need to change her life, she had settled on mission work. This decision had not come easily and had required compromises from her and her family. Having committed herself and traveled across the country, she could not easily leave the work no matter how difficult she found it. Any second thoughts a missionary might have upon arriving at her assignment were checked by WEC policy. If a woman decided she could not fulfill her obligation and do the work, she had to pay for her return

---

[75] Michael Shapiro, *Child's Garden: The Kindergarten Movement from Froebel to Dewey* (University Park: Pennsylvania State University Press, 1983), p. 79; Barbara Beatty, "Child Gardening: The Teaching of Young Children in American Schools," in *American Teachers: Histories of a Profession at Work*, ed. Donald Warren (New York: Macmillan, 1989), p. 72.

[76] Shapiro, *Child's Garden*, p. 94.

trip; she would not be reimbursed.[77] To renege on her commission would also call into question her professed desire to do "God's work." Wood would have to make do despite the limitations she encountered. Should the limitations prove intolerable, there were few options that she could pursue short of quitting. She could complain, as Delia Hills and Salome Verbeck did, and be transferred, hoping that in a new location the circumstances would be more favorable.

As originally conceived, a missionary's success was to be measured by the numbers she converted, but as Mariette Wood had said, converting people was not an easy task. When they set about pursuing their larger religious goals, missionaries worked to assess the needs and resources available in the community to which they were assigned and set about making a place for themselves. The act of making a place for herself and opening her school forced the mission worker in the field to become more openly concerned with issues of professionalism. She would learn to write "begging" letters to supporters in the East asking for money, books, and clothes.[78] She could take a year's leave of absence to gain additional training, as Josephine Orton did when in 1913 she went to Oregon Agricultural College to study domestic science.[79] A missionary would learn how to speak publicly on behalf of the work when she returned east for vacations. She would quickly map the community to which she was assigned to identify who was most influential and who she must court if she was to gather students. A successful home missionary learned to identify the various forces, groups of people and institutions, that shaped her work. She became a skillful negotiator. Initially a sense of self-sacrifice had led women to mission work, but performing the work, ironically, led to a heightened emphasis on self as the home missionary placed herself at the center of a complex set of social forces. In her desire to create a new order, both for herself and her clients, she seized the opportunity offered by the home mission enterprise and created a public role for herself.

[77] The WEC paid for a missionary to return home for a visit after three years of service but only if she planned to return to the work, and she had to pay half of her round-trip fare. Only after five years of service were transportation costs both ways paid. See Faith Haines to Cassie Riddle, March 25, 1884, RG 105, Box 2, Folder 10, PHS.

[78] Mission teacher Mary Stright characterized her letters to eastern mission societies in which she pleaded for financial and in-kind support as "begging letters." See Mary L. Stright, Diary, entry for November 3, 1882, Information File, MHL.

[79] Josephine Orton Biographical File, H5, PHS.

CHAPTER FOUR

"I Am Part of All I Have Met": Women Home Missionaries in Hispano New Mexico

That Hispano New Mexicans welcomed Presbyterian mission teachers into their villages at all seems, at first glance, remarkable. Except for the constant support they received from a small group of Hispano Protestants, mission teachers were, at the outset, more often than not welcomed hesitantly, viewed with a healthy skepticism, or scorned. Presbyterian teachers might preach that Hispanos and Anglo-Americans were part of the same national family, but that partnership required Hispanos to divest themselves of their cultural symbols without a similar sacrifice by the Anglo teachers. Both the Catholic Church and the courts were issuing policies that took away more from Hispanos than they protected, and New Mexican Hispanos had little guarantee that Presbyterian teachers would not do the same— use their work and presence in northern New Mexico to their own advantage and neglect the needs of the population.

Hispanos had rejected the overtures made by male home missionaries for just this reason. Conversion to Protestantism demanded that Hispanos make the change; it did not require the minister to provide anything to the community in return. When mission teachers entered the same communities in which ministers had met resistance, they too had an imperialist agenda, but they also offered a service that Hispanos desired. They could provide a relationship that, from the perspective of Hispanos, offered the possibility of mutual exchange. Teachers did not require students to be Protestant, nor did they insist that they convert to attend their schools.

If Hispanos understood their own position in the larger society to be in flux, so did the Anglo women who moved into their communities. An examination of the impact of the meeting between these groups on mission women illustrates the bargaining relationship that developed between the two groups and suggests a process that generated multiple stereotypes.[1] Even as mission women came to understand that their success depended on deemphasizing conversion and stressing secular skills and as they came to recognize the many "admirable" qualities of Hispano culture, they continued to portray Hispanos as a dependent people. These stereotypes served several purposes: they allowed these women to challenge traditional conceptions of domesticity and to define a central role for themselves as cultural mediators. Over the years, missionaries would use that role to educate their Anglo supporters about the integrity of Hispano culture.

This dual concern with issues of ethnicity and work can be seen in the dramatic first impressions of New Mexico and mission women's descriptions of Penitente activities. Prospective missionaries accepted their assignments to New Mexico with little knowledge of the territory. One missionary, assigned to Arroyo Hondo, wrote to the Woman's Board that she "[supposed] the population is Spanish speaking."[2] Once in New Mexico, most were disconcerted by the conditions they found. Bertha Leadingham recalled that she had left her home "rather hurriedly and had no time to gain detailed information regarding the work." She did not know "what was meant by plaza work." "It never occurred to me," she wrote, "that the plazas were the remote places, the Mexican villages made up entirely of adobe houses of mud and clay and situated from six to sixty miles from a railroad." With her belongings stacked on the back of wagon, Leadingham set off from Santa Fe for Embudo, over hills so "steep" that she had to "close her eyes" out of fear that she would "go headlong" over the front of the wagon. At her destination, in the two rooms that were to serve as her living quarters, she unpacked her dishes,

---

[1] The concept of a bargaining relationship is inspired by Linda Gordon's analysis of social workers and clients in her study of domestic violence, "Family Violence, Feminism, and Social Control," *Feminist Studies* 12 (Fall 1986): 470.

[2] L. C. Galbraith to Emmeline Pierson, November 15, 1899, Galbraith Biographical File, H5, Department of History and Records Management Services, Presbyterian Church (U.S.A.), Philadelphia (hereafter PHS).

cooking utensils, table, and chairs—"as small a supply of furniture as I could possibly get along with." Alone, with no knowledge of Spanish, she began to acquaint herself with this new culture. The houses were made of adobe, the floors of mud; the food consisted mainly of beans and tortillas. The outlook was a "lonely and desolate one," and she was "three thousand miles from home."[3]

The isolation and alienation missionaries felt in these remote places was compounded when they confronted Penitente rituals and processions. Their impressions of the Penitentes provide the most vivid illustration of the cultural divide these women encountered. The immediate effect of these descriptions, which were read by their supporters throughout the country, was to reinforce the differences between Hispano and Anglo culture. They implied that there was something sinister, at the very least strange, about these rituals far removed from the bounds of genteel Anglo society. The rituals fascinated, perhaps even titillated, but they did nothing to ameliorate the misunderstandings about Hispano culture or to promote acceptance of this culture that had been brought under United States dominion.

Mission women's reports on Penitente activities played a critical role in perpetuating the dominant stereotypes of Hispanos as little more than pagans. Early missionary descriptions of the Penitente rituals were dramatic, expressing deep horror and distaste for the Hispano culture. Matilda Allison, stationed at Santa Fe, described Penitentes as a "sect of the Roman Catholic Church, numerous in New Mexico, who believe that by self-torture they atone for their sins and become holy." Allison, like most missionaries, overlooked all service functions of the brotherhood in her reports and focused on the practice of self-flagellation, describing in gory detail the intricacies of the penances performed:

Their bodies are bared and scored with sharp stones until their backs stream with blood . . . the whips [used in self-flagellation] are of cactus or of thorny soapweed, and the blows are laid on with force. Light whipping is allowed; and if anyone falls from exhaustion the whip is taken by one of the attendants and the blows continued. Some carry heavy crosses, which are sometimes driven full of nails and bound to the body. Others crawl on bare knees the entire distance, the way being

---

[3] M. Bertha Leadingham, "The Plaza and Its Hope," *Home Mission Monthly* 18 (September 1904): 267–77.

strewn with stone and cactus. The torture is so great that death sometimes results."[4]

Allison summed up missionary impressions of the Catholicism practiced by Hispano New Mexicans when she called it "but a round of ceremonies and image-worship."

Missionaries saw nothing but unregenerative pain in Penitente rituals. One woman defined New Mexican Catholicism as a religion of "somber hue—a terrified conscience cunningly played upon by avaricious priests."[5] One of the first mission teachers to work in New Mexico, Jennie Flott, expressed the sentiments of the group when she wrote: "Having never even heard of such a religion before coming to this country, it seemed one of the most awful sights a human being could witness."[6] After observing a Penitente procession, another missionary wrote that the spectacle "was such that I never want to see the like again."[7]

Still others spoke of having to look away, unable to bear the sight of the blood running down the backs of the men in the procession.[8] Flott, in a letter to the Ladies' Home Missionary Society of New York City, described in detail the activities of the Penitentes in Taos on Good Friday. She told of the whipping and cutting that the sixteen men who made up the procession inflicted on themselves. They were dressed in "nothing . . . save a pair of white cotton drawers." At the end of the ceremony all sixteen men appeared to be "one mass of blood, from their necks to the very bottom of their drawers." She lamented that "these men think they have thus secured pardon for all the sins they may commit during the following years" and assessed the ritual as "human butchery." She asked her readers to pardon her for writing of these terrible events. She warned that they "may seem disgusting to you," but she could not overlook them because they "made such a deep impression on my mind." That these activities took place within United States boundaries particularly distressed Flott. She could perhaps understand if they occurred in India, but "the cruelties of Hindoo worship to the idol

---

[4] Matilda Allison, "Mission Work in New Mexico," *Home Mission Monthly* 1 (September 1887): 250–51.

[5] "Monthly Concert—The Mexicans," *Home Mission Monthly* 1 (September 1887): 245.

[6] Jennie Flott, "Report from Taos," *Rocky Mountain Presbyterian* 2 (August 1873): 2.

[7] Marion Le Duc, "The Penitentes of Truchas," *Home Mission Monthly* 23 (November 1908): 7.

[8] Elizabeth Rowland, "Shine and Shade," *Home Mission Monthly* 10 (November 1895): 11.

Juggernaut appears no more cruel than this horrible system of purifying from sin."[9]

Penitente rituals reaffirmed the unity of the Hispano village, emphasizing the solidarity of the community. Missionaries, however, saw these ceremonies as reinforcing the foreign qualities of Hispano culture and as anti-American and regressive. For most missionaries the Penitente rituals were the most powerful reminder of the cultural gap that separated them from their Hispano clients. Mission women could see only pain and blood and could think of the ritual only in terms of the suffering experienced by the individual participants. For many it was a challenge to their own religious ideas, especially their belief in a gentle, loving, and all-forgiving God.[10]

Although the most obvious interpretation of mission women's accounts is that they expressed the seemingly irreconcilable cultural difference they felt from Hispanos, these accounts must be seen as part of a more complicated process of self-definition. In this sense, their descriptions of Penitente rituals helped missionaries shape a larger public role for themselves. Concerned with their standing in the larger society and searching for work that was satisfying as well as useful, they understood their mission work to be a form of public service. Missionaries quickly learned that the success of their work depended upon contributions from middle-class women in other parts of the country. Their reports containing the descriptions of Penitente rituals were a way to inform and educate their supporters about the scope of their work. In describing Penitente rituals, mission women were creating stereotypes of themselves as much as of their Hispano clients.[11]

---

[9] Flott, "Report from Taos," p. 2.

[10] Victor Turner has argued that a meeting of these two different religious traditions reveals a contrast between "celebratory processes that stress sacred 'things' and those that focus on the moral, philosophical, and religious worth of 'persons.'" Essentially, he suggests that Hispanic Catholicism stresses idol worship whereas Anglo-Protestantism attempts to purify religious values by abandoning idols. In this case, where Protestant missionaries were attempting to Americanize Hispanic Catholics, the contrast in religious values presented problems because the evangelical Protestant emphasis on the "word," literacy, and education "often accompanies the emergence of the notion of the individual-in-general rather than the corporate group as a main unit of ethics and judgment." See Turner, ed., *Celebration: Studies in Festivity and Ritual* (Washington, D.C.: Smithsonian Institution Press, 1982), p. 216.

[11] Joan Brumberg makes a similar analysis in her study of the descriptions provided by foreign missionaries of social conditions in the cultures to which they were assigned. She finds that they provided a standard by which middle-class Anglo-Protestant American women could define their own social position ("Zenanas and Girlless Villages: The Ethnology of American Evangelical Women, 1870–1910," *Journal of American History* 69 [September 1982]: 369).

Procession of Penitentes (Department of History and Records Management Services, Presbyterian Church USA)

These reports on the activities of Penitentes appeared in the *Home Mission Monthly*, the most important connection between missionaries and the larger population of Anglo women who supported their work. In the magazine they appealed for aid and educated their readers about the lives of the Hispanos who were their neighbors and students. At face value, the frequency and consistency with which mission women reported on Penitente activities would suggest that through the duration of their tenure in New Mexico they remained faithful to the anti-Catholicism and enthnocentrism that had inspired the home mission movement. But this seemingly obsessive concern with the Penitentes may also have served different purposes depending on the length of time the women had worked in the Southwest. At the outset of their assignment, their reports may have been a genuine statement of their alienation. Over the years they may have come to serve a seemingly contradictory function; they reminded supporters that Hispanos were outsiders but also helped mission women win ongoing support.

By doing work with a foreign culture that male missionaries rejected, Protestant women found that they could move beyond the gender limitations placed on their religious work as well as participate more fully in public life. Working with Hispanos may have allowed them to improve their social status, but they did not want to be confused with their clients, fearful that they would somehow be linked with the display of religious excess in the self-flagellation practiced by Penitentes. In her study of anorexia nervosa, Joan Brumberg has suggested that nineteenth-century Protestant Americans were fascinated as well as concerned with the religious excesses displayed by middle-class adolescent girls. Young women who starved themselves, for instance, garnered a tremendous amount of attention and publicity, but their activities also allowed critics to depict women "as the primary actors in the pageant of the miraculous" and to "[associate] them with outmoded systems of belief and with a spirit of mental dillusion unfit for the progressive life of the nineteenth century."[12] In condemning Penitente rituals, mission women were not just separating themselves from Hispano Catholics but also from members of their own class who engaged in religious excess. Through their descriptions they could assert that they were completely within the mainstream Protestant tradition and reassure their followers that they did not condone and were not attracted to this form of religious activity.

At the same time, missionaries may also have taken a lesson from the attention surrounding the "fasting girls" as they used the gory details of the Penitente rituals to fashion their own sensational tale by which to publicize their work and raise the material support that the Woman's Board of Home Missions could not provide. No doubt missionaries were horrified and saddened, even disgusted, by the rituals, but the frequency with which sensational descriptions of flagellation and bleeding appeared in *Home Mission Monthly* articles and the repetition of language used to describe the events of the ritual suggest that the act of telling the story became a ritual in and of itself.

Just as missionaries discovered the financial benefits of their vivid descriptions, it appears that Penitentes began to practice self-flagellation sporadically with less dramatic physical damage than that described by missionaries. By the latter part of the nineteenth century, the Catholic Church had moved to suppress the more dramatic aspects of the ritual by discouraging self-flagellation. Those who continued to practice self-mortification did so more often than not in secret, far from the eyes of watchful missionaries and other Anglo-Americans.[13] In some villages

---

[12] See Joan Jacobs Brumberg, *Fasting Girls: The Emergence of Anorexia as a Modern Disease* (Cambridge, Mass.: Harvard University Press, 1988), pp. 76–77. The passages quoted refer specifically to the work of William Hammond, a Presbyterian minister and author of *Fasting Girls: Their Physiology and Their Pathology*. Hammond was particularly critical of the fasting because, he warned, it produced hysteria which allowed emotion to rule over intellect or will.

[13] As early as 1885, Penitentes were ordered by church authorities to end public flagellations and cross-bearing. See Marta Weigle, *Brothers of Light, Brothers of Blood: The Penitentes of the Southwest* (Albuquerque: University of New Mexico Press, 1976), p. 59. Mission teacher Alice Hyson also noted the attempt on the part of the church authorities to stop flagellation,

the ritual may have proceeded unchanged. Some of the more remote villages remained without resident priests to impose penalties for participating in the rituals or had priests who turned a blind eye to the more dramatic parts and did not impose the bishop's directives. There were Presbyterian mission teachers in some of these smaller villages who might have seen the practices. In the larger towns, however, where priests were more aggressive in their attempts to repress the activities, such as in Taos, Santa Fe, and Las Vegas, it is doubtful that the rituals took place within easy view of mission teachers.

If the ritual itself underwent changes during these years as the Catholic Church sought to repress the more dramatic practices, the details provided in mission accounts remained remarkably uniform over the period. For instance, the images of blood dripping down bare backs, thorn-encrusted ropes, and blood juxtaposed to white "drawers" (trousers) were favorites in mission reports.[14] What did change in the mission accounts was the tone of the rhetoric. The early descriptions of the rituals express shock, dismay, anger, and fear. In later years the distaste remains, but the observations seem more neutral and are less central, preempted by reports about other customs (such as making adobe houses) and the material conditions of their clients' lives.

This shift in tone came when women missionaries downplayed their religious convictions—especially the emphasis on conversion—and stressed the more secular aspects of their work. As mission women built their schools and extended their activities into the community, the drama of the Penitente ritual became one among a variety of activities. The confrontation between Catholic and Protestant, the imperative to convert as many Catholics as possible, was no longer central to the mission experi-

---

writing that the bishop had forbidden Penitentes to whip themselves in public ("Words from Workers," *Home Mission Monthly* 3 [September 1889]: 251).

[14] The near nakedness of many of the men in the Penitente processions was of great curiosity to mission women and almost always elicited comment. Josephine Orton referred to "a single white garment, little more than trunks," in "The Penitentes," *Home Mission Monthly* 23 (November 1908): 6; Elizabeth Rowland wrote of "no clothing except white muslim trousers," in "Shine and Shade," *Home Mission Monthly* 10 (November 1895): 11; Jennie Flott described adherents "with nothing on save a pair of white cotton drawers," in "Report on Taos," *Rocky Mountain Presbyterian* 11 (August 1873): 2; Sue Zuver referred to "a scanty supply of clothing," in "Zeal of Mexican Romanists," *Home Mission Monthly* 15 (November 1900): 7; and Prudence Clark commented on the "nearly naked ones of their numbers lashing themselves with whips," in "Religious Rites in an Isolated Plaza," *Home Mission Monthly* 16 (November 1901): 9.

ence. When mission women's professional concerns expanded, they focused on the institutions they had created and the activities they initiated and oversaw.

† † †

Alice Hyson was one of the most successful missionaries assigned to New Mexico. Originally from Stewartstown, Pennsylvania, she was sent to Ranchos de Taos in 1884, when she was twenty-three, and did not leave there until she was critically ill with cancer thirty-one years later, in 1915.[15] When Hyson began her work, she complained of limited resources, warning the Woman's Executive Committee that the dirt floors and drafty conditions of her rooms would cause respiratory disease and other damage to her health and well-being.[16] She was not generous in her assessment of the Hispano people with whom she lived and worked. She disapproved of the larger ceremonial aspects of their lives, such as patron-saint observances and Penitente Holy Week processions. The Penitente rituals were, to her, the "most heathenish practice called religion, in the United States." She "dreaded" the commencement of Holy Week. She criticized the smallest details of her neighbors' lives, hesitating to eat dinner with them because she thought they prepared their meals under unsanitary conditions.[17]

When asked in 1894 whether she could see "any improvements or fruits" from her labor, Hyson responded that she was "encouraged" even though she had not converted great numbers of villagers. The improvements she cited were material not spiritual; she noted, for instance, increasing "industry" among her students and their parents. By far the most noteworthy change she reported was that Taoseños were welcoming her into their homes. "They are glad to see me," she wrote. In the early years of her assignment, she remembered, "they would come to the door and instead of asking me in, would see if I wanted anything; one would be obliged to say 'I came to visit you,' and then do all the talking besides.[18]

Hyson proved to be a popular teacher. In time, her presence was

---

[15] Alice Hyson Biographical File, H5, PHS.

[16] Faith Haines to Alice Hyson, June 25, 1885, RG 105, Box 2, Folder 11, PHS.

[17] Alice Hyson, "Words from Workers," *Home Mission Monthly* 1 (December 1886): 14–15.

[18] Alice Hyson, "Improvements," *Home Mission Monthly* 8 (September 1894): 258.

accepted not just by the converted Presbyterian Hispanos but also by Catholics. By 1894 hers was the largest day school in the territory, having enrolled five hundred pupils over the ten years it had been open. In her years as teacher and principal of the school, the enrollment averaged ninety-five students a year. Proud of the progress she felt her students had made, she boasted that she had taught several generations of families. She continued to correspond with many former students after they had left Ranchos de Taos.[19] Committed to the community in which she worked, Hyson had become a part of Ranchos de Taos.

Although initially she was antagonistic and suspicious, over the years Hyson settled into her work, built up her school, and, perhaps demonstrating a sign of her intention to remain in Ranchos and make it her home, she cultivated a garden.[20] She never ceased her attempts to proselytize among her pupils and neighbors, but as the years passed, converting Hispanos was overshadowed by community work. She found that her Hispano neighbors responded more enthusiastically when she focused her energies on providing such basic services as education and rudimentary health care. Hyson explained the switch in emphasis as a change in her conversion strategy. She believed that by educating children and providing medical assistance she was showing the people how Protestant faith benefited the community.[21]

Hyson's career path was not unique; it illustrates what another missionary, Alice Blake, would describe as the "universality of experiences" common to those mission teachers who spent many years in New Mexico, which involved an elaborate negotiation between missionaries and their Hispano neighbors.[22] After their early denunciations of Penitente

[19] Hyson, "Words from Workers," *Home Mission Monthly* 8 (September 1894): 258. Yearly enrollment figures for mission schools appear in Board of Home Missions, Presbyterian Church in the U.S.A., *Annual Report.*

[20] Annette Kolodny, in her study of women and the frontier, finds that whereas women employed metaphors of cultivation to explain how they overcame the frontier, men used metaphors of conquest. She argues that women on the frontier were often preoccupied with cultivating gardens and that the desire to grow a garden may represent their attempts to put down roots and to feel settled (*The Land before Her: Fantasy and Experience of the American Frontiers, 1630–1860* [Chapel Hill: University of North Carolina Press, 1984]: 35–54). For a description of Hyson's efforts in cultivating her garden see "Looking Backwards, Ranchos de Taos," *Home Mission Monthly* 26 (November 1911): 22.

[21] Alice Hyson, "Ranchos de Taos," *Home Mission Monthly* 21 (November 1906): 12.

[22] Quoted in Cheryl Foote, "'Let Her Works Praise Her': Women's Experiences in the Southwest, 1846–1912" (Ph.D. diss., University of New Mexico, 1985), p. 178.

rituals, mission women were surprised when members of the Penitente brotherhoods enrolled their children in Presbyterian schools. Initially villagers were hesitant to send children to the schools. Teachers went out and recruited, visiting families, encouraging them to send both sons and daughters, and even offering adult classes at night. They began with a small group of students, usually the children of Presbyterian converts, and as they established a reputation the numbers grew.

Mission teachers distinguished between Catholic and Presbyterian Hispanos, acknowledging that without the support and continued presence of native evangelists, their work would have been stymied. One missionary told how, shortly after her arrival, the priest wrote a slanderous article about her and circulated it throughout the village. The townspeople gathered at her door and angrily warned her to leave town that very night. She played on their sympathies, explaining that, as a woman, she could not travel over the mountains alone at night, and, as a cripple, she could not physically do so. They relented and decided that she could leave in the morning. She was saved by a "Mexican Protestant," who, when told of the danger she was in, "traveled all night long . . . as fast as he could," reaching her by daylight. He explained to the people that the article was untrue and thereby secured her a place in the community.[23]

Catholic priests were the most often cited cause of the antagonism against mission teachers.[24] Teacher after teacher reported on priests' efforts to break up their schools. They threatened parents with excommunication, refused to hear the confessions of families whose children were enrolled in Presbyterian schools, and said they might not baptize and confirm children. Other priests were accused of libeling mission teachers. After a campaign by the priest, teachers sometimes opened school to find few, if any, students. Home missionary E. M. Fenton, in Mora, explained that when these campaigns happened, "sometimes a

---

[23] Miss Dox, "Words from Workers," *Home Mission Monthly* 7 (July 1893): 209.

[24] The Catholic journal *La Revista Católica* reserved harsh words for Protestant mission women. Likening their style to that of "el hombre" (the man), the editors questioned their understanding of theology, especially their contention that Catholicism, with its emphasis on the Virgin, was "empty." The only emptiness was "en aquella misma cabecita" (in that same little head), contended the editors, pointing out that Mexicans were Christians. In praying to the Virgin, believers were asking Christ to forgive their sins. The editors argued that the goal of Protestant missionaries was to induce converts to give up their money. Protestant intentions, they concluded, were corrupt. See "Miss E. V. Lee y los Mexicanos," *Revista Católica*, June 14, 1896, pp. 282–83.

stampede will occur among the people and the school will be broken up in a day. And all we can do is just to hold on our way until the spell is broken and they return."[25]

Believing that the Catholic Church was an autocratic and oppressive institution, mission teachers did not hold the townspeople responsible for these flights of faith. The setbacks teachers experienced as a result of the resistance posed by the priests confirmed their belief that the people had to be liberated from the tyrannies of Roman Catholicism. Teachers wrote sympathetically of the difficulties and contradictions faced by Hispanos when they sent their children to Presbyterian schools. One teacher said, "It must needs take the spirit of a martyr to deny the established religion, the forms and ceremonies of which have been for generations a part of the customs of the people."[26] Another, writing of Hispanos who had converted, noted that she had never realized the courage required "for these people to stand up against all the manners and customs of the church in which they were born and bred, and in the face of all their relatives declare themselves Christians."[27]

As they came to realize what a radical step it was for Hispanos to convert, teachers became less aggressive in their attempts at conversion. Mrs. Dilley at Mora recalled one father who brought his daughters to the school and had the children kneel while he "devoutly crossed them." Having learned her lesson earlier, Mrs. Dilley "immediately decided that it would be folly to meddle with their religious views, so [she] dressed them warmly and made them as comfortable as [she] could." The case that had served as Dilley's lesson was that of a small girl whom she encouraged to join the Presbyterian Church. Soon thereafter the child was taken from the school and whipped. Dilley resolved after this incident that if any of her students wished to convert she would counsel them to wait. She noted with irony that the child who had been removed from the school reappeared a year later with her father and mother, and they offered themselves as members of the church. "So," recalled Dilley, "after I had learned my lesson, I found it was the wrong one."[28]

Although mission teachers did visit homes to evangelize and started programs that might appeal to adults, such as night classes, they discov-

[25] E. M. Fenton, "Words from Workers," *Home Mission Monthly* 3 (January 1889): 61.
[26] "Words from Workers," *Home Mission Monthly* 5 (September 1891): 276.
[27] Annie Granger, "Words from Workers," *Home Mission Monthly* 2 (April 1888): 132.
[28] (Mrs.) S. V. Dilley, "Words from Workers," *Home Mission Monthly* 3 (April 1889): 131.

Parents bringing students to Allison School, Santa Fe, 1898 (Menaul Historical Library of the Southwest)

ered that molding the minds of the children was far more effective. Dilley's is but one example of the generational conflict missionaries inspired. There are few explicit reports of ruptures in families. One must read between the lines of reports that lament the alienation suffered by Hispano converts. When tension was reported, as in the example of Dilley, the stories generally ended happily, with reports of the family remaining intact and joining the Presbyterian Church. Slowly teachers made inroads into the communities, impressing people with their own dedication and service and building personal loyalties. As they did so, they evangelized by handing out Bibles, which people graciously accepted and displayed in their homes.[29] Missionaries reported that the Scripture cards children read in the classroom were taken home and hung as decorations on the walls. Thus symbols of Protestant religious culture found their way into Hispano Catholic households. Challenged by teachers with statements like "you may as well pray to that map . . .

[29] Alice Hyson, "Signs of Promise," *Home Mission Monthly* 10 (November 1895): 17.

as to a picture of a saint," children learned lessons that preached the evils of "idol worship" and wrote compositions in which people prayed to God, not to saints.[30]

As they watched the numbers in their classrooms increase, mission teachers reported more extensive changes in the life-styles of their Hispano neighbors. Missionaries argued that before the home mission movement intervened, the "average Mexican" had been "thriftless, unprogressive, ignorant, and superstitious." These old habits were disappearing; "Many are seeking for light. There is a spirit of inquiry among the Mexicans and a readiness to read the printed page." Mission teachers gleefully reported that Hispanos were imitating American customs.[31] The most dramatic change they noted was not in the numbers converted but in the material conditions of the community. The children were cleaner and more neatly dressed, and the houses were tidier. Chairs and tables were appearing in homes where previously one was forced to sit on the dirt floor, and villagers were eating with knives and forks.[32]

Missionaries might have wanted to take credit for introducing these articles of modern life, but the spiritual revolution they had sought to provoke paled in comparison to the commercial changes taking place in the territory as it became absorbed into the larger industrial economy. Hispanos remained poor; growing numbers of men and boys left the villages to go to "Colorado to work on the railroads or to herd cattle and goats."[33] Increasingly, missionaries commented on the conditions that caused Hispano impoverishment: "They receive so little for their labor," wrote R. S. Wysong from Chaperito. "I have long wished that the people might have more land to cultivate. With a good system of irrigation, and a good leader they would be encouraged to do as well as any people. But from three to five and ten acres provide for only a humble living at best."[34]

Having largely failed to win converts to Protestantism but having proved themselves able and popular teachers, missionaries cast about to

---

[30] Alice Hyson, "A Visit to Our Mexican Mission," *Home Mission Monthly* 7 (November 1893): 7.

[31] M. A. Allison, "Mission Work in New Mexico," *Home Mission Monthly* 1 (September 1887): 249.

[32] See letters from Leva Granger, Sue Zuver, and E. M. Bryce, "Hopeful Progress," *Home Mission Monthly* 12 (November 1897): 15.

[33] Alice Hyson, "Hindrances to Overcome," *Home Mission Monthly* 15 (November 1900): 14.

[34] R. S. Wysong, "Hopeful Progress," *Home Mission Monthly* 12 (November 1897): 15.

redefine the standard by which to measure their success. The diptheria and smallpox epidemics that raged through New Mexico and southern Colorado in the late 1880s and 1890s drew mission teachers out of the schoolhouse and into people's homes. As they nursed the sick and dying and helped to prepare bodies for burial, mission teachers experienced the lives of Hispano New Mexicans as never before. Their concern with the impoverished conditions of Hispano New Mexico and the environment in which the people lived grew to new proportions. When Mollie Clements wrote of the emotional hardships of nursing people through epidemics and watching others die, she lamented, "I cannot tell you what a sad, sad time it has been."[35]

Whereas previously the lack of concern with standards of cleanliness had been discussed as a moral aberration or a character flaw, smallpox epidemics impressed upon missionaries that there was a material basis for the hardships suffered by their neighbors. Mission teachers began to lobby for sanitary reforms along with preaching the Word. Indeed, it was more imperative to teach the importance of washing oneself after visiting an ill neighbor or relative than to talk about the saving grace of Jesus. The epidemics had two consequences: they expanded teachers' sensibilities about the conditions under which people lived and they allowed teachers to enhance their own reputations. Rather than abandon school and village as they were often advised to do by the Woman's Board, many teachers chose to remain in place, closing the schools to nurse the people. They also sought out whatever smallpox vaccination they could obtain to inoculate residents. When they could not combat the epidemic effectively, they joined the community of mourners.

Missionary reports during these periods of disease and sickness exhibit the anxiety they felt about their success as teachers. They worried that townspeople would superstitiously attribute the disease as God's punishment for supporting a Presbyterian school, undermining the institutions teachers had struggled to build. Alice Blake, at Rociada, was happy to report that she no longer met with "fanatical intolerance" but hesitated to say that there had been any "great religious awakening among the people," adding that they seemed increasingly to appreciate the value of education. Referring to the incidence of epidemic in the surrounding villages, she was thankful that Rociada had been "spared the deaths that [had] plagued other towns." During the period of illness the ninety-first

---

[35] Mollie Clements, "Words from Workers," *Home Mission Monthly* 8 (January 1894): 64.

Psalm had become her refrain as she repeated to herself, "Thou shall not be afraid of the terror by night, nor the arrow that flieth by day; nor for the pestilence that walketh in darkness; nor for the destruction that wasteth by noon-day. A thousand shall fall at thy side, and ten thousand at thy right hand but it shall not come nigh thee." Worried that death would be explained as a curse "imposed on account of the Protestant schools," she felt that her neighbors could not help but be impressed "by this escape from evil."[36]

The experiences of teachers who did report numerous deaths reveal that Blake had nothing to fear. Those who wholeheartedly joined in the effort to fight the epidemic and nursed sick people for days without sleep were rewarded for their efforts. They gained entrance into the homes of people who previously had nothing to do with them. If their work as teachers had made them suspect, nursing gained them respect.[37] In situations that might have caused them to flee to preserve their own lives, they continued their work and offered their knowledge and services in other capacities. They had proven their willingness to cast their lot with the others in the village.

Encouraged by the reception their limited nursing skills met, teachers began to expand their "mission" to introduce new and more explicitly secular lessons in domestic arts and manual skills that addressed material concerns. The boarding schools added industrial and home economics departments and offered preparation for the state teachers' exams. By 1925 Allison-James, the boarding school for girls, was offering commercial classes, as well as courses in "home hygiene and child care." In the plaza schools, more attention was given to agricultural education, home improvement projects, and health programs.[38] As the public school system expanded, the mission schools were closed so as not to compete with the public system. The number of plaza schools decreased, and more emphasis was placed on the boarding schools and on providing secondary education. Some schools were converted into community centers, hospitals were opened, and visiting nurses were sponsored.[39] These

36 Alice Blake, "Words from Workers," *Home Mission Monthly* 5 (November 1890): 12.

37 See Leva Granger, "Bright Gleams Here and There," *Home Mission Monthly* 15 (November 1900): 16, and her report in *Home Mission Monthly* 17 (August 1903): 240.

38 Ruth K. Barber and Edith Agnew, *Sowers Went Forth: The Story of Presbyterian Missions in New Mexico and Southern Colorado* (Albuquerque: Menaul Historical Library of the Southwest, 1981), pp. 93, 104, 108. See also Marion D. Dutton, "Educating the Educators," *Women and Missions* 2 (May 1925): 54.

39 See, for example, Eleanor Tilford, "Presenting Chacon," *Women and Missions* 2 (May

developments drew both the teachers and students, missionaries and clients, away from the emphasis on the Word at the core of evangelical Protestantism. Certainly, conversion remained a main goal. Lessons continued to be drawn from the Bible, and the school day was opened and closed with prayers. But teachers were encouraged to draw parallels between biblical lessons and the lives of their students, which required them to study the dynamics of the village.

The most successful teachers transformed their schools into rural settlement houses and insinuated themselves into all facets of village life. Prudence Clark, for example, found that her success hinged on being a "leader and teacher in every sense of the work, not only in affairs religious and social but even in legal questions of the plaza."[40] Clark, who originally came from Eden Prairie, Minnesota, taught in Chimayó from 1902 until 1912. During her tenure she styled herself an informal ethnographer, publishing articles in the *Home Mission Monthly* which described the geography, climate, and agricultural products of Chimayó.[41] She told of the tradition of blanket weaving which marked Chimayó as an artisanal center of the territory.[42] She related the intricacies of Hispano social life by describing the marriage rituals practiced by her neighbors.[43] When she moved to Chimayó she had brought with her a sister, Jennie, who acted as her housekeeper. Jennie died in 1907 of tuberculosis. Her death impelled Clark to seek solace and support from her neighbors in Chimayó. When she left the mission movement in 1912 it was to build a new family, this time with Teofilo Ortega, a Hispano New Mexican from Chimayó, whom she married.[44]

1925): 69; Grace Russell, "Health Campaigns in Truchas," *Women and Missions* 2 (May 1925): 66; Jessie Lewis, "Brooklyn Cottage Hospital," *Women and Missions* 6 (May 1929): 57–58.

[40] Alice Blake, "Memoirs of Alice Blake: Interviews with Missionaries, Teachers and Others in Northern New Mexico," p. 140, manuscript, Menaul Historical Library of the Southwest, Albuquerque.

[41] Prudence Clark, "New Mexico, Location, Climate and Products," *Home Mission Monthly* 24 (November 1909): 4–5.

[42] Prudence Clark, "Blanket Weaving," *Home Mission Monthly* 18 (November 1903): 10–11.

[43] Prudence Clark, "Mexican Marriages," *Home Mission Monthly* 16 (November, 1901): 11–12.

[44] See Prudence Clark Biographical File, H5, PHS. Ortega, a Hispanic convert and lay evangelist, and Clark served after their marriage in Jemez before returning to live in Chimayó. Clark's successor, Pearl English, also married a Hispano church member, Anastacio Trujillo. She too remained in Chimayó and was remembered for her command of Spanish and her

By their actions missionaries gradually contested the limits as well as the assumptions that had shaped women's home mission work when the WEC was originally conceived. The Reverend Bain had implored women to "go everywhere and do everything," and they did just that. By the first decade of the twentieth century, the mission worker was no longer simply using her domestic skills to work with other women. As their descriptions of Penitente rituals and their many reports suggest, converting the "heathen" required missionaries to broadcast their findings to build the public support necessary to sustain their work. The work demanded that they articulate a public persona. Instead, women in the field came to envision themselves as not bound by traditional gender roles but transcending the private sphere to fill a public position of prominence and responsibility. One missionary even suggested that they take as their inspiration Ulysses and adopt as their motto his "I am part of all that I have met." Indeed, one woman went so far as to argue that the work she performed resembled that of a politician. A missionary, she advised, should represent her constituency and "work with them to mutual advantage, in developing the best interests of all classes and conditions of society within the State's boundary, and at the same time grow in wisdom and grace."[45]

In describing their ideal missionary, mission women who had been in the field for many years drew a portrait of a composite person who played a central and important role in the community to which she was assigned. Interestingly, this ideal was neither male nor female but a blend of the virtues and skills ascribed to both men and women. Nellie McGraw wrote that "my ideal missionary is a man in strength and authority and achievement; a woman in gentleness and ingenuity and persuasive powers; a Jack of all trades and virtues and talents, and a master of every one of them; a sort of Swiss Family Robinson man who turns every obstacle to service, who sees possibilities in every stick and stone and creature, and converts those possibilities into realities; who knows nothing of pessimism or discouragement; whose sense of duty is so completely wrapped up in love and willing service that it is entirely lost in the sweeter joys of life and who, out of the useless decrepid

---

translating skills. See Carolyn Atkins, ed., *Los Tres Campos, The Three Fields: A History of Protestant Evangelists and Presbyterians in Chimayó, Cordova and Truchas, New Mexico* (Albuquerque: Menaul Historical Library of the Southwest, 1978), pp. 38–40.

[45] Florence Stephenson, "The Ideal Missionary," *Home Mission Monthly* 23 (August 1909): 234–35.

wrecks along the shore, builds veritable castles for the indwelling of God's love."[46] McGraw's enthusiastic and ambitious description was echoed by other missionaries, among them Frances Goodrich, who argued that this ideal sounded "mythical" but that is was not "altogether a fancy portrait."[47]

While this ideal assumed piety, it did not require women to wait until after they died for their reward. By their own definition, mission work was empowering. It compelled women to think of themselves as activists and demanded that they consider issues of social justice. McGraw's ambitious portrait of the missionary was not a description of the work per se or a discussion of the day-to-day details of mission work but, rather, a description of a particular form of political consciousness. As mission women expanded the scope of their work, adding the role of nurse and community worker and ultimately cultural mediator to their teaching duties, they began to construe their social responsibilities more broadly.

Historian Sarah Deutsch has argued that missionaries had little effect in subverting Hispano traditions. Instead, they introduced new rituals and new organizations that "complemented" rather than "competed with traditional gatherings."[48] Deutsch has attributed to mission women the role of "social director," arguing that Anglo-Protestant society "allotted" them the "role of social control and cultural bearer."[49] Certainly missionaries would have liked to exert control over their Hispano neighbors, but they were never fully to meet this goal. At first, they organized programs they hoped would lead Hispanos to convert. When Hispanos evinced no interest, missionaries introduced a different strategy, which consisted of the various social services and programs that complemented the schooling they offered. The mission movement had assumed that over time Hispanos would assimilate and follow the example provided by the home missionary. Thus these missionaries exemplify the extent to which the social experience of community is an interactive

---

[46] Nellie Tichenor McGraw, "An Ideal," *Home Mission Monthly* 23 (August 1909): 232–33.

[47] Frances Goodrich, "The Ideal Missionary," *Home Mission Monthly* 23 (August 1909): 233–34.

[48] Sarah Deutsch, *No Separate Refuge: Culture, Class, and Gender on an Anglo-Hispanic Frontier in the American Southwest, 1880–1940* (New York: Oxford University Press, 1987), p. 83.

[49] She also argues that it was left to Hispanic women villagers to "adopt" the roles of "social integrator and cultural and community maintainer" (ibid., p. 85).

process, always in the making. Whatever community was created was derived from mutual interaction among all the parties involved. Mission teachers could not simply pass along customs and manners without themselves being changed in the process. By deemphasizing conversion as a critical part of the Americanization process, missionaries adopted a secular conception of what it meant to be American, thereby taking a significant step away from the evangelistic commitment that had originally led them to the movement.

As Hispano culture in New Mexico changed in these years, both resisting and adapting to the encroaching Anglo-dominated culture, so did Anglo culture. Indeed, the ability of Anglo culture to adapt to the resistance it encountered resulted in part from the way mission women redefined their role. The failure of Hispanos to convert compelled mission women to change their definition of success, to reassess their initial impressions of Hispano culture, and to fashion new methods by which to maintain their position, both in their assigned stations in New Mexico and in the larger mission enterprise. The result was that over time the early imperialist goal and agenda—to ensure a Protestant citizenry—was replaced by an ethic that recognized the validity of the surrounding Hispano culture but retained a central role for missionaries as mediators between the two cultures.

Though they stopped short of embracing cultural pluralism, mission teachers' growing acceptance of the legitimacy of cultural diversity reflects one way the movement shared the larger social and political concerns of its Progressive contemporaries. Both movements used much the same language to describe their goals. Just as Progressives active in the settlements drew on the "language of social bonds" and talked of family and community, so too did missionaries.[50] Like liberal Progressives, mission teachers came to espouse a concept of humanitarian social democracy which helped to pave the way for the more pluralist ideology and politics of the 1930s.[51] Rivka Lissak has hesitated to call Progressives "pluralist," arguing that at the height of their political power and influence, they were not able to reach a consensus on issues of assimila-

---

[50] Daniel Rodgers, "In Search of Progressivism," *Reviews in American History* 10 (December 1982): 125.

[51] Rivka Shpak Lissak, *Pluralism and Progressives: Hull House and the New Immigrants, 1890–1919* (Chicago: University of Chicago Press, 1989). See also Mina Carson, *Settlement Folk: Social Thought and the American Settlement Movement, 1885–1930* (Chicago: University of Chicago Press, 1990), pp. 101–9.

tion or pluralism.[52] Instead, they balanced ambivalently between those Anglo-Americans who called on immigrant groups (or those deemed foreign) to acculturate and acquire the dominant Anglo values and representatives of immigrant groups who espoused Israel Zangwill's concept of the "melting pot" or Horace Kallen's ideas of "cultural pluralism."[53] Unable to resolve the tensions between their own commitment to social unity and the cultural diversity that flourished in the immigrant communities around them, Progressives expressed contradictory ideas simultaneously, speaking of "mutual esteem and respect of variety and in favor of cross-fertilization."[54] Though they wavered, Lissak finds that their "opposition to the compulsory eradication of differences, their insistence that immigrant cultures be tolerated, contributed to the redefinition of liberalism in the 1930s."[55] The most important role they played in this process of "redefinition" was not working with immigrant cultures but in acting, as did missionaries, as mediators, interpreting the immigrants to Anglo-Americans.[56]

† † †

Missionaries who were in the field for many years were quite conscious that their impressions and their understanding of Hispano culture had changed. After seven years in the enterprise, missionary Delia Hills —who was stationed in Raton, New Mexico, for eight years—declared that the "novelty of strange sights and sounds" had worn off. "There is nothing new, nothing strange, everything is familiar," she wrote. Lest readers interpret her comments to suggest that the same level of support was no longer required, Hills claimed that "familiarity" did not "lessen the amount of work to be done; it only increases the opportunities for work, and the work that I do in different channels is only limited by my strength."[57] What is impressive about missionary reports from the field is the degree to which the missionaries themselves rather than their Hispano clients are the subjects. Published in the *Home Mission Monthly*, these reports provide insight into mission women's changing

[52] Lissak, *Pluralism and Progressives*, p. 4.
[53] Ibid., pp. 145–49.
[54] Ibid., pp. 8–9.
[55] Ibid., p. 184.
[56] Ibid., p. 123.
[57] Delia Hills, "A Package of Letters," *Home Mission Monthly* 7 (November 1893): 7.

self-consciousness about ethnicity, cultural differences, and social diversity.

Delia Hills found it difficult to write about her work because it had become so much a part of her. She said that reporting on her activities was like "writing about one's own family duties, family cares, and family perplexities." After many years in Raton, she did not feel that that the community called forth the "same comment" it had early in her career. She no longer saw "national peculiarities" and argued that they had "disappeared, completely" in some instances. One can read Hills's comments to mean that she had succeeded in subverting Hispano culture and Americanizing her students. She reported, for instance, that "the children are taking delight in American ways and American customs," though she did not specify these ways and customs.[58] Another reading, however, that is far more plausible is that with time and experience Hills had stopped classifying Hispanos as "other." Indeed, in proclaiming her commitment to the community to which she had been assigned, Hills confessed that though she did "often yearn for the companionship of some American friend . . . I feel that it would be a decided novelty to be suddenly placed among American people and in a school of American pupils." "I am afraid," she concluded, that "I should be continually asking 'Do you understand?'"[59]

Little is known about Hills except what impressions can be garnered from the excerpts of her reports published in the *Home Mission Monthly*. By 1894, Hills had worked in Raton for seven years and was enrolling 170 students in her school. Her school seems to have been one of a very few educational alternatives available to Hispanos in Raton. Raton was one of the larger towns in the region, located just south of Trinidad, Colorado, on the Santa Fe Trail. Its population was roughly divided between Hispanos and Anglos, and the latter seemed to be in charge of the city government. A reading of the local newspaper in the late 1880s suggests that there was one public school on the predominantly Anglo west side of town. The newspaper also reported a Presbyterian mission school in the predominantly Hispano or east side of town, where classes were taught in both English and Spanish.[60]

The school was opened because Hispano children refused to attend

---

[58] Delia Hills, "Schools and Teachers," *Home Mission Monthly* 10 (November 1895): 17.
[59] Hills, "A Package of Letters," p. 6.
[60] "Report from the Superintendent of Schools—Colfax County," *Raton Independent Weekly*, December 31, 1887, p. 1.

Teacher, evangelist, and pupils at Raton, New Mexico (Department of History and Records Management Services, Presbyterian Church USA)

the predominantly Anglo public school. While the public school enrolled sixteen Hispano children, the mission school reported seventy-one in its first year of existence in 1887. Newspaper accounts suggest that the mission school served as an advocate of Hispano children. There had been complaints that "Mexicans could not send their children to school on this [west] side because the American children picked on and abused them."[61] The mission school provoked a storm of criticism when Anglos maintained that it was the source of expanded political claims made by Hispanos. In denying these charges, the Reverend J. M. McGaughey did suggest that he could say a "word . . . in regard to the treatment of Mexican and colored children in Raton" but that he did not care to discuss those issues.[62] Even if he did not want to elaborate on the discriminatory treatment of Hispanos, McGaughey made his disapproval clear.

Delia Hills must have been in the middle of these debates, but she did

---

[61] "School Issue Becomes a Controversy," *Raton Independent Weekly*, September 29, 1888, p. 1.

[62] "Correspondence," *Raton Weekly Independent*, October 6, 1888, p. 6.

not write about them or any other political controversies. Her reports focused on her work but, unlike those of other mission women, Hills's accounts remain intensely personal. They lack the patron or professional qualities evident in other women's accounts. Hills's experience illustrates, however, that part of the process whereby mission women came to substitute their Hispano friends and neighbors for family that was distant or dead. Mission teachers looked first to Presbyterian converts for support and assistance in organizing their activities. They spoke enthusiastically of these Hispanos, finding them to be a source of support during difficult and trying times. Initially, mission women drew their new "families" from among this group.

For many missionaries the friendships they established with Hispanos played a significant role in changing their impressions. One is struck by how deeply Hills cared for those Hispanos who became her friends. When her mother, who was also her companion, died, Hills wrote that "for more than twenty years my mother and I had not been separated for more than one week, and for sixteen years at least, we had not been separated a single night. And in the daytime, if she was not with me, when I had to leave home for an hour or two, she was waiting my return with the the words, 'I am so glad you have come, my child.' And now, I come and go alone."[63] Despairing over her mother's absence, she turned to her friendships with the Hispanos in Raton. She found a source of support from a group of Presbyterian Hispana women she had organized into a Home Missionary Society. Writing about this group one year after her mother's death, Hills noted sadly that the treasurer, Savinista Padilla, had died. Padilla, Hills remembered, was the "first Mexican woman with whom I became acquainted and I loved her."[64]

Missionary reports illustrate a wide range of relationships with their Hispano neighbors and are evidence that the evolution of a more pluralist ethic was by no means uniform. Some missionaries, such as Hills, preferred to discuss their experiences in familial terms. Others maintained a more formal demeanor, defining their position with Hispanos as that of a mentor or patron. Mollie Clements taught in the San Juan Valley in southern Colorado for thirty-one years beginning in 1891, after teaching in Albuquerque for three years. She described her work as caring for people's minds, souls, and bodies. Though she put schoolwork

[63] Delia Hills, "Words from Workers," *Home Mission Monthly* 7 (November 1893): 137.
[64] Delia Hills, "Synodical and Presbyterial Items," *Home Mission Monthly* 8 (May 1894): 166.

first, she was distressed by the impoverished conditions and felt that she should make a greater contribution. She rounded out her days by leaving the schoolhouse to nurse the sick, to help sew clothes, and to settle accounts for the men. She refused to think of herself only as a teacher, choosing to define her role broadly, supposing to "know all that is desirable, and make it a rule to try and satisfy all the applications for assistance."[65] She took very seriously the board's admonition that missionaries act as role models. Clements lived a public life and felt that she must take "pains to draw back the curtains from my little windows at night, that passers by might look in." She remembered that "they could not comprehend how a single woman like myself could live alone, a good life, so I lived openly before them, striving to make my life and motives clear."[66]

Clements's descriptions of the Hispanos with whom she worked were not without racial stereotypes. She could, in one sentence, call Hispanos "sickly and immoral" but then in another assert that they were "bright, uncomplaining, and naturally sympathetic." Unlike Hills, Clements did not define her success in terms of erasing "national peculiarities"; instead, she favored some form of cultural exchange, recognizing that Anglo-Americans did have lessons to learn from Hispanos. She contradicted commonly held assumptions among Anglos about the nature of sexual relations among Hispanos. Young men and women were never permitted to be alone, she reported; parents closely supervised all meetings.[67] Clements's reports also show an increasing balance between spiritual and material concerns. In 1893 she indicated that she had begun to wonder how the poor in her community lived. Rather than comment on the state of their souls or reflect on the reasons for their impoverishment, she took a practical view, wishing that she could give her poorer students "one good substantial meal a day."[68]

Clements's attempts to address the stereotypes held by Anglo-Protestant supporters suggests a repudiation of ideas that the spiritual, intellectual, and social gulf between Anglos and Hispanos was a result of innate physical differences. Another longtime teacher, Matilda Allison, went to great lengths to disabuse her Anglo supporters that the "backwardness" of Hispanos was innate. She described the girls in the Santa

[65] Mollie Clements, "A Package of Letters," *Home Mission Monthly* 7 (July 1893): 9.
[66] Mollie Clements, "La Maestra," *Home Mission Monthly* 10 (November 1895): 6–7.
[67] Ibid., p. 6.
[68] Clements, "A Package of Letters," p. 8.

Fe boarding school as "children capable of becoming intelligent and useful citizens," just like the "average American child." She reported that the domestic education she had introduced into the school brought her the "greatest satisfaction" and that "our girls can now do housework better than most American children of the same age."[69] Mission teachers took pleasure in reporting that Hispano children were capable of doing the same schoolwork as Anglo children. Their job description had pointedly stressed a woman's ability to act as a disciplinarian, but few of the teachers reported discipline problems. Instead, children were described as docile, kind, respectful, even ambitious to learn English.

Peggy Pascoe has argued that home missionaries were "antiracists" because they "anticipated" the distinction that would be made in this century between "biologically determined race and socially constructed culture," but they were not cultural relativists; they believed their own mores and habits to be superior and expected their clients to be transformed.[70] Mission teachers preferred to believe that the issue was one not of "race, but grace."[71] The belief that Hispanos could be transformed was what initially spurred missionary attempts at conversion. To have subscribed to a doctrine of innate racial inferiority would have cast a shadow of doubt over the legitimacy of the mission work. A mission teacher's job was secure only so long as her school remained open, and the Woman's Board was not keen to support schools in which teachers reported little change in students' habits and behavior. This attitude predisposed mission teachers to believe in the possibility for improvement and change among Hispanos. They may have realized that it was self-defeating to report that conditions were unchanged. Lacking converts, however, missionaries became aware of the many factors influencing Hispano life, from the Catholic Church to the deteriorating environmental and economic conditions.

[69] Matilda Allison, "Words from Workers," *Home Mission Monthly* 3 (February 1889): 84.

[70] Peggy Pascoe, *Relations of Rescue: The Search for Female Moral Authority in the American West, 1874–1939* (New York: Oxford University Press, 1990), p. 143.

[71] Michael Coleman, "Not Race, but Grace: Presbyterian Missionaries and American Indians, 1857–1893," *Journal of American History* 67 (June 1980): 41–60, prefers to call missionaries ethnocentric rather than racist, arguing that they did not adhere to the nineteenth-century doctrine of racism, which held that there were innate physical differences among different peoples and Anglo-Saxons were superior. He suggests that "racism struck deeply at the missionary understanding of human nature" (p. 60). This understanding was based on a scriptural interpretation that each individual had a special relationship with God and was fused with an eighteenth-century Enlightenment faith in the unity of mankind and the sameness of human nature.

† † †

Upon her arrival in Rociada, Alice Blake had been quick to condemn the townspeople as "so corrupt in their moral nature that they would scorch the soul of an angel." So immoral were the people, so like animals, that they lived in a "prairie dog town." Adobe houses appeared to be "mounds of earth," and there was "nothing green, except, perhaps, an occasional straggly tree, looking lonesome amid the general barrenness." The state of the village was, concluded Blake, "symbolic of the lives of the people." In hindsight she tempered her evaluation. This young woman, who described herself as being from a "traditional New England home," even though she did not travel to New England until after she was well into her career, came to understand that the "barrenness" served a purpose. "Every stray bit of grass and unevenness is eradicated in the patio, for the purpose of eliminating the encroachment of insects, and to keep the patio in readiness for the spreading of mattresses when the weather is favorable," she related. Hispanos were "not by any means a primitive race," but they had been rendered a "backward" people by the Catholic Church.[72]

Alice Blake, a missionary for forty years, remembered that at the outset of her career in 1889 she had felt that she had been assigned to "Sodom and Gomorrah."[73] Yet as she came to understand the extent of the poverty in which Hispanos lived, she changed her initial judgment; individual Hispanos were not responsible for their impoverished conditions. Casting about for other explanations, she initially blamed the Catholic Church, but over the many years she spent in the field she came to a much fuller appreciation of the forces shaping her Hispano neighbors' lives. Blake's unpublished memoir provides insight into the nature of the political self-consciousness that mission women developed and illustrates the many roles they took on and the professional mind-set many developed about their work. This overview of her life and career also illuminates the dilemmas and contradictions mission women encountered as they found their ideas about both work and ethnicity changing.

Although the Woman's Board of Home Missions hailed her as a mod-

---

[72] Blake, "Memoirs," pp. 215–16.
[73] Ibid., p. 216.

el and applauded her many years of mission work, at the end of her career Blake was of two minds about it. Her memoir, or history of the home mission enterprise in New Mexico (which was not published by the board in part because the reviewer said "it is not well balanced," and the "thing is decidedly top-heavy on the side of the work carried on by the women"), is a troubling and ambiguous document.[74] Neither wholly positive nor negative in its judgment of the mission work, Blake's analysis has no clear voice. The book is the story of women missionaries who came to New Mexico to be spiritual leaders and to bring a better way of life to people they believed were "backward." It is a document charting change—changing mission policies, changing attitudes on the part of Anglo missionaries and their Hispano clients, changing material conditions for Hispanos, and finally the changing consciousness of one woman. If mission women had expected to initiate change and exert control over the changes that occurred, Blake's conclusions suggest another story, that of a mission enterprise whose success was oftentimes deceiving.

After her birth in Iowa in 1867, Alice Blake's family lived in Kansas and Texas before settling in Las Vegas, New Mexico. Blake described her father as a "health seeker."[75] He may have suffered from tuberculosis as Las Vegas had earned a reputation as the "heart of the well country" for its hospitals specializing in the treatment of this disease.[76] In 1883 the family visited the Tercio-Millennial Exposition in Santa Fe, where Alice remained to attend the Presbyterian Academy (the only mission school established for the children of Anglo settlers, it was short-lived). Here she became acquainted with the Presbyterian home mission movement. After attending the academy, she left the territory for Kansas City, where she attended high school, remaining to attend Episcopalian

[74] Blake had hoped that her memoirs would be published. She had first proposed the idea for a book about mission efforts among Mexicans in 1914 (see Blake to Marshall Allaben, February 4, 1914, Blake Biographical File, H5, PHS). The memoir was not completed until after she retired. In reviewing the manuscript, Robert McLean thought it was not of publishable quality. He suggested that Hermann Morse might rewrite it, but in the form Blake had submitted it, "it is valuable source material, to be filed away in manuscript in the Board rooms and made available for those who want to use it for source material" (McLean to Warnshuis, October 14, 1935, Blake Biographical File, H5, PHS).

[75] Blake, "Memoirs," p. 215.

[76] Ralph Emerson Twitchell, *The Leading Facts of New Mexican History* (Cedar Rapids, Ia.: Torch Press, 1917), 4: 227.

Alice Blake (Department of History and Records Management Services, Presbyterian Church USA)

Bethany College in Topeka. In 1888, after completing college, she returned to her family in Las Vegas.[77]

Like the other women who became home missionaries, Blake found that few options were open to her in Las Vegas. She did what many young women in her position did: she taught in the public school. It was a precarious life because public schools in New Mexico were open for only a few months of the year, and teachers were paid only for those months school was in session. Additionally, the public schools in New Mexico were highly politicized. Religious and political organizations

[77] Blake, "Memoirs," p. 218.

argued over the content of education, in many places effectively under-cutting the school. Blake could not have been immune to these troubles. The home mission movement was an attractive alternative: she had attended a mission school, and unlike other women coming from the East, she had firsthand experience with the nature of the work. At the age of twenty-two, after a year teaching in public school, Blake was commissioned by the home mission movement.

Over the course of her career, Blake was assigned to teach in four communities. Her first assignment, from 1889 to 1895, was in Rociada, northwest of Las Vegas in the Sangre de Cristo Mountains. Blake described the village as being "between two small, swift streams where the canyon widens into an amphitheater about two miles wide in diameter." It looked "northward toward a low divide which [separated] it from Cebolla Valley." Las Vegas was the nearest large town and trading point. Here she encountered tremendous resistance from both the local priest and the Penitentes. Even though she managed to build up enroll-ments so that at the end of five years she counted fifty students, the school was closed. Blake moved on to Buena Vista, twenty miles north of Las Vegas. There was no real village, only a "thickly settled farming community," located near La Cueva. In 1897 she agreed to replace a retiring missionary at El Aguila/Chaperito, southeast of Las Vegas, on the Gallinas River. When this school was closed in 1902, Blake moved on to her last station, at Trementina. Here, forty-six miles east of Las Vegas on Trementina Creek, Blake remained until her retirement in 1931.[78]

In her memoirs, Blake's description of her first impressions suggests how critical she was initially of Hispano culture: "We would not say that there was nothing attractive about this priest-ridden people, nor that they did not have the same underlying instincts as others." Later in the same paragraph she admitted that "when environment and traditional influences became better known to me, I came to see that there were extenuating reasons for this state of affairs." Her conclusion was that the people with whom she worked were not "unmoral, but weakly immoral. There is nothing in their habits or philosophy of life to develop self-control." She preferred to think of the people as children in need of training, echoing President Benjamin Harrison's sentiments that this was

[78] Ibid., p. 215, 220–22, 226–27; see also T. M. Pearce, ed., *New Mexico Place Names: A Geographical Dictionary* (Albuquerque: University of New Mexico Press, 1965), pp. 137, 21, 31, 169.

a "child race, who have less self-control than other children of six years of age."[79]

Even at the outset in Rociada, Blake's original impressions and initial stereotypes were challenged. In early reports from Rociada to the *Home Mission Monthly* she argued that Hispanos were "not by any means a primitive race," and yet she assailed the cultural forces in their lives as backward and standing in the way of individual advancement. She reported increasing support for the school. She could not claim any converts, but she was pleased with her work. Her growing concern with the living conditions of the people came at the same time she began to question the guiding principle of the mission enterprise, religious education and conversion. Blake realized, she recalled, "as many in authority did not, that our task was to inculcate new moral standards, even a new interpretation of religious terms." Rather than fill church rolls with people who did not understand the expectations of the church—a practice she believed would lead to misunderstanding and alienation—Blake argued for a slower process. The church must establish itself, make a presence in the social life of the village, before it could expect converts. She did not elaborate on what she meant by her call to inculcate a "new interpretation of religious terms," but she seemed open to modification of theological fundamentals.[80] In addition, she seemed to imply that the mission movement must not limit itself to spreading the Gospel, to preaching, but involve itself in all aspects of daily life. Her position is not surprising; it was one which supported her work. The liturgical role she could play was limited. To emphasize the building of church membership at the expense of community-related activities, like the school, might undermine her efforts.

After her short tenure at Rociada, Blake was transferred to Buena Vista, where she worked for a year, and then was told that the Woman's Board could no longer afford to support the Buena Vista mission. She took a position teaching in the public school in Las Vegas. She returned to mission work the following year at the urging of an elderly missionary, Miss Wysong, who was looking for someone to replace her at her school in El Aguila/Chaperito. Support for this school was guaranteed by a patron, Frances Bray of San Jose, California. At her death, the First Church in Morristown, New Jersey, took over as principal supporter.

[79] Blake, "Memoirs," p. 216.
[80] Ibid., p. 221.

This church was to pay Blake's salary, first at El Aguila and then at nearby Trementina, until her retirement thirty-two years later.

During her three years in El Aguila, Blake encountered the political and economic conditions that were dramatically altering the lives of her Hispano students and neighbors.[81] "The people," she remembered, "were facing serious difficulties in the tenure of their land." She described the destruction of the community:

> First, the wool washing, and the pickling plants that had been established in Las Vegas, were contaminating the water of the Gallinas River so that a scum was left on the plants after irrigation, and they were not producing as well as formerly; and then word came that the most noted land grabbers of the day had succeeded in getting a title to all of the land of the grant, on which these people were living above the irrigation ditch, and the people were ordered not to take wood from this land and not to use it for the pasture of their stock. This was a death blow, as no man could make a living from the little strip of irrigated land he called his own. The people began to move away, some to the public lands beyond the grant lands where pasture and fuel were assured, and where there were hopes for a crop of beans and maize if the season should prove feasible. Others wandered away so that they would not even return during the winter months for the sake of the school.[82]

As a result, the church and the school that home missionaries had built at El Aguila had to be closed. The very economic and political forces the mission enterprise had been meant to support now threatened the foundation the missionaries had struggled to build. In the nearby town of Los Valles, residents were facing similar conditions. Stream arroyos along the canyons of the lower part of the Conchas and Trementina were rich pasture lands. What little land was available abutted the Red River Cattle Company's holdings of the Juan Montoya Grant, limiting any opportunity for future expansion, but the former inhabitants of Los Valles began to bring in small herds of sheep and cattle to graze.[83] On this land, in a town called Trementina, the people would gain a small reprieve from worsening economic conditions. Blake divided her time

---

[81] Village lands, located on the Antonio Ortiz Grant, could no longer support farming. See Alice Blake, *La Aurora*, March 28, 1902.

[82] Blake, "Memoirs," p. 226.

[83] Ibid.

between Trementina and El Aguila, thirty miles apart. El Aguila was soon a ghost town, and Blake became firmly established in Trementina. Trementina was a unique case among the mission stations in New Mexico. It was a new village, geographically isolated and sparsely populated, and inhabited principally by Presbyterian converts. The Catholic Church made few attempts to proselytize in the area.[84] Blake was now free of the cultural challenges the Catholic Church presented to other home missionaries.

Trementina and its people's needs occupied the last thirty years of Blake's career. Originally the settlement had two or three families; it grew to include thirty families, who raised corn, beans, chiles, watermelons, and sorghum cane on the land along the Trementina creek. Every family kept a few horses, cows, sheep, and goats. What little cash the people had came from processing the sorghum into molasses and selling it in the larger towns of Las Vegas, Mora, and Chacón. But residents recalled that "nobody had money." Instead, the molasses was bartered. A former resident of Trementina remembered, "It was all barter. Often when we traded for wheat, we had it ground on shares at the Sanchez mill in Mora." Some earned cash by working as cowboys at the nearby Big Bell Ranch, but this was seasonal work and did not provide a steady income.[85]

In this setting Blake opened yet another mission school. The school served as a unifying force in the community by bringing together the young people from the area. No children were turned away, and Blake reported large enrollments. After establishing her school, Blake branched out into other community activities. She proposed digging a well so that women would not have to walk to the stream one mile from town for water. She was the moving force behind establishing a post office and then acted as postmistress. She campaigned for improved sanitation and hygiene. When a saloon was opened nearby, she spearheaded the campaign to have it closed. When ministers were unavailable, she conducted worship services. She introduced the celebration of Thanksgiving and made it a major holiday.[86]

As her memoir makes clear, Alice Blake changed with the times. In the

---

[84] Foote, " 'Let Her Works Praise Her,' " p. 188.

[85] S. Omar Barker, "Trementina: Memories of a Mission Village," *Albuquerque Journal,* September 23, 1980, p. 11.

[86] Cheryl Foote, "Alice Blake of Trementina: Mission Teacher of the Southwest," *Journal of Presbyterian History* 60 (Fall 1982): 234.

1880s, when she began her work, her strategies emphasized religious convictions and teaching. With her mandate to inculcate new "moral standards," she set about to change the patterns of daily life. She stressed booklearning and organized book clubs, libraries, and literary societies. When she organized a literary society and library in Rociada, she reported enthusiastically that "the idea of getting an education and learning English is growing to be a mania. . . . They will not let any business in Spanish interfere with the hour for English."[87] But these activities did little to relieve or even to address what Blake called the "need of these poor people." In an effort to ease the burdens of daily life, she introduced services which she hoped would have a long-lasting effect. Blake hoped to avoid the mistakes of one of her predecessors, Ella Bloom, who had tried to "alleviate the present need" of her Hispano neighbors by purchasing "all the eggs people brought to her at a higher price than they could get for them" in a nearby market.[88] Instead, Blake set about to improve sanitary conditions, support vocational training, organize projects to build water wells, and campaign for preventive health care.

In keeping with the general profile of the home missionary experience, Blake grew particularly sensitive to health-related problems. She pleaded for expanded medical services and toward the end of her career was certified as a public health worker. In her description of Rociada, she recalled that year after year she had students from the same families, but the individuals were often not the same because mortality rates were so high. She explained: "Although a large number of children were born to a family, usually from twelve to twenty, yet only a few survived. The high mortality was due to the manner of living, and in the handling of contagious diseases. At that time, smallpox decimated the family about every seven years, and measles and Septic sore throat were nearly as bad."[89]

Blake's search for an explanation led her to conclude that baptismal practices were a leading cause of death among infants. "It was customary," she remembered, "to break the ice in the baptismal font and pour this water over the head of the infant, which was usually less than eight days old. The clothing was loosened about the neck in order to make the sign of the cross on the chest and back. A teaspoonful of salt was put in the mouth of a male child and half a teaspoonful into that of a female.

[87] Alice Blake, "Words from Workers," *Home Mission Monthly* 7 (May 1893): 161.
[88] Blake, "Memoirs," p. 222.
[89] Ibid., p. 220.

After the ceremony the child would often be taken home without properly replacing the clothes." She added that "the latter was due to ignorance and poverty."⁹⁰ Gradually, the problems she had originally attributed to individual immorality were ascribed to ignorance and poverty.

As long as she worked in communities where the Catholic Church played a prominent role, Blake could believe that people's "moral standards" or religious beliefs must change for material progress to occur. At a location like Rociada, she could easily link poverty with ignorance. The incidence of disease could be blamed on the practices of the Catholic Church. When she moved to Trementina and worked in a community that had a large number of Presbyterian converts, however, the causes of poverty could not be tied to spiritual ignorance. Converting offered few rewards. In fact, as she herself admitted, conditions grew worse. She could no longer blame high infant mortality on the baptismal ceremony, for instance. She had to confront the reality of the economic circumstances faced by the majority of Hispano New Mexicans, as well as the racial stereotypes that she came to believe hindered their advancement.

Blake came to realize that Americanization was not necessarily in the best interests of the Hispanos. She argued that they had become "thoroughly American-minded in their patriotic allegiance." They had supported the Union in the Civil War, participated as Rough Riders in the Spanish-American War, and volunteered to fight in World War I. She concluded that the revision of land grant laws had had a negative effect on them. Earlier, she argued, the laws were "simple and adequate," but under United States rule they "gave rise to many a law-suit." The result was "heartache" caused by "land-grabbing" Americans. It sometimes had, she conceded, "a material effect on the missionary work." She admitted that the impressions of "newcomers" to New Mexico were "unfair," for example, derisive comments about mud floors and adobe houses. Building these floors was a complicated process, she explained. Hispana women "took the making of their floors very seriously."⁹¹

Twenty years into her career, the Woman's Board of Home Missions lauded Blake as a model home missionary. The *Home Mission Monthly* carried many of her reports, updated readers on her activities, and in 1910 invited her as one of several missionaries to address the Woman's Board at its national convention. She wrote of her accomplishments,

⁹⁰ Ibid.
⁹¹ Ibid., pp. 1–11.

explaining to readers of the *Home Mission Monthly* that "we [she and the other residents of Trementina] have laid out a town site, and nine houses have been built from no other incentive than that offered by our school. We have built a large chapel, schoolhouse, and have put in a town well and windmill and also established a post office which supplies this precinct and one adjoining. . . . Do you realize that we are a city set on a hill?"[92]

Blake told readers of the mission journal, the supporters of her mission, that she was playing a central role in the community; she was mother, patron, and professional all bound into one. She was pleased when villagers referred to her as the "mother of us all," saying that "one comes to feel one's self so much a necessity that it is hard to go away ever for the needed vacation." When she prepared for a vacation, her neighbors urged her not to stay away so that when she did leave she felt like a "deserter till safely back at work again."[93] These "vacations" were often trips east to speak to mission societies that supported the home mission work.

In these talks she tried to convey a sense of Hispano culture, the environment in which she lived, and the problems she encountered. She debunked statistical studies as a good indicator of the "Progress" and "direction" of mission work. In her descriptions of her own work in New Mexico, she relied heavily on cultural analysis. She urged her audiences to consider the difficulties of people facing a transformation of the customs they had known for centuries. "Think for a moment," she said to the annual meeting of the Woman's Board in 1910, "what it must mean to those people, who have lived for centuries entirely isolated from the world . . . to be brought suddenly to the portals of the twentieth century, and to be told that they must change their life, even their mother tongue; that in a day they must teach their hands new cunning in order to seek their livelihood under entirely new conditions." Blake asked her Anglo-Protestant audiences to put themselves in the place of her Hispano neighbors. She defined her role as "helping them to find and to adjust themselves." Ever the teacher, Blake advocated guidance over imposition. She saw the "duty" of the mission enterprise as threefold. First, it must be true to its religious roots and "convince of a full and free

[92] Alice Blake, "Advantages of Isolated Districts," *Home Mission Monthly* 24 (November 1909): 12.

[93] Alice Blake, "Trementina, N.M." *Home Mission Monthly* 26 (November 1911): 17.

salvation through sacrifice of the Cross." Second, it must promote the national interest by making "true American citizens, intelligent and enthusiastic supporters of our institutions." Finally, she urged that a technical education be added to a moral education to "enable them [Hispanos] to cope with the social temptation and problems of the twentieth century."[94]

Blake was one of the most successful of the missionaries in New Mexico. Her career was long, and she was remembered with affection by her Hispano neighbors and students. A former student recalled that she would stop at nothing to seek support for the mission. He told of Blake setting out for Santa Fe in the midst of a snowstorm with huge drifts to attend a presbytery meeting "to seek better support for her mission school." Although she was considered a strict disciplinarian, she also organized social events, even dances. "She didn't much favor dancing," recalled a former student, but "well behaved *bailes* were not forbidden. Lots of times, practically everybody old enough and not too old to walk would dance for hours to the music of guitars and fiddles."[95] She was pleased that after she retired to Colorado she continued to receive cards and letters from the people in Trementina. Yet in the course of her career, Blake had grown disillusioned, and she left mission work with certain misgivings. She wrote to the board in 1943 that she "wondered whether you thought that I had not enjoyed the life I had led for more than 40 years— Enjoy is such a funny word, as most words are just comparative. But I did get a great deal out of that life anyway."[96] It is an odd note, with a tentative, perhaps even melancholy, undertone.

By the time she retired, Trementina was virtually deserted, victim of the drought, soil erosion and successive crop failures that gripped the state in the 1920s and 1930s. As in other villages in northern New Mexico, the Hispanos of Trementina had been lured away by the opportunities and wages promised in bigger cities such as Albuquerque, Denver, and Los Angeles or had joined the ranks of migrant laborers working in the sugar beet and coal fields of Colorado.[97] Blake had strived to introduce "moral standards" and had worked to achieve a better stan-

---

[94] Alice Blake, "A Fifteenth Century Survival," *Home Mission Monthly* 24 (July 1910): 204–5.

[95] Barker, "Trementina," p. 12.

[96] Alice Blake to Edna Voss, January 13, 1943, Blake Biographical File, H5, PHS.

[97] Deutsch, *No Separate Refuge*, pp. 87–199.

dard of living. Unfortunately, after thirty years in one community, there was little to show for her work. Material conditions, she had to admit, had deteriorated rather than improved.

A letter she wrote to Edna Voss of the Board of National Missions (which succeeded the Woman's Board) suggests that Blake had been defeated by the worsening material conditions of Trementina. Writing at the height of the Depression, she observed that "Trementina has been very hard hit through the drought and depression. I lived with their poverty for 30 years, it had a great deal to do with breaking me down, I know I could not have lived through the past four years." Relief had been provided by the government, and "the outlook is better now. There is government road building and the big reservoir whose site was surveyed 10 years ago is being put in 10 miles below the town." In the short term, living conditions were difficult, she explained. "Very little relief had come in before the holidays, it is still barely enough to keep the families alive." She was bolstered by letters she had received; in the face of worsening economic circumstances, the townspeople had maintained the religious and patriotic rituals she had introduced. She wrote that "the people are doing all they can to keep up the precedents that I established." She was most touched by the continued observance of holidays such as Easter, Thanksgiving, and "X-mas."[98]

At the end of her career, she called for greater government support for welfare.[99] Her sympathies seemed attuned to the assumptions that gave rise to New Deal programs. These sentiments are not explicit in her memoirs; they must be extrapolated. Her memoirs are barely self-conscious. In the end, she was unable to explain her part in the changes that had modified her original goals, her own life, and the lives of the people with whom she had worked.

Blake's dawning realization that her work was handicapped by forces over which she had little control was a blow to her professional self-esteem. She questioned her usefulness, complaining that she was weakened by bad health and suggesting that perhaps she was too old or that the mission would be better served if she took medical training. She wrote to the board that "after 20 years of working alone one feels rusty in spite of every effort to keep up through School Journals, etc." She had visited other schools to "observe the work, methods, etc.," and she had

---

[98] Alice Blake to Edna Voss, January 9, 1936, Blake Biographical File, H5, PHS.
[99] Blake, *Memoirs*, p. 233.

taken a six-week course in manual training, feeling that she was qualified to teach only sewing and cooking. She asked the board to send an additional teacher who might conduct classes in manual and vocational skills. Blake felt isolated and professionally stifled. She wrote that she felt the "need of contact with people who are doing things as much as I do the technical study. I simply need brushing up." She suggested an exchange or a summer at a city mission, perhaps Chicago or New York. She considered changing jobs completely and had spent two summers working in a hospital "doing the regular ten hour stint of a nurse on duty." Although she planned to take courses at the Colorado Normal School, in the summer of 1904 she began summer courses at the University of Colorado, working toward a certificate in public health.[100]

Nearing fifty years of age, Blake began to have health problems. Her letters to the board mention surgery to extract a tumor, as well as bouts of neuritis. In 1918 she resigned from missionary work and took a position as matron at East Las Vegas Hospital.[101] That same year she volunteered to work with the Children's Bureau of the Labor Department to weigh and measure the state's children and traveled throughout the northern villages to do so.[102] Informing the board of her resignation and position at the hospital, she noted that the work was "strenuous" but not a "circumstance to what I would have faced in Trementina." She was tired and glad to be away from exposure to bad weather; it was pleasant not to have to get her own meals.[103] However close she may have felt to her neighbors and clients in Trementina, the Woman's Board's invocation of familial imagery could not change the fact that she and the people she worked with were not family.

Blake's isolation magnified her professional crisis. Indeed, it threw into question the work she had performed and her own abilities. Speaking of Trementina, she wrote that "the people expect as much of me now as they did 15 years ago. I am now 50 years old and feel that under favorable circumstances I would not be able to keep up with the work there for a great while. . . . I have felt since my breakdown that I was not doing justice to myself nor to the work but held on under the impression that my place would be hard to fill." She even questioned

---

[100] Alice Blake to Fraser, March 23, 1912, Blake Biographical File, H5, PHS; Foote, "'Let Her Works Praise Her,'" p. 188.

[101] Alice Blake to Marshall Allaben, November 29, 1918, Blake Biographical File, H5, PHS.

[102] Foote, "Alice Blake of Trementina," p. 234.

[103] Blake to Allaben, November 29, 1918.

whether it was work a woman could perform successfully, claiming that it was her duty to get out because it was "a man's job." Furthermore, the opening of the public school undercut the need for a teacher. The greatest need she asserted was for a medical missionary.[104] After several years away from mission work, during which she worked for the Children's Bureau and the Las Vegas Hospital, Blake returned to Trementina. Through a combination of correspondence courses and summer residency at New York University she gained a certificate in public health.[105] It satisfied her need for a change of pace and was the credential required by the state of New Mexico enabling her to continue her informal medical work.[106] Her last ten years in Trementina were spent undertaking community development projects, not teaching.

Throughout the period in which she expressed the disillusionment with the job, she maintained her commitment to the Hispanos with whom she lived; she did not leave New Mexico until her retirement, and only then to live with her brother and sister in Colorado. Ironically, with Trementina rapidly becoming a ghost town, she joined her neighbors in their geographical migration to Colorado.[107] The epilogue to her memoir is an impassioned defense of the state of New Mexico and its people. Blake warned of "how many people there are who are wont to bolster up a prejudice with any passing impression that would seem to justify it." She took issue with a friend passing through New Mexico, who had said, "'Of all the places I have seen, New Mexico is positively the most worthless. It is nothing but a great desert.'" In reply, Blake quoted another missionary who sang New Mexico's praises, pointing to the "beautiful and wonderful everywhere." She argued that the Hispano people should be seen in this light, and she concluded that "a casual visitor might easily note only what seems to him uncouth and unpromising; where one who had had the opportunity of knowing them inti-

---

[104] Ibid.

[105] See "Editorial Notes," *Home Mission Monthly* 36 (January 1922): 65, for the announcement that Blake had completed a course in public health at New York University. She received her diploma from the Public Health Association, Bellevue Medical College; see "Board Reports," Presbyterian Church in the U.S.A., *Minutes of the General Assembly*, 1922, p. 26.

[106] She aided the half-time county health officer by vaccinating people in the Trementina area. For a discussion of her ongoing medical work, see Alice Blake, "Visits and Visitations," *Women and Missions* 4 (July 1927): 147.

[107] Cheryl Foote notes that many of her students and neighbors settled in Denver and that Blake continued to see them ("'Let Her Works Praise Her,'" p. 194).

Health campaign babies at Trementina (Department of History and Records Management Services, Presbyterian Church USA)

mately will have discovered many beauties of character and admirable attributes."[108]

Even as she engaged in seemingly secular activities, Blake turned to the religious language invoked for so many years to decry the moral standards and religious values of Hispano culture, arguing instead for the inherent goodness of the local peoples. She wrote:

> As in the land there are sections that are too dry or too wet to bring out the best that is in the soil; so among the people there are arid souls, and souls that are over fervent with an alkaline deposit of false doctrines and wrong ideas that must be eradicated through the power of the Spirit as it is in Christ Jesus before they can grow into the fullness of the stature of their Lord and Savior. If we have taken you through the arid portions of this particular human vineyard of the Kingdom, we hope that we also may have demonstrated the beautiful possibilities that may be realized through proper husbandry as well as the inherently fine qualities possessed by this people in company with all others who were created in the image of God.

[108] Blake, "Memoirs," Epilogue, unpaged.

Blake preached understanding, stressing that Hispano New Mexicans were not the "other" but a people who had been denied the fruits of the environment.[109]

Unlike Josiah Strong and others who had warned of the dangers of Hispano Catholic culture and likened the mission movement to an army advancing to defend the glories of democracy, Blake employed images of cultivation. Certainly, one cannot dismiss the patronizing tone of Blake's conclusions. Clearly, she was writing to those who, like herself, had thrown over "alkaline deposits of false doctrines" and recognized the power of the "Lord and Savior." But the people of whom she writes are not portrayed as threatening. She was careful to stress to her audience the "fine qualities" of the people she had worked and lived with, qualities which she believed Hispanos had in "company" with all others. The environmental analogy is revealing, for it suggests that Blake understood the people's "backwardness," either spiritual or material, to be the result of years of habit or of forces beyond their control. Implicit in her comments was the assumption that people like herself should remain in control. She may have emphasized growth rather than conversion, but in advocating "husbandry," she was calling for an ethic of management. The Christian "standards," "valuations," or dynamic as home missionaries in Blake's position understood it should not entirely repudiate paternalism.

† † †

For Blake, Clements, and Hills, the goal was to maintain their central position in the endeavor and to convince supporters that mission work was essential in promoting understanding between two very different cultures. Mission women did not relinquish their belief in the importance of conversion to Protestantism, nor could they completely renounce racial stereotypes. They did not see Hispanos as their equals, but by entering into these small Hispano villages they had become familiar with a culture they could not quickly or easily cast out for being "other." Unable to convert Hispanos or to remake them in their own image, mission women settled for promoting "understanding," "cooperation," and "social harmony" between Anglo and Hispano cultures.

What did it mean to mediate between the two cultures? First and

[109] Ibid.

foremost, one did not want to alienate students. Missionaries changed how they conducted their classrooms. If they had learned early on in their tenure to temper their emphasis on conversion, they also learned that their secular skills were welcomed. They took this lesson back into the classroom. As early as 1895, teachers were being encouraged to allow the "children's everyday experiences" to be their guide for planning lessons rather than impose a predetermined Christian curriculum. At the meeting of the First Institute of Presbyterian Mission Teachers in the New Mexico synod, teacher Mary Dissette delivered a talk in which she urged teachers to find points of similarity. She urged teachers not to draw "sharp contrasts" and to find a "common ground instead of antagonizing them [the students]."[110]

If finding a "common ground" was intended to win support of Hispanos in hopes that they might convert or become more like missionaries, this goal also led missionaries to modify their own behavior and ideas about culture. Classes were supposed to be conducted in English, but many missionaries in the plaza schools found this was not practical.[111] Instead, they taught in both English and Spanish, dividing their days between the two languages or teaching in Spanish until individual students had learned English. Celia Morgan reported that she conducted lessons in Spanish so as to gain the support of parents; later, when the child was attending school, she would introduce English.[112] Their goal was to make English the primary language, but in the process many of them became familiar with a language they had originally condemned as alien.

As mission women learned about Hispano culture, they passed their lessons on to their Anglo-Protestant supporters. Articles about the much dreaded Penitentes continued to appear in the *Home Mission Monthly*, but supporters of the mission enterprise could also read about the more mundane aspects of Hispano life. Missionaries provided detailed descriptions about the preparation of Mexican food, courtship and marriage customs, and the production of the "fine" blankets of Chimayó.[113]

[110] Mary Dissette, *Home Mission Monthly* 9 (June 1895): 175–76.

[111] The use of Spanish in the classroom was restricted to the plaza schools. The boarding school teachers insisted on English being spoken at all times, in the classroom and in the domitories. Students in the boarding schools were reprimanded and punished for using Spanish. As the only Anglo, or one of few, plaza school teachers did not have the authority to insist on English.

[112] Celia Morgan, "Words from Workers," *Home Mission Monthly* 1 (January 1887): 62.

[113] "Mexican Cookery," *Home Mission Monthly* 16 (November 1901): 6; Prudence Clark,

MEXICAN WOMAN MAKING TORTILLAS.

Published in the *Home Mission Monthly,* November 1900 (Department of History and Records Management Services, Presbyterian Church USA). Beneath the caption was this description: "Tortillas are thin cakes the size of a breakfast plate, made from a stiff dough of flour, salt, and water, baked in the open fireplace. A quantity of this dough is usually kept ready mixed to be baked each meal" (p. 5).

Missionaries not only taught the Hispanos they lived among; their reports informed a larger group of mission supporters. The *Home Mission Monthly* became the vehicle through which Anglo supporters could

"Mexican Marriages," *Home Mission Monthly* 16 (November 1901): 10. Prudence Clark, "Blanket Weaving," *Home Mission Monthly* 18 (November 1903): 10.

learn about Hispano culture; the magazine allowed people to "travel" to New Mexico without being there physically. Articles provided overviews of the geography, bibliographies listed references for those who wanted to do more reading, maps of New Mexico marked the locations of mission stations, and Spanish words were written so as to indicate the proper pronunciation.[114]

By stating their desire to bridge differences and to find "common ground" between Anglos and Hispanos, missionaries called on Anglo-Protestants to educate themselves about other peoples living within United States boundaries. By arguing in favor of cooperation to find common ground, missionaries called into question Anglo ethnocentrism. They suggested that it was not just Hispano culture that was in need of revision but also their own. This shift in mission women's thinking away from an ethnocentric to a more pluralist ideal proved to be advantageous. Their concern was not to develop an new egalitarian ethic; mission women believed that, vis-à-vis the Hispano community, they were rightfully in a position of authority. Rather, it was an attempt to assert their own power within the larger mission enterprise. They could not deliver the large numbers of converts the Presbyterian Church desired, but they could become "experts," so to speak, on the conditions and problems facing Hispanos. Instead of imposing the imperialist agenda, which had led to the formation of the enterprise, mission women learned that a more complex ethic was necessary if they were to reach their students and build careers for themselves.

[114] Prudence Clark, "New Mexico Location, Climate, and Products," *Home Mission Monthly* 24 (November 1909): 4; "Mexicans in the United States—Bibliography," *Home Mission Monthly* 21 (November 1906): 18; "Stations among Mexicans in the United States," *Home Mission Monthly* 23 (November 1908): 17; "Pronunciation of Names of Stations," *Home Mission Monthly* 16 (November 1901): 10.

CHAPTER FIVE

At the Heart of the "Cause": Hispano Mission Students and the Meaning of Faith

When Alice Blake's Hispano neighbors in El Aguila and Los Valles lost their land and moved to Trementina they were pushed to the edge of that part of New Mexico known as the Hispano heartland. To reach home Trementinos had to travel forty-six miles east of Las Vegas, far from the upper and middle valleys of the Rio Grande watershed, across a vast plain that ends as abruptly as the mesa upon which it is located. There is a drop of over one thousand feet as one descends from land dotted with windmills and grazing cattle to what seems the bottom of othe earth. From the comfort of an air-conditioned car, traveling over well-paved roads, the trip is exhilarating, the views breathtaking. But one has only to survey the distant dirt road on leaving the mesa and step out of the car into the hot, dry air that blows through the piñons and scrub oak and across the red clay earth to understand how difficult it would have been to eke out a living on a small parcel of land in this remote location. In its heyday, at the turn of the century shortly after Blake and her neighbors had moved to Trementina, the town boasted some twenty-five to thirty families. In addition to the mission complex, it had a post office, a general store, two saloons (the bane of Alice Blake's existence), and a stage line that ran through the town connecting it to the rest of the territory. Today, Trementina is a ghost town; the foundations of the old houses that remain sit on privately held land— "no trespassing" signs prominently displayed.[1] Like Trementina, the rest of the Hispano heartland has fared badly. The villages in the Rio Grande watershed which were home to mission schools remain, though they are the poorest in the state of New Mexico, with 32 percent of their residents living below the poverty line. Residents survive by combining small-scale agriculture, out-migration, and seasonal employment with welfare benefits.[2] These conditions are the result of changes that began in the nineteenth century and policies that alienated residents from their land and restricted their access to publicly held grazing lands.

Even though Anglo-Protestant women missionaries gained greater sympathy for cultural differences and an awareness that private social service agencies could not meet the needs of Hispanos, they could do little to alleviate the deteriorating material conditions of their Hispano neighbors. Instead, their political self-consciousness was restricted by a contradictory set of expectations which mandated that they be concerned primarily with the souls of their subjects. Although they politicized the deteriorating conditions of their neighbors by publicizing their plight in the national mission literature, their own political activism seems to have been largely confined to local issues which they believed would impede the moral development of their subjects. Hence Alice Blake led spirited campaigns against the saloon keepers in Trementina.[3] The goal, as missionary Marion D. Dutton summed it up, was to "train Christian leaders, educational, political, and religious, for the future of the Southwest."[4] Hispano students were supposed to convert, renew their faith in God (a Protestant God), take up work that expressed their faith, and set aside selfish desires for the good of faith and country. One young convert, Charles Córdova, captured this sentiment when he wrote about his mission school experience: "I went to Menaul a poor ignorant child and came out a Christian young man." Just as his teachers had

---

[1] "Trementina," *New Mexico Magazine*, September 1978, p. 35.

[2] Suzanne Forrest, *Preservation of the Village: New Mexico's Hispanics and the New Deal* (Albuquerque: University of New Mexico Press, 1989), pp. 151–80.

[3] See articles in *La Voz del Pueblo* concerning the censure of R. B. Gomez for operating a cantine in Trementina, (October 28, 1899, p. 3; November 18, 1899, p. 3; December 3, 1899, p. 3). Cheryl Foote reports that in one instance Blake wrote letters and pestered the governor to have the saloon closed because it had been opened illegally ("'Let Her Works Praise Her': Women's Experience in the Southwest, 1846–1912" [Ph.D. diss., University of New Mexico, 1985], p. 186).

[4] Marion D. Dutton, "Educating the Educators," *Women and Missions* 2 (May 1925): 54.

learned by their own experience, he too learned that "there was no royal road to success but the way they themselves were following—the master's way of self-sacrifice and service for others." He cast aside the desire for riches, arguing that a wealthy man did not necessarily have "vision," or "character." "Your success," he advised younger students at the Menaul school, "will lie in the fact that you have been *faithful* while making a man of yourself."[5]

Missionaries were well aware, however, that vision, character, and faith would not carry students far if they did not have the means to support their spiritual beliefs. When Alice Blake contended that her job was to introduce twentieth-century ideas into a society stuck in the fifteenth century, she was speaking about introducing a rural agricultural people to a mechanized and increasingly urban society. Yet the most successful graduates of mission schools did not rely in the long run on the vocational and domestic skills that missionaries struggled to introduce; they did not work with their hands. Instead, they followed directly in the footsteps of the missionaries. When public schools superseded the mission schools, they often hired former mission students as teachers. Native evangelists were ordained and took over the churches that had been built by Anglo ministers. They joined the community programs instituted and advocated by missionaries and moved into administrative positions within the school system and various social welfare programs or sought out work in other government agencies such as the post office.

The purpose of mission work was to engage in a protracted struggle for souls. As long as the "faithful" were seeking out and attempting to convert others, the endeavor would be ongoing and could not fail. This emphasis on religious experience as transformative was not unique, for the Catholic Church had been seeking converts in New Mexico some three hundred years before the arrival of Protestants. By moving into a culture in which conversion had long played a central role, Protestantism may not have offered a particularly new or unique religious experience to Hispanos, but it did offer other social services that had the power to transform people's social experience. For the majority of Hispanos who came into contact with missionaries, the secular uses of their Protestant experience (whether it entailed just a few years in a plaza school or conversion) proved as important as any spiritual benefits gained. Hispa-

[5] *Sandstorm Yearbook* (Albuquerque: Menaul School for Boys, 1914), p. 45.

no New Mexicans became consumers of religious services from both Protestant and Catholic churches, and they switched allegiances depending upon what each institution could offer.

The relationship between Anglo missionaries and their Hispano neighbors was never static. Just when missionaries believed that they had achieved a measure of influence which allowed them to exercise control over students and parents (if not the larger community), they would find their authority questioned and challenged anew. The challenge might come from a new Catholic priest, or from renewed attempts to usurp title to community lands, or from an outbreak of typhoid or influenza. Missionaries could never be sure of the nature of the authority they exercised, if any, or of its durability. In her study of a Methodist mission hospital in El Paso, Vicki Ruiz has contended that "Mexican clients, not missionaries, set the boundaries of interaction." She found that most Mexican women who availed themselves of the medical services offered recognized Houchen Hospital not as a "beacon of salvation but a medical and social service center run by Methodists. They consciously decided what resources they would utilize and consciously ignored or side-stepped the settlement's ideological premises." Ruiz believes that we must see this process—the meeting between missionaries and Hispanos—as one of "cultural coalescence." "Immigrants and their children pick, borrow, retain, and create distinctive cultural forms," she argues, "there is not a single heuristic Mexican or Mexican-American culture but rather permeable cultures rooted in generation, genders, region, class and personal experiences." Although the Anglo mission women set out to create what they believed would be a "new type," their students would not easily be cast into a particular mold. Even the most "faithful" of students—those who converted—"picked" and "borrowed" from among what Ruiz calls "the cognitive construction of missionary aspirations and expectations" to construct their own Hispano-Presbyterian culture.[6]

Mission literature contains many testimonials from Hispanos who converted and made a new life for themselves within the Presbyterian Church. Certainly one can question the validity of these expressions of faith, even dismiss them simply as the construction of missionary mentors or as an example of false consciousness on the part of those Hispanos who did convert, but these statements also evince a growing Hispa-

---

[6] Vicki Ruiz, "Dead Ends or Gold Mines? Using Missionary Records in Mexican-American Women's History, " *Frontiers* 12 (1991): 50–51.

no presence (albeit small) within a mainline (and predominantly white) Protestant denomination. While Hispanos who converted took on much of the language of the enterprise, asserting time and again their "faithfulness," for example, they also played a role in redirecting mission priorities. Gradually they asserted a stronger voice, countering discriminatory treatment, asserting the legitimacy of their cultural heritage, eventually rewriting mission history such that they were not the victims of the mission enterprise but arbiters or brokers of a new culture.

† † †

Clearly, the small number of Hispano converts to Protestantism indicates that most Hispanos did not desire or intend to convert when they sought out the services provided by missionaries or sent their children to mission schools. For many, the act of sending their children to Presbyterian schools was simply one more defensive strategy by which they might countermand the conditions that threatened their livelihood. Suzanne Forrest has suggested that the mission schools attracted Hispanos who had "upwardly mobile ambitions." From these schools, she argues, "emerged an elite corps of teachers, lawyers, politicians, and businessmen," who "formed the nucleus of a new professional Hispanic middle class and paved the way for others to follow in their footsteps."[7] The patriotic and religious lessons the mission movement had originally conceived of as being at the center of their enterprise were of secondary importance to Hispanos. Being literate, gaining a mastery of the English language, and learning the niceties of being middle class (Anglo-American style) were among the more constructive of lessons "successful" Hispanos later remembered.

The impact of this educational experience on Hispano students varied. Obviously, mission schools had the most far-reaching influence on that small group of students who converted to Presbyterianism or Protestantism. These Hispanos would be the recipients of whatever largesse the mission enterprise had to reward in this field. They were introduced to a network of people who would see to it that they had the resources to continue their education and who could then provide work. Among this group, the elite of the mission system, distinctions were made based on gender. The educational and economic favors the church had to reward

---

[7] Forrest, *Preservation of the Village*, p. 29.

went primarily to Hispanos; Hispana Presbyterians found their subordinate status reinforced not simply by a male-dominated church hierarchy but also by the Anglo-American women who served as their teachers. The impact on those who remained Catholic is more difficult to measure. When the enterprise boasted that the mission schools had served as the training ground for the majority of the territory's (later state's) Hispano teachers, for instance, it did not matter whether students had remained Catholic or converted. Those who converted were celebrated; those who did not were believed to have been improved by their contact with the movement. The enterprise satisfied itself by proclaiming that it was playing a crucial role in creating a "new type," a general category of person who was a "mixture of old-world and new."[8]

Gabino Rendón was one example of this "new type" produced by the home mission movement. He converted to Presbyterianism as an adult, taught in a mission school, served as a lay evangelist, and eventually was ordained as a minister.[9] Rendón's conversion story is typical: integral to it is an emphasis on conversion as a route to individual transformation and social mobility. Like Rendón, other Hispanos who availed themselves of mission education were not immune to the changes in the material conditions of territorial residents. Their hometowns disappeared, and their families were dispersed. Although they suffered the economic disruption common to Hispano New Mexicans, those enmeshed in the network of mission schools found themselves cushioned by a safety net of sorts. The Hispanos who sought out Presbyterian mission education in the early days of the home mission movement were availing themselves of a higher-quality and more accessible education than that provided by the public schools or the Catholic Church. They recognized that English-language skills would be a benefit in a society in which economic conditions and political structures were rapidly changing.

Gabino Rendón's first encounter with the Presbyterians came in the early 1870s, when his devoutly Catholic parents enrolled him in one of the first mission schools opened in the territory, an attractive alternative to a public school run by a drunken teacher who was notorious for beating his pupils.[10] Indeed, what most impressed the young Rendón

---

[8] Katherine Bennett, "Editorial Notes," *Home Mission Monthly* 26 (March 1912): 110.

[9] Gabino Rendón, as told to Edith Agnew, *Hand on My Shoulder* (New York: Board of National Missions, Presbyterian Church in the U.S.A., 1953).

[10] Rendón describes his public school experience in "Schools and Church Schools in New

Gabino Rendón (Menaul Historical Library of the Southwest)

about the mission school was not the Scriptures read by the Reverend John Annin or even the "wasted" attempts to teach him English, but rather the friendliness of the two young teachers, Laura and Rebecca Annin, daughters of the minister. Laura Annin made it a point to remember the names of her students, and Rendón recalled that she "was able to connect them with our faces, and even knew us when she met us on the street."[11]

Mexico," p. 5, unpublished paper, Gabino Rendón Information File, Menaul Historical Library of the Southwest, Albuquerque (hereafter MHL).

[11] Rendón, *Hand on My Shoulder*, p. 21.

Rendón's attendance at the mission school was sporadic. Unwilling to antagonize the local priest or call into question their Catholic faith and fearing that their son's enrollment in a Protestant school might result in excommunication, Rendón's parents withdrew Gabino from school after the birth of each of his younger sisters until the new baby had been baptized, when he would return to the mission school. Until he left school at age thirteen, Rendón divided his time between the mission school and public schools.[12] Later he attended the newly opened St. Michael's College, run by the Jesuits and built on land donated by Rendón's father. At St. Michael's he came to realize how much he enjoyed learning and vowed to pursue his studies. He graduated the following year, having lived up to his mother's premonition that he would be "different," recognizing that the opportunities for education he had had not been available to his parents and believing himself to be a "real credit" to both his teachers and his parents.[13]

The Rendón family was of modest means but closely knit. His parents—his mother, the daughter of a tavern keeper, and his father, a buffalo hunter and trader—recognized that their son could not escape the changes taking place as Las Vegas grew to be New Mexico's commercial and trading center. His parents' emphasis on education was the result of their recognition that their children would gain their livelihood by different means than they had. After Rendón tried his hand at his father's trade, buffalo hunting, with little success, his mother encouraged him, advising that "it is all right *mi'jito*—my little one—the days of buffalo hunts are passing. We have spoken of it, your father and I. You are going to be something different. What that will be, God knows—but it won't be the life of a hunter."[14]

In 1878, the year Rendón enrolled in St. Michael's, his mother died, throwing the family into a crisis. Her death had been slow and painful; the family had employed every resource available to cure her. Hundreds of prayers had been offered and every herbal remedy tried. Rendón felt

---

[12] Many Hispanos followed this pattern. In the biographical dictionaries of prominent New Mexicans of the turn of the century, one finds that among the small number of Hispanos mentioned many of the biographies list an education gained in both Catholic and Protestant parochial schools. Ralph Twitchell listed seven Hispanos among the "prominent" men of Taos County. Of these, six had attended mission schools; three listed their religion as Roman Catholic and two were Presbyterian (*The Leading Facts of New Mexican History* [Cedar Rapids, Ia: Torch Press, 1917], 5: 460–70).

[13] Rendón, *Hand on My Shoulder*, pp. 33–34.

[14] Ibid., pp. 13–14.

that the family had been betrayed by both faith and tradition. Furthermore, his father, in his sorrow, had stopped trading to nurse his wife and had failed to plant crops, taking on short odd jobs instead. "I cannot tell you, and unless you have had the same experience," recalled Rendón, "you cannot know the despair and grief that settled over our house. All around was wailing and confusion. The long mirror was turned face to the wall. My grandfather gathered up the images to which we had prayed and, crying aloud for his only daughter, he threw the saints out the window, shouting '*Estos santos de Neuvo Mejico no sirven para nada.*' [These New Mexican saints do not work for anything.]"[15] His father disappeared, and Rendón was left to care for his two younger sisters.

"Nothing would be the same," Rendón wrote, because this turn of events meant that his desires and dreams would have to be deferred. He went to work doing manual labor on a construction crew, his frustrations compounded by the arrival of the railroad, which reminded him of the possibilities he had dreamed of in school. By the time he was nineteen, the family that had nurtured him as a child no longer existed. His beloved grandfather had died as well. Rendón cast about for steady work, trying his luck in business, selling liquor and later wood. One day Annie Speakman came to visit him, hoping to interest him in reenrolling in the Presbyterian mission school. The school that he had originally attended had been closed but was about to be reopened by Speakman. Speakman visited the families of former students, trying to rebuild a student body. Rendón turned down Speakman's offer, saying that he was too old to go back to school. Instead, he enrolled his younger sister Petra, who did exactly as mission teachers hoped their students would do—she showed Gabino her books. She did so "out of pride," remembered Rendón. Jealous and worried that his sister might soon be far ahead of him and wishing to acquire the knowledge that Petra was learning, Rendón returned to Speakman's school.[16] Speakman, welcomed him, tutored him, and gave him special encouragement.

Shortly after he returned to school, Rendón had an experience that sealed his commitment to the pursuit of his education. While he was visiting with old friends in a local store one afternoon, a man entered and asked the proprietor to fill out a piece of paper for him, but it had to

[15] Ibid., p. 37.
[16] Ibid., p. 37, 45.

be in English. "In English! we stood around attentively while the shop-keeper found pen and ink, smoothed out the order form, dipped the pen, and held it poised over those blank spaces," recalled Rendón. "Would he be able to fill them up in English?" Slowly and carefully, the proprietor did his task, much to everyone's surprise and generating great respect. This was Rendón's moment of enlightenment, his realization that his desire for education had a practical application. If asked to do a similar favor, "I could not do it. For the life of me, I could not do it." Filled with newfound determination, he vowed to learn English. "Even if they jeer at me," he told himself, "I am going to study that English language until I learn to write it, and even to speak it, to some extent."[17]

Hispanos attended mission schools principally to learn English. Initially, Rendón did not turn to Speakman for spiritual guidance but rather to exploit her skills as a teacher, understanding that knowledge of English gave the possibility for social mobility. It might enable him at last to fulfill his mother's prediction. In the process of teaching him the language, Speakman became his mentor. As his studies continued, Rendón was introduced to other Presbyterian Anglo-Americans within the mission enterprise, including his future wife, Amelia Brill, matron at the mission house. This new circle of acquaintances and the association with Speakman (with whom he continued to correspond long after both of them had left Las Vegas) brought into question a set of assumptions which had previously governed his life. He recalled that his definition of "truth" changed when he realized that he did not have to turn to others to be told what was "truth," that he could know for himself. In this assertion of his individuality, he also expressed his dissatisfaction with the impoverished conditions in which he lived, his impatience with traditional authority figures, and his longing for his life to be different.

Recounting his own conversion, Rendón told the story of Benito, the Catholic boy who converted when he found that "Jesus Christ himself was truth." For years he had believed that "only priests knew the truth," that it was "beyond common folk like him." Jesus, he discovered "was impatient with prayers said by rote. He quarreled with priests and turned upside down their notions of rank and position. What was within the simplest person mattered more than all the temple rites; the poor were better off than the rich, the weak would outlive the powerful." This knowledge turned Rendón's "whole world of ideas . . . topsy turvy."[18]

[17] Ibid., pp. 45–46.
[18] Ibid., p. 50.

As he underwent the process of conversion, Rendón was caught between the ideological demands of two cultures. He remembered his mother taking him through the Stations of the Cross, as well as his first communion and confession. He recalled the pride he had felt in his work at St. Michael's College and the priests whom he had considered friends. He admitted that "my memories pulled me in one direction—my convictions in another."[19] He dreaded telling his father of his confusion, but his father, who had returned to head the family, did not criticize him. This support made Rendón's decision to convert easier. Even so, as he made the transition, he continued to pray to the Virgin Mary, not wanting to relinquish all the trappings of Catholicism.

Conversion did bring Rendón the measure of social mobility he sought. As a teacher and minister Rendón would live a life of modest means; conversion would not bring him financial success. Instead, Rendón used religion to achieve status in an Anglo-American culture that otherwise would have excluded him. At age twenty-one, Rendón became a member of the Presbyterian Church; later he became an elder in the local church. Speakman arranged for him to attend a meeting at which he learned Robert's Rules of Order. Later he would credit this knowledge with his success in organizational duties and administrative bodies, claiming that these skills helped him to be elected as the first Hispano moderator of the Synod of New Mexico. Trained as a native evangelist, Rendón moved from Las Vegas to a series of small towns, working as a mission teacher until he was ordained. He married an Anglo woman and claimed that with her encouragement he practiced the "Protestant ethic of self-improvement." He refused to settle into his job as a schoolteacher, desiring not to be "tagged as a country schoolteacher, or an untrained local evangelist" for the rest of his life.[20] By becoming a Protestant and joining the mission movement, Rendón had not simply gained a new theological outlook but had acquired a new measure of respectability.

† † †

For residents in the small towns of northern New Mexico the Presbyterian mission schools continued to represent prosperity even after the public school system was well established and widespread. Administra-

[19] Ibid., p. 51.
[20] Ibid., p. 67.

tors of the Presbyterian women's home missions curtailed their educational activities in New Mexico not because the community stopped supporting the schools but because they hesitated to interfere or in any way impede the development of the public school system. Indeed, mission teachers believed that their schools would serve as models for the public schools. In the period covered by this study, the Presbyterian home mission movement opened schools in sixty-three locations throughout southern Colorado and New Mexico. The peak years were between 1885 and 1906, when an average of twenty-five schools were in operation yearly. When New Mexico achieved statehood in 1912, the number of mission schools in operation had begun to decline and would continue to do so. After 1912 only fourteen schools remained open.[21]

During this period, the public school system grew steadily, supplanting mission schools. Between 1890 and 1901, for example, the territorial school superintendent reported dramatic increases in school enrollments, from 12,397 to 42,925 students. The number of public schools grew from 407 to 726, and the number of teachers increased from 407 to 1,046. School terms were short, however, averaging 4.5 months, and teachers were paid an average salary of $54 a month. Parochial schools provided better services. The Presbyterians boasted skilled teachers and schools that were in session 9 months of the year (as were Catholic schools).[22] After the territory became a state, the quality of public education, if measured by the number of months of the year schools were open and the quality of the teaching staff, began to catch up to that of

---

[21] Ruth K. Barber and Edith Agnew, *Sowers Went Forth: The Story of Presbyterian Missions in New Mexico and Southern Colorado* (Albuquerque: Menaul Historical Library of the Southwest, 1981), Appendix I, pp. 159–60.

[22] Figures on enrollments, numbers of teachers, and length of school terms are from New Mexico (Terr.) Superintendent of Public Instruction, *Annual Report* (Santa Fe: New Mexico Printing Company, 1891, 1893, and 1901). Slightly different enrollment figures are reported in U.S. Department of Interior, Bureau of Education, *Bulletin*, 1920, no. 11, "Status of State School Systems, 1917–1918," pp. 95–99 (Tables 23–25). This bulletin reports the numbers of students enrolled in school in New Mexico as follows: 1870–71, 1,320; 1879–80, 4,755; 1889–90, 18,215; 1899–1900, 36,735; 1909–10, 56,304; 1917–18, 85,677. This steady increase can be attributed both to the influx of immigrants to the territory/state and the expansion of the public school system. Lois E. Huebert, "A History of Presbyterian Church Schools in New Mexico" (Master's thesis, University of New Mexico, 1964), reports that the school year in rural areas was no longer than four months, usually averaging two to three months (p. 25). By contrast, Catholic and Presbyterian schools averaged ten and nine months respectively. Enos García, "History of Education in Taos County" (Master's thesis, University of New Mexico, 1950), found that schools in Taos were open an average of four months in the 1890s. See Table 3, p. 58.

the parochial systems. Indeed, the Presbyterian mission administrators were proud to boast of their graduates who went on to teach in the public school system. These graduates turned teachers were looked to as the people who would make the needed improvement in the public system, who would professionalize the system.[23]

Of the nine Presbyterian schools remaining open after 1920, two, the Menaul School for Boys in Albuquerque and the Allison-James School for Girls in Santa Fe, were boarding schools that provided instruction beginning in the seventh grade. When the primary, or plaza, schools were closed or began to emphasize other services, mission resources were concentrated in these two schools.[24] The mission schools (indeed, the parochial system both Catholic and Protestant) offered secondary education to Hispanos who otherwise might not have had the opportunity. Of the 85,677 students enrolled in 1918, only 3,760 attended secondary school, and, of these, 734 were enrolled in private and parochial schools.[25] In 1912 1,472 students had been enrolled in public high schools and 237 in private high schools, one Presbyterian (Menaul), one Baptist, and five Catholic. Although it is difficult to be precise as to the ethnic breakdown because of the way Hispanos were classified in census materials, it is interesting that of the twenty-five public high schools in the new state only five were in towns located in the traditionally Hispano or northern part of the state. All of these five schools were in towns that had significant Anglo populations (Raton, Wagon Mound, East Las Vegas, Santa Fe, and Albuquerque).[26] For instance, Raton graduated its first high school students in 1887, but it was not until 1908 that the first student with a Spanish surname was graduated. Others graduated in 1911 and in 1918, with a gradual increase thereafter.[27] The private

[23] Lois Huebert quotes Ruth Barber, the last principal of the Presbyterian Allison-James School in Santa Fe, who boasted that "during those first years at Allison-James, a girl's school, the eighth grade graduates took the state examinations. Many of them went out to teach in little adobe schools, which were poorly lighted and poorly equipped. These eighth grade graduates of our school were better qualified than many of the rural teachers because they could speak English well. When two years of high school were added, about 1914, some of these young teachers returned to Allison-James to continue this education. Later they returned to teaching" ("History of Presbyterian Church Schools," p. 34).

[24] Barber and Agnew, *Sowers of the Seed*, p. 108.

[25] See U.S. Department of Interior, Bureau of Education, *Bulletin*, 1920, no. 11, "Status of State School Systems, 1917–1918," pp. 95–99 (Tables 23–25).

[26] See U.S. Department of Interior, Bureau of Education, *Bulletin*, 1912, no. 22, "Public and Private High Schools," pp. 14, 27, 36, 192.

[27] See Carson Crecey, "A History of Public Schools of Raton, New Mexico" (Master's thesis, University of New Mexico, 1941), Appendix.

secondary schools, three of which were located in Albuquerque, two in Santa Fe, one in Las Cruces, and one in Alamagordo, graduated 25 students in 1912, 19 from Catholic schools and 6 from the Presbyterian school. Of the 139 students who graduated from the public schools, 90 had prepared for college. Three students graduating from private schools were listed as having prepared for college; all were graduates of the Presbyterian Menaul School.[28]

In the long run, missionaries were most successful in providing students with minimal skills with which to cope with the economic conquest of the territory and the resultant changes, which undermined subsistence farming. Mission teachers in New Mexico had brought the message that progress was good, but all they had was the Word. They were unable to build the economic conditions in rural New Mexico necessary to support the progress they advocated. Instead, they taught their students English and prepared them for a variety of service jobs in the larger towns and cities. They facilitated entry for a few students into high school and college, at institutions such as the Menaul and Allison-James schools, which took students out of their hometowns to the larger commercial centers of New Mexico.

Helping students to move away from farming was an unintended consequence of mission education. Although mission educators spoke extensively about the need for programs in vocational education, home economics, and farming (presumably to strengthen family farms), their primary contribution was not to modernize or make agriculture profitable. By the 1920s it was estimated that one member from each family in northern New Mexico was employed in an out-of-state wage labor job.[29] Income from agricultural production was meager. By the beginning of the Depression most households gained their income from wage labor, supplemented by selling homegrown produce.[30] Overgrazing, timber cutting, overdivision of lots, loss of water rights, and loss of land had led Hispanos to reorganize their economy. The railroad facilitated outmigration. People left their families on a seasonal basis, searching for work in the sugar beet fields in Colorado or rounding up cattle on large

[28] See U.S. Department of Interior, Bureau of Education, *Bulletin*, 1912, Table 35.

[29] Kenneth Weber, "Rural Hispanic Villages Viability from an Economic and Historic Perspective," in *The Survival of Spanish American Villages*, ed. Paul Kutsche (Colorado Springs: Colorado College Studies, 1979), p. 82.

[30] Nancie L. González, *The Spanish-Americans of New Mexico: A Heritage of Pride* (Albuquerque: University of New Mexico Press, 1967), p. 120.

Chimayó pupils at Menaul School for Boys (Menaul Historical Library of the Southwest). Handwritten on the back of the photograph was the following note: "Our pupils after a little further training at Menaul. The one at the left in the upper row is Melecio Trujillo, ready for college and wishes to go. He feels that he needs more preparation that he may do the most he possibly can to help his people. He is an earnest Christian. His mother is a widow and can not help him, but with a little help, he will help himself, and make good use of his opportunities."

ranches. In the face of these larger economic changes, mission proposals to build model farms were an anachronism.

A drought in the 1920s wiped out the crops that had been the basis of the barter economy in many small New Mexico communities. To the inhabitants of these villages it was increasingly clear that small-scale farming was unfeasible. These developments, coupled with a desire to enjoy the benefits of "progress," led to the depopulating of villages like Trementina. As Blake's student Abelino Estrada remembered, the residents of Trementina welcomed progress; for instance, horse-drawn wagons were replaced by cars. But cars required gas, which had to be purchased with cash. The need for jobs that paid cash wages led to outmigration as individuals voluntarily moved away and families followed.[31]

The students who attended the boarding schools in Albuquerque and Santa Fe came from the most isolated communities in New Mexico. Almost half had attended plaza mission schools. They came from large families; one survey taken in 1935 indicated that the average family contained 5.3 living children. Most students reported that their parents had had little education; the majority had not gone beyond fifth grade. One teacher at Allison-James in the early 1930s wrote about her students: "Most of the children come from poor homes, they live on small farms of from eight to ten acres perhaps. Their cash income is very small, often not more than a few hundred dollars a year. They have what they can raise on their little farms, which is very little." Twenty students in one class of twenty-three came from agricultural communities. Only two reported that their families owned tractors and mowing machines. The teacher who gathered this information also reported that she was surprised to discover that her students did not see motorized agricultural tools as necessities but rather as "work-lessening inventions." Most of the work done on garden patches and fields was done with hoes, rakes, and other hand tools.[32]

Indeed, the Presbyterian schools appeared a prosperous alternative to the poorly maintained public schools, which were often overcrowded and understaffed or staffed by teachers with little education.[33] One of the few plaza schools to remain open after 1920 was the Presbyterian school in Chacón. Sociologist C. D. Bohannan, hired by the church to survey conditions in the town in 1927–28, found that the area was served by four schools, which enrolled a total of 247 students. One-third of the students were enrolled in the mission school. Bohannan described the public schools as consisting of "an unpretentious wooden structure, of the ordinary type, one of them being in such a state of repair that we were informed that it had been condemned for school use and that

[31] S. Omar Barker, "Trementina: Memories of a Mission Village," *Albuquerque Journal* 23 (September 1980): 12.

[32] See survey of Allison-James student body, 1935–36, Information File, Allison-James School, 1866–1959, Statistics, 1926–57, MHL.

[33] In a student survey conducted in 1939, of 103 students enrolled at Allison-James, 58 noted the reputation and quality of the school as their reason for attending. Fifty students listed themselves as Presbyterian, 48 as Catholic. Many of the Catholic students, in particular, noted that Allison-James was a "better school," or offered "better advantages," or that "AJ was better than public school." See 1939–40 School List for Allison-James, Information File, MHL.

classes had been held in various buildings in that district during the previous school year." Most of the public school teachers had no more than two years of high school, and they conducted classes in Spanish. In contrast, the mission school was more generously endowed. He described it as a solid structure with playground space and equipment. The staff included two teachers and a principal, who also served as community worker and nurse.[34]

Most of the students in Chacón did not go beyond the fifth grade, and after that point the numbers of students attending school dropped dramatically. Because there were no public high schools in the area, students who wished to go beyond the seventh grade had to leave town and board away from home. The mission school sent its graduates to Menaul or Allison-James. Allison-James reported students from forty different communities in New Mexico, while Menaul counted representatives from fifty-five different communities.[35]

Its role in promoting education was the most enduring legacy of the Protestant mission enterprise in New Mexico and became the focus of the many appeals that emanated from the field. Correspondents never tired of claiming that mission schools had served as a model for the public system. By the 1920s, the principal role of the enterprise was to "educate the educators." As Marion D. Dutton reported, mission students could best use their skills and exercise their power and influence by becoming educators. To this end, Menaul seniors were given a course in educational pedagogy, which included "planning and equipping a building and playground," as well as organizing the classroom. Students were taken into classrooms throughout Albuquerque to observe teaching, and they learned the "modern methods" for teaching various subjects. In the graduating class of 1925, eight of ten students reported that they intended to teach.[36]

Ironically, although the mission schools educated generations of public school teachers, this also proved to be one of the factors that led to the demise of the enterprise. As the public system expanded, employing mission graduates as teachers, the need for mission schools could no longer be justified. No longer could it be argued that the public system

[34] C. D. Bohannan, "Report on the Survey of Chacón, NM Community," for Board of National Missions of the Presbyterian Church in the U.S.A., January 1928, pp. 11–13, Chacón, N.M., Information File, MHL.

[35] Ibid., p. 23.

[36] Dutton, "Educating the Educators," pp. 54–55.

was not doing its job in Americanizing Hispano students. In a 1957 report the Board of National Missions found that the four mission schools studied were redundant, and that many of those villagers active in public school activities were graduates of mission schools, if not Presbyterians. In Holman the principal of the public school was a Presbyterian and a graduate of Menaul; of the nine teachers employed, four had attended Menaul and four Allison-James. In Ranchos de Taos, the public school teacher was a graduate of Menaul. In each of these cases the teachers recommended closing the mission schools so as to increase the enrollment of students in the public system and ensure their jobs. They did not believe it necessary to maintain mission schools where the "public schools [were] adequate." Only in Truchas was it recommended that the mission school be kept open; the public school there did not have room to accommodate mission students. Even there, the principal of the public school was a Menaul graduate, as were all the teachers.[37]

† † †

Of the elite group of Hispanos who went on to Presbyterian high schools, most of those who graduated left behind their hometowns and abandoned the agricultural way of life.[38] The experience was a sharp departure from what they had known in the past; the change in their class status effected a secular conversion perhaps as profound as a religious one. In the 1915 issue of the Menaul school's *Sandstorm Yearbook*, the editors noted that twenty-four students had graduated in the nine years that Menaul had served as the boys' high school in the Presbyterian mission school network. Most students came from families who lived by farming or ranching. Asked how they themselves were making a living, only two of the graduates responded that they were farmers. Of

---

[37] Milton Brown, *Educational Work in New Mexico* (New York: Board of National Missions, Presbyterian Church in the U.S.A., 1957). He also noted that Menaul graduates were active on the county school boards in Rio Arriba and were county superintendents of schools in Mora and Taos. In interviewing ministers (Hispano Presbyterians) in these locations he found that they were discouraged by these teachers' "nominal allegiance" to the church, meaning that they did not regularly attend services or participate in church activities (p. 20). The Anglo missionary who was the executive of the Truchas mission school was more charitable in her assessment. She was reported as active in community affairs and said that "only about 50% of our local boarding school [Menaul] graduates contribute in leadership ways to our church but that their contribution and leadership in the community is much better" (p. 25).

[38] The focus here is on those who did graduate. Many more Hispanos attended Menaul for a year or two but did not graduate and returned to their villages.

these two, one described himself first as a teacher and second a farmer. The other graduate listed as a farmer was responsible for maintaining the farm training component of the Menaul school. Among the other graduates were four preachers, eight teachers, four who ran stores, three who were continuing their education, and one each who worked as a bookkeeper, traveling salesman, boiler maker, and plumber.[39] The 1926 graduates followed a similar pattern. Rather than return to farming or ranching, three had entered public service, three were performing religious service, three were in education, and one was doing technical work. The three who worked in the public sector made their careers with the welfare department and postal service.[40] In the year that he made his study, Bohannan wrote that the thirty-three graduates of Menaul included fifteen teachers, seven college students, and three businessmen. Only three graduates in his survey had returned to the family farm. Of the twenty-four women who graduated from Allison-James in 1926 and 1927, thirteen were working as teachers, three were attending college, two each were working in offices and as domestic workers, and two were homemakers.[41]

The Menaul and Allison-James schools taught Hispano students the niceties of being middle class. They also became enmeshed in a network that provided economic and political support as they made the transition away from an agricultural and rural way of life. The education was not simply book-oriented. The students who went to these two boarding schools were remade. For many of the students, the trip to Albuquerque to attend the Menaul school, for instance, was a trip away from an old way of living. They considered it a brand new beginning.

Alfonso Esquibel wrote that his first trip to Menaul was also the first time he traveled by train. In his memories he coupled Protestant mission education with industrialization, as represented by the railroad, the two being synonymous with modernity; both the train and the school would carry Esquibel away from the farm. Esquibel had come to know of the mission movement through Alice Blake and her work in Trementina. His

[39] Information compiled from the *Sandstorm Yearbook*, 1915.

[40] Golden Reunion (1977), Menaul-Allison Class of 1926 Information File, MHL.

[41] Bohannan, "Report," p. 29. Another study shows that of the 132 students who had graduated from Menaul by 1929, 72 had received some postsecondary education. Fifty-two were working as teachers or school administrators, 34 had entered other professions or were skilled workers, and 6 worked as preachers. Only 16 were listed as unskilled workers. See Anna Elizabeth Falls, "The Place of Private and Church Schools in the Education of the State" (Master's thesis, University of New Mexico, 1929), p. 78.

Cooking class and dinner table of eighth grade girls, Allison-James School, 1934–35 (Menaul Historical Library of the Southwest)

father was a sheepherder who died when Alfonso was sixteen years old. While apprenticed to a local rancher, Alfonso was accidentally shot when working on the ranch. Bleeding badly, he was taken to Blake, who gave him first aid and sent to Las Vegas for a doctor. Later he encountered a local teacher and graduate of Menaul, Reyes Gutiérrez, who convinced Esquibel to attend Menaul. What most impressed Esquibel was Gutiérrez's appearance, especially that he wore a coat and tie. In comparison, his own clothing—he recalled that he was "dressed in an old shirt, dirty pants, boots, spurs, and a big cowboy hat"—deeply embarrassed him. Claiming that he was "too old to learn new ways," he put off Gutiérrez's suggestion for several years until he was twenty years old. Blake helped him fill out the Menaul application, and he entered the eighth grade at the age of twenty-two.[42]

The new ways that Esquibel learned at Menaul were not so much academic as how he should live and what manners he should possess. The teacher for whom he retained the fondest of memories opened her classes with exercises in living. "She taught us how to behave in some-

[42] Alfonso Esquibel, *Vaquero to Dominie: The Nine Lives of Alfonso Esquibel* (Las Vegas, N.M.: N.p., 1978), pp. 12–13.

one's house, how to use a knife and spoon, and other table manners," he recalled. When he graduated from Menaul in 1926 at the age of twenty-seven, he worried about what he would do and considered harvesting wheat or digging ditches for sewer lines. After five years at Menaul, Esquibel still thought of himself as fit only for jobs as a laborer. But the network of which he had become a part had other plans for him and found him a job at the YMCA, which paid $150 a month. This proved to be an interim step. In 1928 Esquibel enrolled at the University of New Mexico, his tuition paid by the church, which also provided a job for him while he attended college. "It was like a dream come true," noted Esquibel. "Only a few short years before I had been an ignorant *vaquero*, tending sheep and cattle on Uncle Sanchez's ranch, little dreaming I would get an education of any kind, let alone go the University." For Esquibel the transition was difficult: "It was hard work for me, harder than the physical labor I had been doing on the ranch. I never had been much of a reader and now all of a sudden here I was, thrust into the world of books, where I had to learn to read to survive."[43]

For other students, attending Presbyterian mission schools, particularly Menaul, would make them feel strangers in the culture in which they had been raised. Antonio Durán found the environment at the Presbyterian schools to be more hospitable, more to his liking, than the Catholic schools he attended. He recalled that he was impressed by Presbyterian townspeople. He entered the mission school in Dixon at the urging of his father's supervisor (he worked for the railroad at the time). Soon thereafter his parents withdrew him from the school at the insistence of the local priest. He was placed in a Catholic school, where he was ostracized because of his attendance at the mission school. Discouraged, he prepared to drop out of school and return to his family. By chance he met a friend who urged him to stay in school and invited him to board with his family. Durán finished the year at the Catholic school, but at the urging of the family with whom he boarded, who were Presbyterian, he returned to the mission school the following year.[44]

Durán's choice to attend the mission school eventually led to a rupture with his family, who warned that his actions would lead to their excommunication. "I told them that from there on I was responsible for my own sins, hell or highwater, and they were not going to stop me." He continued to live with the Lucero family, whose kindness he appreciated.

[43] Esquibel, *Vaquero*, pp. 24, 68, 79.
[44] Antonio Durán, unpublished memoirs, Information File, MHL.

"Those people were nice to me not for what I had to offer them. They were just good dedicated Christians." Disturbed by his distance from his family, he returned home for a reconciliation but came to realize "that the environment in my home village was not the ideal place for me, and I wanted to do something with my life besides being a sheepherder." Alienated from the cultural mores of his childhood, Durán desired opportunities not available in the small rural communities of New Mexico. After he graduated from Menaul the mission enterprise offered him a job as a teacher.[45]

Mission teachers were especially pleased to report on students who were teaching, preaching, or doing some other form of public service. Charles Córdova emphasized that one could not simply "pay" for success, meaning that success was not measured in riches or the amount of money one had. Indeed, Córdova had learned the lesson that women mission teachers had fashioned out of their own work experience, that success was not quantifiable but was best measured in service to the community. In this sense, Blake and other women missionaries brought with them to New Mexico a femininized vision of success which they passed on to their students.

This vision of success is crucial to understanding the mission movement. There were few converts, there were few material gains, communities failed rather than prospered. Mission successes were more subtle, better measured in qualitative terms. Missionaries introduced particular attitudes, a kind of sensibility, a quality of living that they believed would mark Hispano New Mexicans as good Americans and would assure Anglo-Americans that Hispanos, once envisioned as potential traitors, had the best interests of the nation at heart. The missionary conception of what constituted patriotic activity was limited, however. Little was written, for example, about the more traditional political forms by which Hispanos expressed their dissatisfaction at the turn of events in New Mexico in this period.

Mission women did not inform their supporters of the Hispanos' organized resistance to the loss of their land. No mention was made of Las Gorras Blancas (the White Caps) in San Miguel County, who in 1889 began to attack the property of large landholders, particularly cattle ranchers, destroying the fences they had put up to define their lands. Although these actions were largely symbolic, fences represented

[45] Ibid.

the end of communal grazing and the growing power of land speculators. Yet an active group of the Knights of Labor represented members
of Las Gorras Blancas when some of them were arrested and tried. Nor
was there any mention of El Partido del Pueblo (the Party of the People),
an independent Hispano political party organized in the early 1890s. It
called for ethnic unity and sought to organize the supporters of Las
Gorras Blancas. In San Miguel County in 1890 the party captured each
office with an average of 60 percent of the vote. It was particularly
popular in communities located on disputed land grants.[46] Furthermore,
no mention was made of the unions Hispanos joined in attempts to
improve their working conditions as they began to migrate out of their
communities for seasonal employment in other areas.[47]

Mission women seemed to view all forms of political activity in New
Mexico, particularly party politics, with suspicion, making only oblique
references to them and representing them as corrupting forces.[48] Like
their sisters in other reform movements, the missionaries' political ethos
stressed social policy over partisan politics. Paula Baker has argued that
this pattern among women reformers at the turn of the twentieth century
constituted a "domestication" of politics.[49] Along with their feminized
vision of success, they championed a "domestic" political ethic that
emphasized social responsibility over laissez-faire. Even though many of
their students obtained their teaching jobs within the public system
through the patronage of party politicians, mission women preferred to
highlight more abstract and less pragmatic forms of patriotism that

---

[46] See Robert Rosenbaum, *Mexicano Resistance in the Southwest: The Sacred Right of Self-Preservation* (Austin: University of Texas Press, 1981), pp. 99–139.

[47] See Robert Kern, *Labor in New Mexico: Strikes, Unions, and Social History, 1881–1981* (Albuquerque: University of New Mexico Press, 1983); and Sarah Deutsch, *No Separate Refuge: Culture, Class, and Gender on an Anglo-Hispanic Frontier in the American Southwest, 1880–1940* (New York: Oxford University Press, 1987), pp. 87–106.

[48] John Gass, in "Mexicans as Citizens," *Home Mission Monthly* 25 (November 1910): 4–5, expressed missionaries' sentiments when he warned that Mexicans were being swayed by "political boss[es] with plenty of money or whiskey." Alice Blake faulted local politicians for prolonging racial divisions, writing that "the Mexican politician seeks very covertly, but none the less assiduously, to keep up race feeling in order to hold for himself the solid race vote. He is probably sincere in his arguments, as he regards an American invasion in office to be as great a danger to his people as to himself. I will do him justice to say here, that on the whole, I consider he makes as good an officer as the average American" ("Encouragements and Outlook among Mexicans in the United States," *Home Mission Monthly* 22 [November 1907]: 3).

[49] Paula Baker, "The Domestication of Politics: Women and American Political Society, 1780–1920," in *Unequal Sisters: A Multicultural Reader in U.S. Women's History*, ed. Ellen C. DuBois and Vicki L. Ruiz (New York: Routledge, Chapman, & Hall, 1990), p. 78.

focused on the life of the nation. Fourth of July celebrations were noted and commented on, and the large Hispano contingent of soldiers serving in both the Spanish-American War and World War I were hailed as indicative of how deeply committed Hispanos were to the United States.[50]

† † †

How should we measure the impact of the mission enterprise on its Hispano students? Ruiz suggests that the missions served a largely practical purpose, providing Hispanos with otherwise limited social services. In the typology she presents, the meeting between missionaries and Hispanos exemplifies "cultural permeability." She finds that there was little assimilation or change in the culture. Mario García, in his study of second-generation Mexican-Americans, offers a more linear typology, calling the generation that emerged in the 1930s one "that on the whole began to understand that it was part of U.S. society and that it had to compromise between its ethnic roots and full incorporation and assimilation into American society." This generation did not achieve full assimilation or deethnization but a form of cultural pluralism or "pluralistic integration." They advocated integration and acceptance but did not forsake their culture; rather they sought to maintain their Mexican heri-

[50] Mary McWhirt, stationed at Ocate, told of planning a Fourth of July celebration for the "poor." Only the wealthier members of the community had ever celebrated the holiday. See "A Patriotic Picnic," *Home Mission Monthly* 13 (November 1898): 18–19. In her memoirs Alice Blake recalled that at the outbreak of the Spanish-American War there was fear that Hispanos would sympathize with Spain. "On the contrary," she noted, "they seemed to come to themselves, and really to realize that this is their country, and that they truly belong to the American Republic." She went on to assure her readers of the deep patriotic sentiment felt by Hispanos: "It is true that they are intensely loyal to their faith and their mother tongue. But when they realize a clash between the first, and the interests of their country, we may depend on their asserting themselves; as when, during the World War, a German priest tried to create sympathy, and secure financial aid for his friends in his Homeland, the people rose against him and insisted on his removal, as a Pro-German" ("Memoirs of Alice Blake: Interviews with Missionaries, Teachers and Others in Northern New Mexico," p. 60, manuscript, MHL.) The Allison-James school even went so far as to divide the school up as if it were a city, with wards, overseen by a council. Officers to the council were elected from among the student body. Also chosen were a mayor, clerk, and heads of police, sanitation, and fire departments. The student officers were also required to take an oath. Teacher Mabel Tillman explained, "Thus we are trained for a larger service when we reach the voting age" ("Their Alma-Mater—Allison-James," *Women and Missions* 4 [July 1927]: 68).

tage.[51] More specifically addressing the situation of Hispanos in New Mexico, or "Americans of Mexican origin," Mario Gamio has argued for the emergence of a "third culture." Of the population of Mexicans who had been longtime residents in the Southwest he wrote, "This civilization is American nominally, and exhibits the principal material aspects of modern American civilization, but intellectually and emotionally it lives in local Mexican traditions."[52]

In none of these scenarios is a culture lost, and Hispano culture was not lost or undermined in New Mexico, even among those who converted to Protestantism. This is especially evident in the reluctance of converts to give up all vestiges of their Catholic faith. Rendón continued to pray to the Virgin Mary even after he converted. Perhaps because the Protestant churches could not offer them anything better, or because they hoped to keep their options open, women seem to have been more hesitant than men to convert. In many instances husbands joined the Protestants while wives remained faithful to the Catholic Church. In his report on the Penitentes, Charles Loomis noted that one of the adherents in the procession behind the crucifix was the wife of the local lay evangelist.[53] José Inés Perea, an early convert, played a crucial role in laying the foundation for later Presbyterian efforts, but his first wife remained Catholic.[54] A husband and father's decision to attend the Presbyterian Church could cause tremendous friction. Fulgencio Romero remembered that the conversion of his father, Cesario, led to a temporary separation between his parents, even though Cesario assured his wife that she could continue to "believe what she wanted to."[55] Some wives joined the Presbyterian Church only to return to Catholicism later in their lives.[56] These examples suggest a fluidity in the experience of con-

---

[51] Mario García, *Mexican-Americans: Leadership, Ideology, and Identity, 1930–1960* (New Haven: Yale University Press, 1989), pp. 10, 18, 34.

[52] Quoted in Carey McWilliams, *North from Mexico: The Spanish-Speaking People of the United States* (Philadelphia: Lippincott, 1949), p. 212.

[53] Of the procession Loomis recalled that "tallest among the women was the Mexican wife of the Presbyterian missionary" (Charles Fletcher Loomis, *Land of Poco Tiempo*, quoted in Twitchell, *Leading Facts of New Mexico History*, 5: 483, n. 9).

[54] Mark Banker, "Missionary to His Own People: José Inés Perea and Hispanic Presbyterianism in New Mexico," in *Religion and Society in the American West: Historical Essays*, ed. David Guarneri and David Alvarez (Lanham, Md.: University Press of America, 1987), p. 84.

[55] Jane Atkins Grainger, ed., *El Centenario de la Palabra: El Rito Presbyterian Church, 1879–1979* (Albuquerque: Menaul Historical Library of the Southwest, 1980), p. 95.

[56] An example is Cassandra Martínez Brown, the mother of Lorin Brown, a fieldworker for

version made necessary by the very small numbers of converts. As Anglo missionaries and Hispano lay evangelists discovered, the risk in demanding greater discipline and orthodoxy was that one might lose supporters.

Even when they converted, Hispanos resisted policies of assimilation that would have made them "Anglo." In particular, Hispanos pursued different tactics in building congregations. Whereas Anglo ministers upheld rigid standards of church discipline, Hispano evangelists and elders proved more flexible. In the early 1870s José Inés Perea served as the principal patron and benefactor of John Annin's small church in Las Vegas; he was also the ruling elder and responsible for maintaining discipline. Perea's task was "made difficult by Annin's rigorous expectations of his parishioners." Perea apparently mediated between Annin and other Hispano followers, and his friend Gabino Rendón remembered that Annin and Perea "did not see eye to eye on the matter of church discipline," suggesting that Perea was more willing to overlook "improprieties" which Annin felt should disqualify congregants.[57]

Nor did Perea seem reluctant to challenge Anglo ideas about propriety when he took as his second wife Anglo-American mission teacher Susan Gates. But he gave his children by this marriage English names and proudly represented the Presbytery of Santa Fe at the church's General Assembly, suggesting assimilation to this Anglo cause. Yet, throughout his career, he advocated that Hispanos retain the Spanish language. Perea's refusal to embrace Presbyterianism in such a way as to divorce himself entirely from Hispano culture had within it a measure of self-protection. Historian Mark Banker argues that relations between Perea and the Anglo ministers with whom he worked were always cordial, but these ministers never considered Perea their equal. Knowing that he would never be fully accepted by the Anglo hierarchy and that some would complain to others about his "miserable Mexican way of doing business," Perea did as women missionaries did; he charted an independent course that gave him a special foothold within the institution. By

---

the New Mexico Writers' Project. Brown's mother converted to Protestantism as a young woman and spent her adult life teaching in rural villages in northern New Mexico. Lorin attended the mission school in Taos. As an old woman, Brown's mother returned to the Catholic Church. When she was buried, the local Cofradía oversaw her wake, funeral, and burial. See Lorin W. Brown, with Charles Biggs and Marta Weigle, *Hispano Folklife of New Mexico: The Lorin W. Brown Federal Writers' Manuscripts* (Albuquerque: University of New Mexico Press, 1978), pp. 5–10 and 255, n. 33.

[57] Banker, "Missionary to His Own People," pp. 86–87.

insisting that certain aspects of Hispano culture be retained, he ensured that there would always be a need for Hispanos within the institution.

The mission enterprise may not have converted as many Hispanos as it educated, but those who did join the church, like Perea, waged ongoing battles against unfair stereotypes and the discrimination they encountered. When the *Home Mission Monthly* published one of Kate Kennedy's first reports from Embudo in which she detailed the "strange customs" of the family with whom she had lived at the outset of her assignment, Gabino Rendón fired off a letter of protest. "Some of us Mexican workers have talked about it [the article] and think it very unjust and untimely," he wrote. "Your grievances with the people should be brought to the proper authority and not before the public." Rendón said that he did not mean to be "unkind," but he had only the "heart of the Cause which we all represent" in mind.[58] A contrite Kate Kennedy wrote to the board immediately, apologizing and insisting that she was "greaved [*sic*] ever since I received Gabino Rendón's letter." She had not meant to make trouble, but the experience had taught her that she could not perpetuate such stereotypes and hope to do her work effectively.[59]

The Woman's Board was often called on to arbitrate instances of racist behavior and discriminatory treatment, even though it promoted larger policies that were inherently biased. For instance, both the Woman's Board and later the Board of National Missions maintained separate churches and schools for Hispanos. Though separation and segregation do not seem to have been the official policy—presumably Anglos could attend Spanish-speaking churches and mission schools (and some did) and Hispanos could join Anglo congregations—in reality there was little crossover. This segregation, reflective of larger social patterns, nevertheless proved a problem. The function of the mission boards was to bring greater numbers of people into the church, but as Anglo women and, later, ethnic and racial minorities were brought in, the hierarchical distinctions were complicated by the racism and sexism of the larger society. Racist standards of the day dictated that Hispanos were subordinate to Anglo missionaries, male or female. The church privileged men over women, however, subordinating women missionaries to ministers.

[58] Gabino Rendón to Kate Kennedy, January 2, 1902, RG 51, Box 2, Folder 16, Department of History and Records Management Services, Presbyterian Church (U.S.A.), Philadelphia (hereafter PHS).

[59] Kate Kennedy to Mrs. Pierson, January 7, 1902, ibid.

As male converts and students became evangelists and then ministers, their position in the social hierarchy vis-à-vis their Anglo and female teachers changed. Anglo women seemed to accept the privileging of Hispano men, proclaiming the successes of their male students, turning to Hispano evangelists for counsel, even accepting the protection of male students.

Because they did not challenge the patriarchal standards of their own culture and largely accepted those of the Hispano culture of their students, Anglo missionaries did not have the same expectations for their female students as they did for the men they taught. The mission enterprise presumed to hold all students, male and female, to the same standards of patriotism, but females were not lauded in the same manner as their male counterparts, nor were they expected to accomplish as much. Although many of the women students went on to be teachers or nurses, Anglo-American mission teachers envisioned very traditional domestic roles for them. Female students were taught domestic skills such as sewing and cooking to prepare them to manage families. They were to be wives and mothers, serving in the "helpmate" role that many mission women themselves would never fill. At the Allison-James School for Girls the teachers emphasized, for example, lessons in baby care, home nursing, and home economics. Anglo teachers recognized that their students filled a variety of occupations, including domestic workers, store clerks, teachers, and nurses, but it was expected that female students would ultimately marry and turn their full attention to housekeeping. The true test of their "Christian character" and "Christian citizenship" was how they ran their homes.[60]

---

[60] See, for example, Ruth K. Barber, "Allison-James Prepares for Home Life," *Women and Missions* 11 (May 1934): 52–53; Ruth Barber, "All Interpreters," *Women and Missions* 6 (May 1929): 52; Teresita Martínez Fernandez, "A Happy Wife," quoted in "Their Alma Mater—Allison-James," *Women and Missions* 4 (July 1927): 68–69. The expectations that Anglo missionaries had for their female students were similar to those of Progressive social reformers who worked with Mexican immigrant women. George Sanchez, in "'Go After the Women': Americanization and the Mexican Immigrant Woman, 1915–1929," in *Unequal Sisters: A Multicultural Reader in U.S. Women's History*, ed. Ellen C. DuBois and Vicki L. Ruiz (New York: Routledge, Chapman & Hall, 1990), pp. 250–61, argues that reformers believed that the role of the Mexican woman "in the creation of a new industrial order would be to transform her own home into an efficient, productive family unit, while producing law-abiding, loyal American citizens eager to do their duty for capitalist expansion in the American Southwest" (p. 261). While mission schools were one type of Americanization program, the difference between the secular programs Sanchez describes and those of the mission enterprise was that the primary intention of the secular programs seems to have been to prepare Mexican

Mission teachers did not shirk from the duties the movement had set out for them. They faithfully did as the home mission movement's literature prescribed—"woman's work for women." But mission women in New Mexico, especially those working in the plaza schools, quickly realized that they could be most effective and wield the greatest amount of power and influence, both in the church and in the larger society, if they reached the men. When one mission teacher wrote early in her career that "my province is of course only among the women and children, but to revolutionize this place the men must be reached," she was expressing her own frustrations with the limited nature of her prescribed role but also commenting on the distribution of power in Hispano culture.[61]

The privileging of male students appears to have set women missionaries in New Mexico apart from their colleagues in other fields, who lavished most of their attention on their female students. This may have resulted from the sex segregation that characterized missions located in other areas. In the overseas missions, for instance, women were more often assigned to work only with other women. Those women assigned to New Mexico who had the most sustained contact with male students and neighbors were assigned to plaza schools and were often the only missionary, and sometimes the only Anglo, living in the village. They did not have to share their work or divide duties with Anglo men, nor were they limited by taboos about relations with men that women in other mission fields faced. It has been suggested that the privileging of men "echoes the partnership" between the women who built the WEC and the maverick Presbyterian ministers such as Sheldon Jackson.[62] This

---

immigrants for domestic labor. Certainly, the mission schools wanted to prepare its women students to work (and domestic labor was one job), but they focused more specifically on the familial duties of women.

[61] "Words from Workers," *Home Mission Monthly* 6 (February 1892): 84.

[62] In the work of Vicki Ruiz, "Dead Ends or Gold Mines," and Peggy Pascoe, *Relations of Rescue: The Search for Female Moral Authority in the American West, 1874–1939* (New York: Oxford University Press, 1990), women missionaries target their efforts toward women clients. In other cases, mission women did work with men. For example, in his discussion of the work missionaries performed among American Indians, Michael Coleman argues that in the case of Sue McBeth, who spent her life among the Choctaw and Nez Perce, the most satisfying work she engaged in was teaching Indian men theology, something she would never have been allowed to do on the home front. (*Presbyterian Missionary Attitudes toward American Indians, 1837–1893* [Jackson: University Press of Mississippi, 1985], pp. 25, 146). I am indebted to Peggy Pascoe for the suggestion that the relations of missionaries to male students "echoed" the partnerships they had had with male mentors.

may well be; certainly the most successful of missionaries exhibited the same pragmatism as their leaders. Just as the original founders of the WEC had sought out male support, so might individual women in the field. They forged relationships that would enhance their prestige and power without challenging the patriarchal ethos of either of the two cultures, Anglo and Hispano, in which they lived. To build the foundation for the church, they tapped those who, within Hispano culture, had traditionally served as educators—the men.

Male students who converted and were later ordained signaled missionary success. While preparing for ordination they were employed by the WEC to teach school and after ordination were given churches and supported by the Board of Home Missions. Hispanas, in contrast, were marginalized within the WEC and by the larger church.[63] The WEC seems to have been reluctant to hire Hispana students, though mission women were happy to recommend their female students for teaching jobs in the public schools. A small number of Hispanas were hired by the Woman's Executive Committee to teach for a short period or to serve as assistants to Anglo mission teachers, but they were paid less and if they worked with an Anglo teacher were often regarded as little more than servants. There is no evidence that any Hispana found long-term employment as a mission teacher. Indeed, Hispanas seemed to have exercised much more influence by using their mission training outside of the enterprise.[64] Because the rules of the Presbyterian Church did not allow women to preach, Hispanas could not serve as native evangelists. Like the Anglo teachers, Hispanas found themselves negotiating two patriarchal cultures simultaneously, but the latitude granted to Anglo women was not initially extended to their female clients. Only when the mission

---

[63] This is not to imply that Hispanas had no role in the church. Many carved out a special role as wives of native evangelists and ministers, aiding their husbands in their ministerial duties, but the Presbyterian Church did not formally recognize this role. For a discussion of the work that Hispana wives in the Presbyterian Church might have performed see Clotilde Falcón NañWez, "Hispanic Clergy Wives: Their Contribution to the United Methodism in the Southwest, Later Nineteenth Century to the Present," in *Women in New Worlds: Historical Perspectives on the Wesleyan Tradition*, ed. Hilah Thomas and Rosemary Skinner Keller (Nashville: Abingdon Press, 1981), pp. 161–77.

[64] In 1927, 50 percent of Allison-James graduates were reported to be teaching, another 20 percent in college, and 10 percent keeping house. See "Their Alma Mater—Allison-James," *Women and Missions* 4 (July 1927): 68. That Hispana graduates of mission schools did more than simply work until they married is evident in Ruth Barber's "All Interpreters," *Women and Missions* 6 (May 1929): 51, in which she recalls a meeting with a former student who had become a "successful storekeeper" and had been a county school superintendent.

enterprise expanded to include medical work did Hispana students benefit; perhaps reflecting their ability to translate an earlier source of power within Hispano society as healers and midwives, they sought and won jobs as nurses to Anglo doctors.

By hiring students or former students as assistants in plaza schools, the Woman's Board hoped to provide extra support to those who had converted, as well as alleviate some of the pressures that teachers complained about. Those employed could not be Catholic, they had to have converted, and they were to assist with teaching or to help with the domestic work.[65] This policy caused no end of problems. Because it was considered inappropriate for mission women to take young men into their homes, those young men hired as assistants helped to run the school, unlike the young women, who often became live-in servants, even though this was not the intention of the board. In their attempts to effect compromises in cases of abuses, the Woman's Board was governed by "propriety," or by its sense of good manners. Missionaries were reminded that these young people were employees; in one instance, for example, missionaries at the Indian School in Albuquerque were chastised for objecting to having to sit at the dinner table with one of their Indian assistants. "Surely this could not harm anyone," wrote Faith Haines to the principal of the school. But she tempered her criticism by agreeing that it was not necessary for this young woman to room with one of the teachers.[66] Expressions of prejudice were not condoned; they were often taken as evidence that a teacher was not suitable for a particular field. The board would remove a teacher for not being "in sympathy" with her students and neighbors.

This preoccupation with "propriety" kept direct challenges to the social hierarchy, which privileged male over female, Anglo over Hispano, in check. Differences were smoothed over; all parties received reprimands. The board was especially quick to act if it heard rumors of romantic alliances. Fears of sexual impropriety and miscegenation demanded that teachers keep their distance from male students. Pearl English was transferred from Truchas to Chimayó when the board learned that she had formed a "sentimental attachment with one of her students."[67] In reality, however, the few mission women who married His-

---

[65] See Mrs. Haines to Reverend Maxwell Phillips, May 15, 1883, RG 105, Box 2, Folder 8, PHS, and Mrs. Haines to Elizabeth Craig, January 29, 1890, RG 51, Box 4, Folder 3, PHS.
[66] Faith Haines to R. Coltman, November 30, 1888, RG 51, Box 4, Folder 1, PHS.
[67] Pearl English Biographical File, H5, PHS.

Prudence Clark and Pearl English (Menaul Historical Library of the Southwest)

pano converts seem to have suffered little public criticism. In Chimayó, Prudence Clark and Pearl English married Hispano men active in the local Presbyterian Church and remained in the village. As Gabino Rendón's biography suggests, his marriage to missionary Amelia Brill was another mark of his Americanization. This discrepancy between the home office's concern and the actions of teachers and students in the field suggests that the social mores, or rules of propriety, varied; mission teachers and their students could rewrite these rules if they wished.

Establishing a close relationship with a mission teacher carried with it a host of potential complications other than romantic ones. A job as assistant to a mission teacher had certain advantages. For some it was the first of a series of jobs they would hold within the Presbyterian Church. In addition, many gained some rudimentary teaching experience which served them well when they moved into the public system. Building close connections with Anglo missionaries had other rewards as well: it could result in being admitted to college with a scholarship to offset expenses. To reap the benefits from this job, though, one had to contend with the demands and desires of the mission teacher, whose expectations were often not shared by her assistant. In 1899 Alice Hyson suffered a "fright" when an intruder broke into the living quarters of the mission teachers at Ranchos de Taos. Seeking to ensure her safety, Hyson asked one of her students, a Mr. Vigil, to live in the mission house with her and Harriet Benham. Hyson held great hopes for Vigil, whom she described as "so able a Mexican evangelist." Her plans for Vigil included a mission appointment as her assistant to prepare him to continue on in missionary work. The board might have appropriated the funds to hire Vigil, but its members were worried about the seeming impropriety of a young man living with two older, and single, women. "We do not wonder that you feel safer with Mr. Vigil in the house," they wrote, "and yet there is a feeling here at headquarters that it would be much better not to have any cause for remark at all." Although Hyson attempted to sway the opinion of the board by arguing that it was not considered improper in Taos, one cannot help but wonder how much this excuse was self-serving and not an accurate reflection of local mores. The object of this debate, Vigil, diplomatically sidestepped both the debate and any hint of impropriety by accepting an offer to work as a public school teacher. His decision left Hyson feeling "disappointed" but not angry, and his move may very well have served to protect both his and Hyson's reputations.[68]

By accepting the offer to work in the public school, Vigil skillfully opted out from under Hyson's authority, all the while maintaining cordial relations with her. For other Hispano assistants, the demands of mission teachers seemed imperious and arbitrary and were contested. Two years after the incident with Vigil, Hyson employed a young woman, Marina, as her assistant. In this instance, the rules governing proper behavior were even more confused than with Vigil. As was the custom, Marina lived with Hyson, and as Hyson wrote, "took breakfast with me every morning, and used my bed and things just the same as though they were her own." Marina's duties were not domestic; Hyson explained to the board that "I never asked Marina to do anything for me in way of my cooking, ironing, or extra work that I had to do." She was to assist Hyson at the school, to help with the teaching as well as perform chores such as making the fire and ringing the school bell. Unfortunately, Marina's age (she was fifteen), her position as assistant in the school, and her place in Hyson's home (Benham had been reassigned this same year) made her, all at once, child, employee, and companion to Hyson. These

[68] Emeline Pierson to Alice Hyson, December 6, 1899, RG 51, Box 4, Folder 15, PHS.

factors, compounded by cultural differences, made for a volatile combination that came to a head when Hyson forbade Marina to attend a dance.[69]

Marina defied Hyson, seeing nothing improper in dancing. More galling to Hyson was Marina's anger when reprimanded and her refusal to apologize (though Marina did apologize to the synodical missionary, the Reverend Robert Craig). It was left to the board, specifically to Rev. Craig, to mediate the situation. His solution was to explain to Marina that as an assistant she was under the direction of Hyson, a situation she must accept.[70] This would seem to have been a victory for Hyson, but her own letters suggest otherwise. She was extremely contrite for having caused trouble. After all, her inability to manage her employee brought critical scrutiny from the board and an implication that she was not in control. Marina's small protest might seem to have had little impact, but comments from others in the mission field suggest that her insistence on going to the dance represented a struggle that also took place at other stations. Remembering the various reasons why he respected his former teacher, Alice Blake, Abelino Estrada recalled that she had permitted dances, "well behaved *bailes*," even though "she didn't very much favor dancing," suggesting that this had not been a common practice among missionaries.[71] The clash between Marina and Hyson is but one example among many of the cracks that would appear in Presbyterian traditions as these two cultural and religious traditions collided. Certainly this challenge did not take place only in the Hispano field but was replicated again and again as missionaries (and other Anglo-Protestant social reformers) confronted competing social systems. The collective impact was to change social mores throughout the society as, in this example, the orthodox and conservative Presbyterian ban on dancing fell by the wayside.[72]

† † †

[69] Alice Hyson to Mrs. J. F. Pingry, October 21, 1901, RG 51, Box 2, Folder 18, PHS.

[70] Reverend Robert Craig to Mrs. John F. Pingrey, October 28, 1901, RG 51, Box 2, Folder 17, PHS.

[71] Quoted by Barker, "Trementina," p. 12.

[72] For another discussion of social reformers' failed attempts to exercise control over the social mores of young working-class girls, in this instance urban young people, see Kathy Peiss, *Cheap Amusements: Working Women and Leisure in New York City, 1880–1920* (Philadelphia: Temple University Press, 1985), pp. 163–84.

When the students of the mission schools formally entered the movement, whether as teachers, evangelists, or community workers, they challenged the idea that Americanization required them to become less Hispanic. Readers of *Women and Missions* learned that students at the Allison-James school were learning traditional Spanish handcrafts such as weaving, carving, and embroidery and were applying Spanish designs in each of these crafts, all under the supervision of a team made up of both Anglo and Hispano teachers.[73] Cosme García, a longtime member of the church and member of the New Mexico State Board of Education, noted, in an article providing an overview of mission accomplishments, that "the whole populace is rapidly becoming bi-lingual." Spanish-speaking children were learning English but were not losing their Spanish; they were learning to belong to two cultures.[74] Daniel Vásquez, a graduate of the state agricultural college, and alternately employed both by the Presbyterian Board of National Missions and as a county agricultural officer, found himself assisting small subsistence farmers, attempting to improve their methods. He confessed that his "modern" ways often could not stand up to the "practical" ways of older, "gray-headed" farmers with more experience; they knew things he did not know. Vásquez became deeply immersed in the lives of the people in the small towns to which he was assigned and started 4–H clubs, organized athletic activities, and conducted manual training classes in addition to his agricultural duties. He was not neglecting the spiritual dimension of the work, he asserted, but he preferred to stress a more "practical Christianity." These people, he argued, would be "better citizens if we try to teach them how to gain a profitable living."[75] Hispano students did not share their teachers' disdain for party politics. They ran for school boards, established their own local systems of political patronage, and awarded teaching jobs to fellow mission school graduates.[76]

All these pieces of evidence point to the permeability of culture, as well as "pluralist integration" and the existence of a "third culture." Indeed,

[73] Ruth Barber, "Allison-James Prepares for Home Life," *Women and Missions* 11 (May 1934): 52–53.

[74] Cosme García, "An Outsider's Estimate," *Women and Missions* 12 (May 1935): 69.

[75] Daniel Vásquez, "A Task Just Begun," *Women and Missions* 11 (May 1934): 69.

[76] Manuel Madrid was elected county superintendent of schools of Mora County in 1911 (Twitchell, *Leading Facts of New Mexican History*, 3:427); when Dora Vásquez applied to teach in the Loma Parda school in 1926, she was awarded the job by Cosme García, who held the job as county school superintendent (Vásquez, *The Enchanted Dialogue of Loma Parda and Canada Bonita* [N.p.: N.p., 1983], p. 9).

Hispano-Presbyterians were in the process of rewriting the history of the mission enterprise in New Mexico. When minister Epifanio Romero reflected back over history, he asserted that Sheldon Jackson had "urged that, as on foreign mission fields, missionaries of this area teach children to read so that they could understand the word of God, and also be better able to hold their own in the advancing culture from the eastern states."[77] The original imperialist designs of the movement had been reinterpreted, this time by Hispano students. Their version held that, in the face of Anglo imperialism, mission efforts had helped Hispanos to "hold their own" or to maintain their culture.

By refusing to relinquish their language and other aspects of their tradition, Hispano-Protestants challenged the social order that the mission enterprise had originally envisioned in which Anglo-Protestantism triumphed. Instead, their experience continually reminded supporters of mission work that cultural traditions were not easily or quickly undermined and would persist even though people changed their religious affiliation. This determination of Hispano converts to maintain their language, to assert a particularly Hispano presence within this Anglo institution, presented the church with a new set of conflicts. Just as the church had responded to women's demands in the 1870s by recognizing separate mission boards, so it addressed the needs of Hispano converts by establishing a Mexican Department (later expanded into the Spanish-Speaking Department) in 1911. This move was meant to make the church more responsive to the problems of Hispano converts by centralizing the administrative aspects of programs intended for Hispanos within the Board of Home Missions. Although women were allowed to run their own organization, Hispano Presbyterians worked under a succession of Anglo administrators who acted as intermediaries between them and the church hierarchy in New York. The policies these administrators pursued expanded the services available to Hispanos, but their very presence as advisers to Hispano evangelists and ministers signaled continuing paternalism on the part of the church. Under Paul Warnshuis, appointed in 1932, the department became a fiefdom in which he managed the entire operation, refusing to give local jurisdictions more responsibility. Rather than install Mexican-Americans as pastors, he undermined their ability to gain the prestige or security of a pastorate by

---

[77] Letter from Epifanio Romero, 1953, quoted in Grainger, ed., *Centenario de la Palabra*, p. 69.

moving them around from church to church. According to Douglas Brackenridge, "Rather than becoming self-sufficient clergymen they were dependent on the Spanish-speaking Department in the person of Paul Warnshuis to sort out their problems and make decisions that normally would have been their personal prerogative."[78]

Ultimately, paternalism as exercised by Warnshuis would be challenged, as Hispanos demanded greater representation, authority, and discussion of their concerns by the church as a whole. By the 1960s the church would be confronted by, among others, its Hispanic members, who demanded a reevaluation of its treatment of minorities and called for an end to the traditionally paternalistic practices, greater emphasis on socioeconomic issues affecting Hispanics, and more coordination between the church and secular political organizations such as the League of United Latin American Citizens (LULAC), the United Farm Workers, and other Mexican-American political groups.[79] The earliest Hispano converts, however, relied on the introductions provided by Anglo mentors to make their concerns known to the larger church. Not surprisingly, both the converts and their mentors preached cultural tolerance. Together, they challenged Anglo stereotypes of Mexicans and Spanish-speaking peoples and pushed the church to address the issue of race relations in the Southwest.

† † †

Though moved by their experience in the field to call for greater tolerance, Anglo mission teachers were unable to translate their changed attitudes into political activism. The most successful mission students, however, did what their teachers could not. They forged a new politics in which the ideal of cultural pluralism was central. Hispano mission students translated the enterprise's emphasis on social harmony into a set of political ideals which underscored their credentials as Americans but, at the same time, fought ethnocentrism. In so doing, they refused to compromise their Spanish-Mexican heritage or to separate themselves from that history, which Anglos had labeled as "backward."

[78] For a discussion of the history of Hispano Presbyterians, with a focus on those who become ministers, see R. Douglas Brackenridge and Francisco O. García-Treto, *Iglesia Presbiteriana: A History of Presbyterians and Mexican-Americans in the Southwest* (San Antonio: Trinity University Press, 1974), p. 171.

[79] Ibid., pp. 197–225.

The efforts of students to make cultural connections and to join the various cultural forces shaping their lives took many forms. In an essay for which he won a prize, for example, Menaul student Julian Durán pleaded for friendship between the Mexican and United States governments. "Do we have to hate Mexico because of our love to our country?" he asked, suggesting that patriotism did not legitimate American exploitation of another people. Mexico's complicity with Germany during World War I had heightened United States anxiety about the Mexican Revolution. Coming to the defense of Mexico, Durán reminded his readers that the United States was not "wholly blameless." Mexico had emulated the United States in its fight for independence from Spain in the 1820s; bitterness toward the United States had grown only after the United States had undertaken an "unjust war" in which it had claimed the northernmost territories. He condemned American exploitation of the Mexican people and resources: "Is there any justice in what oil and mine speculators have done and are doing down there? About eighty-seven per cent of the Mexican people are illiterate. Americans have taken advantage of this pitiable condition and practically stolen the money from the people. Then when they become rich in this shameful way they have come away with all the money they have acquired" without reinvesting in the country itself. Were not Mexico's protests against this exploitation justifiable?[80]

The problem as Durán saw it was that most Mexicans knew only ruthless speculators, not those who represented "Christian America." Though critical of the behavior of U.S. economic interests in Mexico, Durán did not challenge their right to do business in Mexico, only their methods. He defended the increasing number of Mexican immigrants by asserting that their plight was like that of African-Americans; they sought to escape "slavery as our negroes did when they knew they would be free only by escaping North." What was needed in relations between the United States and Mexico was broader fellowship and understanding, not armed intervention. The United States should look to make Mexico a "co-worker," not subdue the country by force. If the disagreement between the two countries could not be resolved peacefully, both should submit to the mediation of outside countries (he called for resurrection of the ABC—Argentina, Brazil, and Chile—committee, which

---

[80] Julian Durán, "Our Relation to Mexico," *Sandstorm Yearbook* (Albuquerque: Menaul School for Boys, 1920), unpaged, MHL.

had attempted to mediate the 1914 United States invasion of Veracruz).[81]

The Mexican Revolution and the exodus of Mexican citizens across the border fueled the xenophobic fears of Anglo-Americans living in the Southwest. Between 1910 and 1920 the Mexican population in the United States almost doubled. In the last three years, 1917 to 1920, more than one hundred thousand Mexicans crossed the border into the southwestern United States fleeing the chaos of the revolution, seeking economic opportunity and stability.[82] Hispanos found their own "peculiar" position highlighted; they were not Mexican, but because of their heritage they too were victimized by prejudice. By acting as cultural mediators, they claimed a measure of power and influence. Durán's commentary on these events was not simply a discussion of current world events but a statement about the special role he and other Hispanos could play in resolving the problems.

Durán's call for mediation, his desire that Mexico be recognized as a "co-worker," was not a call for self-determination. Indeed, Mexicans needed "Christian" America just as he had as a child. Like his teachers, who had invoked images of familial relations to describe the form interactions should take between missionaries and their clients, Durán called for similar paternalistic sentiments. It was the duty of Americans to help "from an elevated position." Mexico required the same aid that Hispanos had received. "Help must come from the outside." Statements such as these also served as evidence to the broader mission movement that it should step up its efforts in the Southwest. Beginning in 1912 an interdenominational Council on Spanish American Work (COSAW) was organized in Albuquerque with the intention of organizing churches and opening community houses to accommodate the new population.[83]

Admittedly, Durán's are the words of a dutiful mission student, yet his defense of Mexico, his call for broader fellowship, and his belief that Mexicans be seen as co-workers suggest the development of a set of political ideals in keeping with the liberal positions that Mario García

[81] Ibid.

[82] McWilliams, *North from Mexico*, p. 163. The Mexican immigration to New Mexico in these years was smaller than that to Texas and California. The Mexican immigrant population in 1910 numbered 125,016 in Texas, 33,649 in California, and only 11,918 in New Mexico. By 1930, 683,681 Mexican immigrants lived in Texas, 368,013 in California, and 59,340 in New Mexico. New Mexico lacked the large-scale agricultural economy that attracted the vast majority of Mexican immigrants to Texas and California.

[83] Durán, "Our Relation to Mexico"; and Barber and Agnew, *Sowers of the Seed*, p. 88.

has argued characterized the "Mexican-American generation" that emerged in the 1930s. In this group he finds a "richness of political struggle, and a deep search for identity."[84] From this generation arose organizations such as LULAC, which embraced a program of "pluralistic assimilation," pursuing such seemingly contradictory goals as adjustment to American values and customs, political socialization, and cultural pluralism.[85] García finds that this generation stressed cultural balance, preached tolerance, and sought to chronicle "cultural authenticity and persistence."[86] They found what Mexican-American folklorist and New Mexican Arthur Campa identified as "cultural coexistence." Campa, the son of a Mexican Methodist missionary, attended the Harwood Methodist School in New Mexico and the University of New Mexico and later taught at that university, Columbia University, and the University of Denver. He believed that "refreshed by contact with Mexico," Hispano culture "could sustain acculturation with Anglo America without being seriously damaged. Mexican-American culture would endure although in an adaptive rather than static form."[87]

This position recognized that these cultural relations were marked by differences and conflicts that could not be resolved. Hispano culture would hold its own, though it would undergo significant change. The

---

[84] García, *Mexican-Americans*, p. 19. Protestant converts in both Mexico and Peru also embraced similar "liberal" principles, advocating greater social justice, especially in education, while championing individualism. Deborah Baldwin, *Protestants and the Mexican Revolution* (Urbana: University of Illinois Press, 1990), argues that Anglo missionaries and their Mexican converts supported what she calls "democratic Christianity." Missionaries believed that their job was to provide the proper environment so that others could grow in the "fullness of the stature of true manhood and womanhood." Eventually, this ideology required missionaries to give way to native ministers who emerged during the revolution, some of whom moved into powerful government positions, especially in the area of educational policy (pp. 162–71). Rosa del Carmen Bruno-Jofre, *Methodist Education in Peru: Social Gospel, Politics, and American Ideological and Economic Penetration, 1888–1930* (Waterloo, Ontario: Wilfrid Laurier University Press, 1988), argues that Methodism embodied liberal principles that appealed to a cross section of Peruvians who opposed the traditional elite. The social vision preached by Methodists was one of a "pure democracy based on the conciliation of antagonistic interests. The role of Christianity is to mediate between those antagonistic interests, to become an alternative to socialism and to preserve the liberal content." Peruvian Protestants, like Hispano-Presbyterians in New Mexico, stressed cooperation and coordination. Progress was achieved by cooperation, not conflict. See pp. 48–59.

[85] García, *Mexican-Americans*, p. 34. Founded in Texas in 1921, the organization included eighty councils throughout the Southwest by World War II.

[86] See García's discussion of three Mexican-American intellectuals of this period, writer Carlos Casteñeda, sociologist George Sanchez, and folklorist Arthur Campa, in *Mexican-Americans*.

[87] Ibid., p. 288.

"cultural coexistence" espoused by Hispano intellectuals of this generation should not be confused with more romantic variations on this theme of cultural pluralism. Other progressive Anglos moving into the area looked at the situation in New Mexico and found in the fragile "cultural coexistence" forged between Hispanos and Anglos the ideal alternative to what they perceived as the "ugly conglomerate produced by the 'melting pot' in other parts of the country." Writing in the *Nation* in 1920, Elizabeth Shepley Sergeant glossed over conflicts between Indian, Hispano, and Anglo to proclaim enthusiastically that "here, if anywhere on American soil, it should be possible to conserve the heritage of the past without limiting the promise of the future." In New Mexico, "God's Country," as she called it, were "vast undeveloped resources, both mineral and agricultural, land enough for everyone to have a comfortable slice, high wage standards, simple standards of living which minimize social distinctions—almost every New Mexican has a horse as well as a ranch and the woman who has lived eleven years in Paris works as hard at her plowing as her humblest neighbor—here are some of the conditions of an ideal community."[88]

Because they were so deeply committed to the ideals of conversion and progress and to making changes, adherents of the mission cause could take no comfort in this Anglo idealization of the "primitive." Whereas Sergeant gloried in the simplicity she saw in the lives of her Indian and Hispano neighbors, missionaries and their students wanted to build something different; they embraced change as positive. Anglo missionaries wanted to remake Hispano society, while their Hispano students wanted the benefits and security they had come to associate with modernization, although they refused to relinquish their traditional culture. Their advocacy of cultural pluralism was marked by certain limits, however, one of which was a rejection of radical political ideas.

García argues that many among the "Mexican-American generation" were anticommunist, and a similar pattern is found among mission students.[89] Out of the process of acculturation and resistance was fashioned a liberal ethic that joined concern for cultural pluralism with such traditional liberal values as individualism and capitalism. Julian Durán, for instance, believed the revolutionary governments that had followed Porfirio Díaz in Mexico were "selfish and corrupt." The efforts by some

---

[88] Elizabeth Shepley Sergeant, "God's Country," *Nation*, July 10, 1920, pp. 39–40.
[89] García, *Mexican-Americans*, e.g., his discussion of Carlos Casteñeda, p. 245.

Cooperative store, Allison-James School, 1944 (Menaul Historical Library of the Southwest)

involved in the Mexican Revolution to carry out a more thorough social revolution, meant to address problems of poverty and repressive government, were seen as failures.[90]

Within the mission enterprise Hispano students equated the idea of revolution with political and moral corruption. In his condemnation of the Bolshevik Revolution, another student, Benigno Romero, wrote that the platform of the Bolshevik movement said, "Away with private property! Away with authority! Away with the state! Away with the family! Away with Government, flag and religion!" He painted a picture of dictatorship which confiscated private property, foodstuffs, and personal belongings and generally tyrannized the Russian people.[91] Like their

[90] Durán, "Our Relation to Mexico."

[91] Benigno Romero, "Bolshevism," *Sandstorm Yearbook* (Albuquerque: Menaul School for Boys, 1920), unpaginated, MHL.

Anglo teachers, Hispano-Protestants believed wholeheartedly in the efficacy of "progress," sharing the mission enterprise's commitment to modernization.[92] They also championed the individual, stressing that change would come with the development of individual capacity. Seeking out a better education, learning English, and gaining new skills were key to enhancing the power of the individual.

Romero was particularly concerned with the effects of the Bolshevik Revolution on people in this country, and in his condemnation he sounds much like Josiah Strong railing against Catholicism. Romero warned that communism was spreading throughout the world and gaining a foothold in America. Like Strong, Romero painted a conspiratorial picture. He wrote of "subsidized agents" and "agitators" infiltrating the unions and promoting labor conflict and strikes. These were not loyal citizens, but foreigners. He asked his readers, "Shall we consent to have in our country people, whose ideas are to do away with our form of government, our right to own property, our homes and families, our religion and our God?"[93]

The solution to this growing problem, believed Romero, was to advocate a constitutional amendment that "ought to demand good knowledge of our English language and the American ideals of liberty, equality, fraternity, and our customs, before she allows foreigners to become American citizens. She should provide schools for children of foreign birth and Americanize them thoroughly." The most potent weapon against communism, as it had been against Catholicism a half century earlier, was the Christian church: "America must show them a Christian church which is a friend of men and an instrument of freedom. Without the Church and Christ's spirit, our efforts toward eradicating this movement will not be successful."[94] Ironically, Romero took a much harder line against communism than others within the mission movement. Administrators at the mission headquarters were inclined, in the early years of the Russian Revolution, to temper their criticism. Charles Stelzle, who was appointed to oversee mission efforts among industrial workers, was

---

[92] In keeping with his argument that the second generation of Mexican-Americans was "mostly liberal," García argues that LULAC's program of "pluralistic assimilation" with its emphasis on adjustment to American values, political socialization, cultural pluralism, desegregation, and education embodied this generation's liberal leaning (*Mexican Americans*, pp. 2, 34–35).

[93] Romero, "Bolshevism."

[94] Ibid.

more sympathetic, pointing out that the Russian people had lived under tyrannical governments for too long.[95]

The parochialism exhibited by Romero is surprising, but his failure to make connections between the situation of Hispanos in the Southwest and immigrants in other parts of the United States speaks to the relationship between the structure of the mission movement and its political message. Anglo-Protestants would remain at the center, moved by the humanitarian impulse to make alliances with the separate groups they deemed foreign. They did not promote alliances among the various groups of clients. Hispanos like Durán and Romero did not overtly challenge the linear model of progress, which placed their mission mentors in a position of superiority. The focus of discussion was not so much on problems that afflicted the nation as a whole but rather on the conditions of specific groups of people. Instead of forging a democratic and mutualistic pluralism that would serve as the basis of a new, more inclusive ideal of nationalism, the mission enterprise served more limited ends. It empowered certain individuals of many different ethnic groups, providing opportunities for them to enter more influential economic and social arenas. Mission students came to the state wary of radical politics; they would take a middle road, avoid extremes, and advocate mediation. They would stress the importance of believing in God; their belief was a sign both of their patriotism and their moral character.

Hispano membership in the Presbyterian Church would remain small. It peaked in the early twentieth century, declined, and has remained relatively steady throughout the century.[96] Yet this small group helped effect important shifts in mission attitudes. Denunciation of the Catholic Church was muted, for instance, as Hispano converts set an example for nonsectarian interaction. After graduating from Allison-James, convert Dora Vásquez went to teach in the public schools of New Mexico and invited the local priest in to say Easter and Christmas mass.[97] She was one of only two Protestants in the community, she explained, and it seemed right to invite the priest to officiate over religious holidays. Because she had been raised within a largely Catholic culture, Vásquez

---

[95] See Charles Stelzle, *A Son of the Bowery: The Life Story of an East Side American* (New York: George H. Doran, 1926), pp. 140–41.

[96] Mark T. Banker, "They Made Haste Slowly: Presbyterian Mission Schools and Southwestern Pluralism, 1870–1920" (Ph.D. diss. University of New Mexico, 1987), p. 415.

[97] Vásquez, *Enchanted Dialogue*, p. 11.

was able to act in a nonsectarian fashion much more easily than had her Anglo teachers.[98]

Not only had the enterprise been forced to acknowledge the continuing influence wielded by the Catholic Church and begin to work with priests, but Hispanos within the church were increasingly vocal about the racism of the Anglos with whom they worked and worshiped. A study by the Commission on International and Interracial Factors in the Mexican Problem in the Southwest, conducted under the supervision of Menaul school superintendent Harper Donaldson, found that most of the Hispanos interviewed believed that the "racial question" had to be faced. Very much removed from the ethnocentric mission rhetoric of the late nineteenth century, this study located the root of the racial problems in the Southwest in the "American ruthlessness in the invasion of the new territory" and the "taking of land." The report cited numerous instances of "unfair treatment" suffered by Hispanos, concluding that the "instances of personal prejudice against Spanish-Americans even in churches are the most serious consideration." The authors insisted that "one ought to be able to expect in the churches a welcome to those who have chosen the church's invitation to its mission school." Included in a long list of suggestions as to how best to address the racial divisions was a call for the end to segregated churches and schools, the teaching of Spanish to Anglos, "a public opinion which would condemn the mutual criticism between the groups in public meetings," expanded educational opportunities for Hispano children in the high schools and colleges, and "religious freedom and tolerance."[99] This dialogue about the realities of racial difference would be expanded as the century progressed and the church took actions that anticipated the larger civil rights reforms of the 1950s and 1960s. In the 1940s, for example, school personnel and

---

[98] Mark Banker notes that as early as 1909 Menaul officials were sensitive to the religious differences among their students. During a two-week series of evangelical services held at the school, the evangelist, who was Hispano, had "preached the truth in a very convincing and forcible way" but had said nothing "that would cause the young men of the Romanist faith to be offended" (quoted in Banker, "They Made Haste Slowly," p. 369). Similarly, Randi Jones Walker argues that between 1850 and 1920 the Protestants in New Mexico moved from a position of "separation" to one of "cooperation" (*Protestantism in the Sangre de Cristos, 1850–1920* [Albuquerque: University of New Mexico Press, 1991], p. 110).

[99] A summary of the commission's findings is included in Manuel Gamio, *Mexican Immigration to the United States* (Chicago: University of Chicago Press, 1930), Appendix III, "Race Relations in New Mexico," pp. 210–15.

pupils were encouraged to participate in interracial conferences, and the policy of operating segregated schools was abandoned.[100]

No longer did the mission enterprise see itself as an army in defense of Christianity, but rather as a force for reconciliation and greater understanding. Yet in 1920 the mission enterprise assessed its contributions in this regard and found itself lacking. "One can hardly say that this contribution has been as great as might have been hoped," reported Donaldson.[101] His disappointment was compounded by growing poverty and worsening social and economic conditions, about which missionaries could do little because of their emphasis on a faith that privileged individual transformation. Women missionaries had been at the forefront of the move away from a purely evangelical message to one that advocated applied Christianity, but it was their students' insistence that "racial friction and misunderstanding" be addressed as well as their nonsectarianism that impelled the church to support more secular approaches to the social problems of the day. The only "speedy and satisfactory" ending to the problems that Donaldson's commission could recommend was to join the work of missionary agencies to that of an expanded public sector, particularly in the areas of public health and education.

[100] Banker, "They Made Haste Slowly," p. 404.
[101] Gamio, *Mexican Immigration*, p. 216.

CHAPTER SIX

From Mission to Social Service: The Rise of a New Creed

By the 1910s, missionaries, once hailed as the exemplars for how women's power might best be harnessed for the "evangelization of the Great West" and applauded for the various social institutions they had built, were being dismissed as obstacles in the implementation of newer, rational, scientific standards of social service. According to critics, the problem with home missionaries was that they exemplified an older tradition of "charity" rather than "philanthropy." They looked to "alleviate human suffering," whereas social workers trained under new philanthropic standards "carried the idea of prevention of distress and the positive promotion of human welfare." Advocates of professional social service saw the home mission movement as a "reform" organization, characterized by "strong sentiment and 'inspired' leadership," as opposed to a social work agency, whose leaders emphasized "organizing ability and expert training." The mission's goal was to "bring about a specific economic or political change" whereas social work agencies were "occupied with the task of meeting existing situations in the lives of particular individuals and groups."[1]

Other critics asserted that social workers were not "usually enthusias-

---

[1] Sydnor H. Walker, "Privately Supported Social Work," in *Recent Social Trends in the United States: Report of the President's Research Committee on Social Trends* (New York: McGraw-Hill, 1933), pp. 1168–69.

tic" about working with Protestant missionaries. At a 1924 interdenominational meeting concerning mission work in the American Southwest, one participant, Druzilla Mackey, presented a paper, "The Protestant Missionary and the Social Worker," in which she urged that "volunteer" missionaries be prevented from entering Mexican communities and that resources be focused on "trained" missionaries chosen with "especial reference to their spirit of tolerance," ones versed in "scientific methods of religious education" but knowing "something of the history, psychology, and social customs of the Mexicans."[2] Mackey's observations echoed earlier sentiments expressed in the report prepared by the Commission on International and Interracial Factors, which had insinuated that mission teachers often held regressive opinions on race and called for the "cooperation of all missionary teachers with the department concerned of the state government."[3]

The role played by the missionary had come under increasing scrutiny as the original intention of the movement, to build a more "moral" state by converting individuals, was being modified. In large measure because of the experience of its missionaries in the field, the movement had already lessened its emphasis on evangelization. Responding to the demands and needs of client groups, it evinced greater interest in issues of social justice, racial equity, and world friendship. The movement now envisioned itself working on two fronts. Individual salvation would remain a priority; however, the movement also proposed that the government should play an important role in promoting "social justice." The national interest would not be strengthened simply by demanding that citizens adhere to a particular set of moral or religious standards; social

[2] Druzilla Mackey, "The Protestant Missionary and the Social Worker," in Minutes of the Thirteenth Annual Meeting of the Permanent Interdenominational Council on Spanish-Speaking Work in the Southwest, Los Angeles, December 1924, pp. 6–7, Department of History and Records Management Services, Presbyterian Church (U.S.A.), Philadelphia (hereafter PHS). Similar pressures were faced by missionaries within the Methodist Church as well. See Virginia Lieson Brereton, "Preparing Women for the Lord's Work: The Story of Three Methodist Training Schools, 1880–1940," pp. 192–93, and Mary Agnes Dougherty, "The Social Gospel According to Phoebe: Methodist Deaconesses in the Metropolis, 1885–1918," pp. 210–14, in *Women in New Worlds*, ed. Hilah Thomas and Rosemary Skinner Keller (Nashville: Abingdon Press, 1981). Home mission workers were not the only religious social service workers to feel pressure from the imposition of new standards. Evangelical women who worked in Salvation Army and Florence Crittenton homes for unmarried women faced similar criticism. See Regina G. Kunzel, *Fallen Women, Problem Girls: Unmarried Mothers and the Professionalization of Social Work, 1890–1945* (New Haven: Yale University Press, 1993).

[3] Manuel Gamio, *Mexican Immigration to the United States* (Chicago: University of Chicago Press, 1930), p. 216.

problems had to be addressed. The church, it was proposed, should work with government to address these problems.

As mission objectives and programs were recast, there was also among leaders of the movement, as one observer noted, the "beginnings of an appreciation of the professional viewpoint," and a new emphasis was placed on "modern training" for volunteer and social work.[4] Church social service groups introduced new administrative techniques aimed at making their organizations more efficient and more "modern." The new methods and strategies employed by the board's leadership, though generally supported by missionaries in the field, who had long complained of the inadequacies of the mission administration, actually had the effect of limiting input from those in the field as well as limiting participation in the enterprise to women with particular skills and training. Gradually the ethic of social service which had appealed to so many of the Anglo-American women drawn to mission work, one rooted in evangelical convictions and voluntarism, was secularized and professionalized. One was no longer a "missionary" per se, but rather a "professional" working for a religious social service agency. Women who continued to work within the movement reluctantly separated the evangelical and spiritual beliefs they held from the work they performed. In the twentieth century, employees of the board would be asked to lend their support to public agencies that sought to tap and use the energy and resources of home missionaries but also subordinated their activities under the aegis of a secular state.

Favoring women who came to the movement with particular skills and training allowed leaders of the Woman's Board to deliver needed social services efficiently and effectively. Hispano Catholic clients of the mission movement benefited from these changes because they no longer had to convert to receive the full benefits of social services overseen by public agencies, even though these services might still be delivered by a Protestant missionary. Among Presbyterians, these developments generated tremendous controversy. Far removed from the original intent of the mission movement, which had envisioned the church and state as equal partners in a quest to build a more "moral" society, the new direction signaled the acceptance of a secular and more dominant state. Fundamentalists within the church complained bitterly that the mission

[4] See C. Luther Fry, "Changes in Religious Organizations," in *Recent Social Trends*, p. 1009.

movement had strayed from its emphasis on individual salvation while liberals argued that the social services being provided by the mission enterprise might be better left to social service professionals. The result was that gradually fundamentalists withdrew their support and liberals transferred their attentions from the social service organizations of the Protestant churches to other nonsectarian and secular groups.

The women who had long supported and sustained the mission movement largely accepted these developments, though they did not foresee the degree to which their work, including its content and quality, would be called into question. In 1923, the Woman's Board of Home Missions ceased to exist as an independent organization within the Presbyterian Church, when it and the other mission boards were incorporated into the Board of National Missions. Women not only lost a platform from which to call attention to their subordinate position within the church, but they lost the institutional foundation for the public role demanded of them by the mission movement. The decline of the women's mission movement undercut the power of a religious and political ethic that joined faith, work, and social action and seriously inhibited one avenue by which to mobilize middle-class Anglo-Protestant women (the employees, volunteers, and supporters who had collectively made up the home mission enterprise) to take action on the social issues that would be at the crux of the emerging welfare state.

† † †

The challenge mission clients presented to the movement's evangelical imperative was compounded by the growing influence and popularity of Progressive reform efforts. Indeed, one impetus behind the professionalization of the mission movement can be found in its relationship with Progressive reform efforts. There is no denying the connections, indeed the overlap in methods and pedagogy, between the mission movement and Progressive reformers, particularly those active in the settlement house movement.[5] The Presbyterian Woman's Board admired and ap-

[5] Historian Patricia Hill has made a similar argument in her study of the home-front support for the women's foreign mission movement, suggesting that the more modern and secular Progressive movement had a far-reaching impact on the fortunes of the mission movement. Hill attributes the decline of the mission movement to the leaders' interest in establishing professional standards and promoting themselves as "experts" in the "science" of missions. By doing this they were following the lead of secular Progressive reformers but moving away from the ideology of "domesticity," which Hill believes had inspired the mission movement, attracting

plauded the work of prominent Progressive reformers; missionaries and their supporters were encouraged to read and learn from the work of such reformers as Jacob Riis and Jane Addams. In 1902, for instance, the board recommended that members read Addams's *Democracy and Social Ethics*, stating that "Miss Addams's superb common sense, her calm, clear, resolute judgement, her grasp of her subject, as well as her sympathy with the people among whom she works and whose point of view she is able to take with sympathy and accuracy, make this volume one of more than ordinary value to the student of civic problems."[6]

Indeed, many settlement houses were affiliated with urban churches and were little more than urban missions. Of the settlement houses in the South, for instance, 70 percent were religious settlements or "modified missions" run by the Methodist Church.[7] Like their counterparts in the mission movement, the majority of the settlement workers were female, in their mid-twenties, and unmarried. What distinguished them from their sisters in the home mission movement was their class background and their higher educational level; most were from moderately well-to-do old-stock American families of the Northeast or Midwest, and 90 percent had received a college education. Many took settlement house work after college before moving into a profession.[8]

Historians have credited Progressive reformers with advocating the secularism and cultural pluralism that became central to modern liberalism, for promoting the rise of the corporate welfare state by arguing for greater government oversight and legislative reform, and for emphasizing the environmental causes of poverty rather than focusing on individual failings. Settlement house workers, in particular, are noted for challenging the ethnocentrism of a hegemonic Anglo-Protestant culture and

---

women supporters by promoting "women's work for women" and promising to remake homes throughout the world to conform to the ideal Christian home. As the movement grew larger and more bureaucratic, the administrative bodies of the organizations lost touch with the ideology of domesticity, which had attracted mass-based support in the past, and were also unable to attract younger women who found the secular Progressive rhetoric of "civic reform" more exciting than the older religious message. Caught in the middle and unable to recruit effectively, the women's mission movement declined. See Hill, *The World Their Household: The American Woman's Foreign Mission Movement and Cultural Transformation, 1870–1920* (Ann Arbor: University of Michigan Press, 1985), p. 4.

[6] See "A Message from Jacob Riis," *Home Mission Monthly* 15 (August 1901): 229, and "Recommended Reading," *Home Mission Monthly* 16 (August 1902): 242.

[7] See Allan Davis, *Spearheads for Reform: The Social Settlements and the Progressive Movement, 1890–1914* (New York: Oxford University Press, 1967), p. 23.

[8] For a profile of settlement house residents see ibid., chap. 2.

for encouraging the dominant culture to recognize the efficacy and inherent goodness of many cultural forms. They may have found in Christianity a personal source of inspiration, but they refused to proselytize among the people with whom they worked, favoring a more subtle approach. They sought to serve by example rather than to convert.

Although as a group they were overwhelmingly Protestant in background, leading Progressives rejected evangelical Protestant rhetoric.[9] Worried about alienating immigrants who did not share a similar religious background, they constructed institutions and employed strategies that would appeal to the broadest cross section of people. They refused to commit themselves to a particular religious doctrine and would not be limited by liturgical strictures or rules established by religious institutions which governed behavior and determined the boundaries of the work they could undertake. Robert Woods, for example, believed that although the settlement house movement owed a debt to religious institutions, "sectarianism in the establishment and direction of the settlement hinders its influence not only in the neighborhood but throughout the city. Possible volunteer assistants and donors hesitate to invest time and money in an organization whose denominational loyalty they do not share."[10] Lillian Wald, founder of Henry Street House, dismissed critics of nonsectarianism by arguing that settlements could attain their full measure of "usefulness" without employing "definite religious propaganda." She wrote:

> It has seemed to us that some thing fundamental in the structure of the settlement itself would be lost were our policy altered. All creeds have a common basis for fellowship, and their adherents may work together for humanity with mutual respect and esteem for the conviction of each when these are not brought into controversy. Protestants, Catholics, Jews, and an occasional Buddhist and those who can claim no creed have lived and served together in the Henry Street house contented and happy, with no attempt to impose their theological convictions upon one another or upon the members of the clubs and classes who came in confidence to us.[11]

[9] Ibid., p. 27.

[10] Robert Woods, *The Settlement Horizon: A National Estimate* (New York: Russell Sage Foundation, 1922), p. 427.

[11] Lillian Wald, *The House on Henry Street* (1915; reprint, New York: Dover, 1971), p. 254.

To reformers such as Woods and Wald, nonsectarianism represented a move away from an older and outmoded style of reform which they identified with religious missions. Settlement house workers were not to be confused with "Lady Bountifuls" dispensing charity. Instead, settlements were to provide a place wherein a new and better society might be built and true democracy realized. Mary Simkhovitch expressed what the secular settlement leaders considered the crux of the difference between religious and secular reform work when she wrote: "The mission is a propagandist effort, religious, political or economic, perfectly proper in its place, but not to be confused with the settlement whose philosophy is that of our government; that is, of a democratic society where all have an equal chance, and where people of every race, color and creed are on an equal footing."[12]

Sentiments like those expressed by Simkhovitch, that mission workers were not the best advocates of a democratic government, must have come as a great shock to those active in religious reform organizations. After all, they had undertaken their activities for the good of the nation; their goal had been to strengthen the very foundation of democracy. Indeed, the mission enterprise, in general, had taken much inspiration from its Progressive and secular counterparts. John McDowell, in his study of missions in the South, finds that Methodist missionaries took the urban settlements of Progressive reformers as their model, including their emphasis on nonsectarianism. Missionaries toned down their religious rhetoric as they confronted the daily and routine problems of their clients. Not only does he find that there was an exchange in the methods and content of their work, but the organizational aspects of bureaucracy and scientific study associated with Progressivism competed with an older style of voluntarism on which the mission movement had been built.[13]

One finds a similar pattern in the Presbyterian home missions. By the turn of the century, the emphasis on conversion had been toned down,

[12] I am indebted to Domenica Barbuto for this quotation. See her study, "The Matrix of Understanding: The Life and Work of Mary K. Simkhovitch" (Ph.D diss., State University of New York at Stony Brook, 1992).

[13] John P. McDowell, *The Social Gospel in the South: The Woman's Home Mission Movement in the Methodist Episcopal Church, South, 1886–1939* (Baton Rouge: Louisiana State University Press, 1982). For a discussion of the impact of religious settlements in two urban areas see Ruth H. Crocker *Social Work and Social Order: The Settlement Movement in Two Industrial Cities, 1889–1930* (Urbana: University of Illinois Press, 1992), chaps. 1 and 4.

and missionaries had come to understand that they must evolve a "bargaining" relationship with their clients if they were to succeed and keep their stations open. But the Woman's Board had not yet made a transition from being primarily concerned with saving the "souls" of its clients to addressing the impoverished conditions in which most of them lived. Nor had the board evolved an organizational structure that was more "professional" in its operations. The most notable example of how the more secular settlement house movement influenced this particular home mission organization was in the choice of Katherine Bennett to succeed Mary James as president. Bennett, the last leader of the Presbyterian Woman's Board of Home Missions, was responsible for negotiating this organization through a period of dramatic change, from a primary concern with individual spiritual salvation to one that addressed issues of social welfare.

Born into a prosperous New Jersey family, Katherine Jones Bennett graduated from Elmira College in 1885. She taught school for several years, but as her membership in the College Settlements Association (CSA) attests, she was more interested in social service. In 1894, when Bennett began working as the national secretary of young people's work at the Woman's Board of Home Missions, she remained active in the CSA, serving on its electoral board. Organized to raise support for settlement work, the board of the CSA stressed that the settlement was neither a "charity" nor a "mission." Rather, it represented the "fairness of the Christian culture." In other religious matters the CSA stressed that the settlement was a "family" that "stood for churchgoing in a nonchurchgoing community." The emphasis on religion was not primary; most important was the "mutual knowledge and mutual confidence born of the sharing of conditions" between settlement house resident and neighbor or the exchange between classes.[14]

For Bennett, the CSA served as a bridge between two eras and traditions of social service and action. The idea that there was a religious foundation, a spirit of ecumenical fellowship, to serve as the basis for social services legitimized the more political and professional directions in which the settlement movement was headed. College Settlement Association Electoral Board reports from the 1890s indicate that discussion of the spiritual issues gave way to increasing interest in establishing a

[14] See the report of the head worker from the New York Settlement and Report of the Electoral Board, Fourth Annual Report, 1892–93, pp. 8–12, College Settlements Association, Sophia Smith Collection, Smith College, Northampton, Mass.

Katherine Bennett (Menaul Historical Library of the Southwest)

cooperative relationship between settlement residents and municipal authorities and demands that "permanent staffs" be favored over "visiting residents" to create a "permanent nucleus" of workers with "larger knowledge," able to wield more power in the neighborhood.[15] As Bennett moved into a position to succeed Mary James as president of the Woman's Board of Home Missions, her years on the CSA board provided the experience she needed to remake the Woman's Board. When she married Fred S. Bennett in 1898, she resigned from her paid position

[15] See Fifth Annual Report, 1893–94, Report of the Electoral Board, p. 6 and Sixth Annual Report, 1894–95, Report from the Philadelphia Settlement, p. 22, ibid.

at the board but was asked to serve on the board of directors. At Mary James's death in 1909, Bennett became president of the board, which she headed until 1923, when the Woman's Board was merged with all other mission organizations to form the Board of National Missions. She remained a vice-president of that board until 1941.[16]

Mary James had been deeply immersed in the evangelical culture of the late nineteenth century. To her mind, the principal concern of the Woman's Board was to Christianize America. Good works, social service, and social activism were secondary to saving souls. Running the Woman's Board was not work but a calling. Bennett, by contrast, represented the modernist in American Protestantism. Her religious sensibility was informed by the Social Gospel, which minimized the importance of personal salvation to stress good works and social activism. Active in a variety of ecumenical organizations, Bennett was a member of the Federal Council of Churches, as well as the Council of Women for Home Missions. While her predecessor spoke of the mission enterprise in domestic terms, comparing it to a family, recreating the hierarchy of the patriarchal family, with minister as father, mission teacher as mother, and the students as children, Bennett's writings emphasize secular concerns such as reforming the structure of the organization and introducing more professional standards. For Mary James, the mission enterprise was a family endeavor, one in which her husband, Darwin, was also active. Little mention is made of Katherine Bennett's husband, Fred; they were clearly not a team in promoting missions as James and her husband had been.[17]

The most significant difference between these two women, however, was in the spiritual message they fashioned to guide supporters of the

[16] Robert T. Handy, "Mary Katherine Jones Bennett," in *Notable American Women, 1607–1950: A Biographical Dictionary*, ed. Edward T. James and Janet W. James (Cambridge, Mass.: Harvard University Press, 1971), pp. 134–35.

[17] Unlike Darwin James, Fred Bennett was not a public servant and seems to have had no connection to the mission enterprise. Katherine Bennett's biographies in *Who Was Who in America* and *Notable American Women* list his occupation as a manufacturer. Bennett is mentioned in a short article in the *New York Times* in 1915 as being an officer in the William L. Burrell Company of New Jersey. Apparently his company was in the business of producing picric acid used in explosives, as dye or biological stain or as an antiseptic. The company was sued in 1915 by a Mervyn Woolff for failure to pay his fees for services rendered in assisting Bennett et al. to close an agreement with the French government for picric acid worth approximately one million dollars, suggesting that the Burrell company was supplying war material. See "Suit over Picric Acid Sale," *New York Times*, July 17, 1915, p. 14. His death was noted in *Women and Missions* in March 1930, p. 454.

enterprise. Katherine Bennett did not celebrate American missions as her predecessor did by heroizing missionaries. Like increasing numbers of missionaries in the field, she encouraged the enterprise to rethink earlier stereotypes of those deemed "foreign." National ills were not the fault of "foreigners" living in this country or of some outside force. Better that mission supporters look at their own lives with a critical eye. The country, she argued, had lost track of its "national ideals." The members of her class had become too greedy, too concerned with profits, too caught up in the commercialism and materialism of the day.[18]

Bennett sought to convince her constituency that they were responsible for the squalid conditions endured by many people in American society. One could not point the finger of blame at "foreigners" or new immigrants. Certainly she did not undercut efforts to convert these populations, but she did not assert that conversion, spiritual salvation, or individual transformation would cure societal ills. Her aim was to arouse in her supporters interest in transforming society. Acknowledging that she might sound pessimistic, she warned that "pessimism is ofttimes accused of being unpatriotic," but she cautioned that "unwarranted optimism is more dangerous than the baldest pessimism, as it preaches a doctrine of *laissez-faire*, a doctrine that wrecks nations as well as individuals."[19]

Bennett believed that conditions were so bad that there was no time to waste disagreeing or debating about which methods would best resolve them. Calling it a "fallacious argument," she set aside suggestions that the conditions facing the poor were the "result of their own weaknesses," suggesting instead that "we [Anglo-Protestant Americans] must free ourselves from prejudice, social, economic, or racial, and each bear a share in the struggle." Standing against the xenophobia of her day, Bennett asserted that the immigrants might remind Anglo-Americans of the national ideals. That immigrants were able to rise above the "sordidness, the meanness, the cheapness of life about [them]" was to be recognized, applauded, and aided. She challenged those who would be critical

---

[18] As Susan Curtis argues in *Consuming Faith: The Social Gospel and Modern American Culture* (Baltimore: Johns Hopkins University Press, 1991), Social Gospelers like Bennett sought to expose and redress some of the worst aspects of industrial capitalism. But Curtis also suggests that their efforts may have backfired. With their passion for science and their desire for economic organization and efficiency, they ended up actually promoting the culture of consumption they had sought to control.

[19] Katherine Bennett, "Conservation of National Ideals," *Home Mission Monthly* 26 (September 1912): 274.

yet apathetic. "To deplore an evil without aiding in the enforcement of a remedy is supine," she argued, "to shift responsibility for existing conditions upon those in authority is shirking our own share in forming public opinion; to stand idly by without giving definite service to right the wrongs we deplore is selfish as well as unpatriotic."[20]

Bennett finally argued that "assimilation of foreigners" did not mean "transforming them into men and women like our fathers and fore-fathers, for that would be impossible." Instead, supporters of the home mission enterprise should look for a "new type. . . . A mixture of old-world and new in the generations to come." Anticipating fears of what this "amalgamation" would mean, she confronted her listeners' doubts by querying, "Shall we lose our inherited Anglo-Saxon ideals? What will be the effect individually, socially, politically, upon our habits of thought, our morals, our institutions?" Rather than deny the existence of cultural diversity and difference, advocates of the mission movement must help save those "redeeming features of these aliens and thus counteract the undesirable characteristics."[21] In her view, Anglo-Protestants should recognize the validity of certain aspects of foreign cultures and even help to maintain them.

Bennett set the tone for the issues that came to dominate the mission literature. Echoing Bennett's sentiments, Mrs. D. B. Wells painted a picture of a society morally weakened by an industrial ethic that pro-moted exploitation when she wrote of the "disintegrating forces" faced by the church social service agencies. The society was marked by a "greed," which produced "child labor, insufficient wages, sweat shops, irritation and antagonism in the working classes." The by-products of greed were "great wealth, ostentatiously displayed, and undue luxury—class distinctions founded upon the accident of birth, wealth, or social position—a growing evil"; "corporate monopolies which force the man of small capital out of existence as an independent worker"; and "low commercial standards of honesty and fair competition in trade." Lesser evils but important nonetheless because they were problems more easily addressed by a woman in her daily life were "indifference to others," which included the "failure to know of what purposes property is rented; whether dishonesty or misfortune and sickness cause the failure to pay rent past due; delay in the payment of wages or money due to servants;

---

[20] Ibid., p. 275.
[21] "Editorial Notes," *Home Mission Monthly* 26 (March 1912): 110.

exaction of over-labor without over-pay," and "over-dress," which created "envy in others and pride in self."[22]

Wells urged that the church not be indifferent to these problems, that it be a "friend to any and all; freely giving advice, assistance, guidance, protection, education, amusement, medical aid and care, sympathy, cordiality, brotherliness." Bennett sounded a more dire warning, arguing that such vast exploitation could only arouse discontent and discord. The "national ideal" as she saw it was the "Golden Rule." She called for her followers to be heroic. She urged that home mission supporters embrace the Golden Rule, "making brotherly kindness a more imperative motive than the claims of commercialism, ranking mentality, morality and spirituality above pecuniary success in the daily judgments of the marts."[23]

The exhortations of Bennett and Wells were meant to instill a sense of responsibility in their followers, to reiterate the importance of personal involvement and commitment. The *Home Mission Monthly* was replete with suggestions as to how home mission supporters could individually assist these new and larger principles of the mission enterprise. Women were encouraged to show "brotherly kindness," for example, to make certain they paid their employees promptly and regularly. In this way they could ease the burdens of the poor while going about the daily routine of their lives. The work and reports of missionaries in the field were to provide the "direct information" middle-class supporters of the enterprise used in redirecting their personal as well as political priorities.[24] In 1910, the board was pleased to report, for instance, that its supporters, the women active in the mission enterprise "head, heart and soul . . . are the women, as a rule, who are also allied, more or less intimately, with community movements that are making for uplift in health and morals, especially in the protection of children and youth—as

---

[22] (Mrs.) D. B. Wells, "Mission Study: The Social Service of the Church," *Home Mission Monthly* 26 (January 1912): 77.

[23] Bennett, "Conservation of National Ideals," pp. 274–75.

[24] In 1901, the Woman's Board had supported two public measures, an antipolygamy amendment and a bill to create a permanent water supply for the Pima and Papago Indians in Arizona. The board downplayed its lobbying role, arguing that "the question of politics in no way enters into the action of the women in trying to influence legislation on such points." They knew their support for these bills to be "right" by virtue of their "direct information from the missionaries." At this point, the board did not encourage its supporters to become politically active themselves, but rather to "bring their knowledge before the men of their households, that voters may exert proper pressure upon Congressman." See Mrs. Frederick H. Pierson, "Annual Report of the Secretary," *Home Mission Monthly* 15 (July 1901): 202.

anti-child labor, juvenile courts, public playgrounds, etc." With the information they had gleaned from years of mission activism, women would "[arouse] the public conscience" about the importance of these social programs.[25]

Homilies reminding individual women of their social responsibilities connected the administration of the enterprise to its churchgoing constituency. The board saw its relationship to supporters—those women who were members and subscribers but not employees—as largely educational. It argued that it could not engage in overtly political action to promote social welfare because it was "constituted for a distinct purpose," which, it was argued, "does not include these [more overtly political] lines of effort."[26] Bennett's purposes, however, were larger than to remind women of their obligation to servants. She urged her mission workers, for instance, to think beyond the problems of individual clients and instead to consider the larger structural reforms that might be made. Missionaries, she argued, must be kept informed and "abreast of the best thought of its age." Educating both her employees and mission supporters to the new social work standards of the day, Bennett wrote that the "watchword" for the twentieth century was "preventative work." Mission workers were to be thought of as social service experts, not just volunteers. To this end, Bennett encouraged missionaries to think beyond their religious calling, to embrace the contributions of the growing field of sociology, in which, she explained, the emphasis was on preventive measures as well as "on supervised playgrounds, on recreation centers, on protected childhood." The goal as she explained it was that there should be no "evil to eradicate." She concluded that "instances of preventative effort are too many to be listed but, in all lines of endeavor, the economy, the savings in bodies and souls as well as in dollars, the unutterable wisdom of such methods is recognized."[27]

To bring about such change, to bring mission workers and supporters into the mainstream of the emergent social work profession, and to imbue in them support for Progressive ideals required that the Woman's Board be restructured. Describing the Woman's Board as a business, Bennett saw her role as instituting "planned growth." To make her case for expansion, she compared the organization to the mighty railroad

[25] "Editorial Notes," *Home Mission Monthly,* 24 (February 1910): 78.

[26] Ibid.

[27] Katherine Bennett, "Annual Address of the President," *Home Mission Monthly* 25 (July 1911): 204.

businesses of the day. Quoting a supporter, Bennett said, "It is as if a railroad were all surveyed, graded, track laid, stations built, trains running, business flourishing, credit sound. It does not need to begin at the beginning in order to enlarge its capacity and to meet its growing business. All the slow, difficult pioneer tasks have been accomplished. It needs to parallel its tracks, double its rolling stock, build branch lines, enlarge its working force."[28] There was a need for "readjustments" within the organization. To do this, the group had to work with government, philanthropic, and other religious agencies to reorganize the "details of its work." She called on members of the local societies, the bread and butter of the institution, to support her. Using a scientific allusion, she asked that members not act as "insulators," defined as "any nonconducting substance, that cuts off the electric current, and refuses to pass it along."

Bennett and her workers in the field might have shared sympathies about the intrinsic goodness of groups that had earlier been suspect and about the need for expanding programs that addressed the social conditions of their students, but there were growing differences about how the work should be done and who should perform it. Bennett's insistence on professionalization and bureaucratization, though a welcome relief to missionaries in the field who had had to scramble for funds and wait for overdue checks, also threatened the personalistic approach that had been the lifeblood of the organization. Beginning just after the turn of the century the board began to emphasize credentials, methods, and pedagogy. To meet this challenge, workers such as Alice Blake struggled to expand their knowledge and to gain additional training. Blake described this period as one of personal dissatisfaction, but her complaints coincide with the debate taking place at the top levels of the organization over the training and professionalism of workers in general. Longtime workers found that the rules and requirements for the work were changing.[29]

---

28 Ibid., p. 200.

29 Barbara Balliet discusses a similar move away from volunteers to professionals in the Women's Educational and Industrial Union, arguing that "hierarchal tiers" were introduced, giving rise to a new structure which provided "greater definition and control of employees and their tasks." See "What Shall We Do with Our Daughters?" Middle-Class Women's Ideas about Work, 1840–1920" (Ph.D. diss., New York University, 1988), p. 267. In his study of social workers employed by Jewish social service agencies, "The Making of a Feminine Professional Identity: Social Workers in the 1920's," *American Historical Review* 95 (1990): 1051–75, Daniel Walkowitz addresses the pressures and dilemmas faced by Jewish social workers in

The dilemma faced by workers is illustrated by the ensuing debate about who workers were to report to. Bennett was advised by the board's superintendent of education to make a distinction between a community worker, who should be "essentially evangelistic," and a schoolteacher, whose work was primarily "pedagogical." The superintendent, Marshall Allaben, insisted that for the sake of efficiency, the direction of the school had to be pedagogical. He urged Bennett to clarify to her teachers that their direction should be taken from the "schoolmen" in charge of the educational departments. At issue for women missionaries in the field was who they worked under, the pastor of the local church, the superintendent of education, or the New York office of the Woman's Board. In his memo to Bennett, Superintendent Allaben admitted that all "Christian work should be related," but he believed there were two "distinct channels," evangelistic and educational. The relationship of the two channels was up to the executive officers of the mission boards, but the "actual local administration should be the function of men whose professional training fits them for the work attempted. Let the school work, then, be administered by schoolmen, the evangelistic work by pastors."[30]

The effect of the measures taken to improve administration and to make the mission movement more efficient, as well as to bring it in line with the demands of "standard making social agencies," was to reinforce male authority. Indications are that women missionaries were increasingly subject to additional layers of male authority, whether that of the minister or the male superintendent of education. As the church moved toward incorporating all of its mission boards for the sake of efficiency, women lost the autonomy and power that a separate organization had afforded them.[31] More important, the evangelical and spiri-

---

the same period. Although he makes no distinction between those employed by secular versus religious agencies, he does find that workers in the Jewish social service agencies organized workers' councils and the Association of Federation Workers. Their goal was principally to control negative stereotypes. Protestant missionaries made no similar effort to organize themselves.

[30] Memo from Marshall Allaben to Katherine Bennett, June 20, 1911, RG 105, Box 5, Folder 1, PHS.

[31] Susan Curtis notes that a crucial aspect of this religious movement in general was the assertion of a "muscular Christianity," as liberal churchmen fought to make religion once again attractive to men, who, they believed, had been discouraged by the "feminization" of religion (*Consuming Faith,* pp. 81, 187). This campaign may have included reasserting administrative authority over women's activities, as Allaben was attempting.

tual content of the work was gradually being separated from the work as a whole. In the process, a host of questions were raised: To whom were women workers responsible? Were they teachers, social workers, or missionaries? Were they working under the ethic that had inspired the movement in the 1870s, by evangelical concerns, or by the secular scientific and pedagogic concerns increasingly demanded in the 1910s?

† † †

The opening of the Brooklyn Cottage Hospital in Embudo, New Mexico, in 1915 appears to have been a logical extension of mission services. Mission teachers, who had served informally as nurses, had long advocated that medical work be undertaken in the area. Assigned to the hospital, nurse Mary Yeats administered vaccinations and saw to basic medical problems. Her work was supervised by a mission doctor, Horace Taylor, whose territory included the small towns and countryside between Santa Fe and Taos. When the state of New Mexico established its Board of Health in 1919, Yeats and Taylor conformed their practices to the new regulations, working closely with the Board of Health to vaccinate children, record births and deaths, and report contagious diseases. But for local customs, the extension of medical work might have continued the pattern whereby a growing number of male workers were privileged with missionary positions that had once been the province of women. But the local Hispano custom of relying on the *curandera* (healer) or *partera* (midwife) secured this as a field for women, as both nurses and doctors. Local mores ensured that Horace Taylor's tenure was short-lived. He made the mistake of attending to a birth without having received the husband's permission. Soon thereafter he became the target of a furious husband, who, angered that an Anglo man had touched his wife, began to harass Taylor, eventually setting other members of his family upon the doctor. The incident made it impossible for Taylor to continue to practice effectively, and he withdrew from northern New Mexico. For ten years the field remained without a doctor. When the board finally assigned a new doctor in 1931, it sent Dr. Sarah Bowen.[32]

---

[32] For the story of Horace Taylor see Ruth K. Barber and Edith Agnew, *Sowers of the Seed: The Story of Presbyterian Missions in New Mexico and Southern Colorado* (Albuquerque: Menaul Historical Library of the Southwest, 1981), pp. 132–35.

Under the leadership of Bowen, and later Dr. Edith Millican, the Brooklyn Cottage Hospital at Embudo thrived, employing a growing corps of nurses and gradually expanding through the 1950s to include surgical, maternity, and children's wards.[33] Bowen and Millican consulted with a corps of private doctors in the area, most of whom were men, but the two women were largely responsible for building the constituency for the hospital. They and the nurses employed at the hospital traveled throughout the northern part of the state conducting clinics and training midwives. When the board closed mission schools, the medical workers took on the larger burden of maintaining connections between the Presbyterian Church and the local Hispano population. Whereas the students of mission teachers had entered and strengthened the public school system, medical missionaries worked simultaneously with church and state, handing out Bibles as they helped midwives to gain state certification, for example.

Bowen and Millican represented a new generation of missionaries. Doctors took over for teachers, signaling the larger shift toward providing more specialized services by more highly trained personnel. Both Bowen and Millican expressed frustration with the board, which they believed did not provide enough support to the Embudo hospital. Bowen submitted letters of resignation numerous times, earning a reputation for being difficult. She complained constantly about the board's reluctance to provide additional personnel, to build better facilities, and to supply up-to-date equipment. In one of her letters of resignation she noted bitterly that the board would have paid more attention to a "male executive." Had there been an "aggressive man in charge," the hospital would have adequate staff, buildings, and equipment, she claimed.[34]

Bowen's comments echo those of Alice Blake when she wearily suggested in her correspondence with the board that a man could better serve Trementina than she; perhaps he might have better luck.[35] Both were acknowledging the limits of their power, not within the community to which they were assigned but within the larger enterprise. Blake had assumed, incorrectly as it turned out, that if she took more training, gained new skills, and became certified in public health, she would be

---

[33] Ibid., p. 137.

[34] See Katherine Gladfelter's summary of Sarah Bowen's correspondence to the Board of National Missions, "Pertinent Items from Dr. Bowen's Personal Folder," November 1936 and June 1937, Sarah Bowen Biographical File, H5, PHS.

[35] Alice Blake to Marshall Allaben, November 29, 1918, Blake Biographical File, H5, PHS.

better able to lobby for the people of Trementina and secure for them a greater portion of mission resources. Bowen's experience indicates how much the power accorded "professionals" within the mission movement was limited by gender. She deeply resented having her hospital evaluated by ministers and administrators who had little knowledge of the community or respect for the work she was performing. "When you have an executive responsible for a station the executive should have a right to expect something from the Board," she wrote. "Is it the Christian duty of a missionary executive to take everything that is handed out and say nothing," she asked, questioning the enterprise's very premise that missionaries should be guided by an ethic of self-sacrifice.[36] Chafing at the central board's attempts to regulate her work, Bowen resented that her professional judgments were scrutinized by others only distantly connected to the work.

Over the years, home missionary women had found themselves constantly scrambling to explain to the board why it should keep their particular stations open. They had invoked a variety of reasons—they were engaged in "woman's work for women," work that men could not do, or the lack of public schools necessitated their presence, and in the case of medical missionaries, the lack of adequate health care required their services. The expansion of a public school system had reduced the need for mission schools, the consolidation of the men's and women's boards in 1923 had rendered the idea of a separate "woman's work for women" obsolete, and the extension of public health programs threatened the medical work. Underlying these changes in the programs and services offered was a more profound change in the ethic of service generally. The women's home mission enterprise had been born of an ethic that likened the work to an act of "brotherly kindness." It called on familial images and metaphors, demanded that Anglo-Protestants do more than simply give money to a good cause, and made performing service a requirement for good citizenship. Most important, this ethic was rooted in voluntarism. Whatever professional credentials one acquired were to complement and enhance this larger sense of service, not take its place.

When the state began to move into the area of social welfare, women reformers welcomed the new programs, seeing them as an opportunity

[36] Sarah Bowen to Alexander Sharp, October 6, 1958, Sarah Bowen Biographical File, H5, PHS.

to expand the services they had been providing for years. Just as they had welcomed each reform in public school laws, mission women in New Mexico applauded the establishment of the Department of Public Health and then the Department of Public Welfare. But they had not thoroughly considered the impact of the rules and regulations promulgated by these new agencies on their own work. By 1920, for example, it did not matter that one might want to join the mission enterprise, having been "called" to God's service to teach Hispano Catholics in New Mexico, if one could not show the teaching credentials required by the state of New Mexico.

A simple desire to serve others would not suffice; state requirements demanding teacher certification, coupled with the mission enterprise's demand for skilled workers, excluded from mission work women who twenty years earlier had been welcomed. Grace Scanland, for example, had worked as a teacher in El Rito, New Mexico, from 1904 to 1909, when she resigned citing ill health. When she reapplied five years later, in 1914, she was assigned the place of matron at one of the mission boarding schools. She declined the job, preferring to teach. In the following years she taught in Oklahoma, worked in real estate, and gave private Spanish lessons. In 1929, she reapplied to the National Board of Missions asking to be considered once again for a teaching position. Scanland's application was denied. The board cited her age (she was forty-three), as well as the state requirements that teachers have twelve course hours of educational theory. Furthermore, she was informed that the mission schools required their teachers to have recent academic training and experience. Because she had not taught for ten years, she was not eligible for the available jobs.[37]

The distinction between volunteer and professional was codified even further when local and state governments took over the delivery of social services. Margaret Reeves, who headed the New Mexico Bureau of Child Welfare for many years, was particularly proud of her staff's credentials and stressed their professional expertise.[38] Writing in 1932 about the bureau, she said that "we have endeavored to build our pro-

[37] Anna Scott to Grace Scanland, April 14, 1931, Grace Scanland Biographical File, H5, PHS.

[38] In 1921, New Mexico organized its State Bureau of Public Welfare to handle functions that previously had been scattered among other state government agencies. See Harold W. Odom, "Public Welfare Activities," in *Recent Social Trends*, p. 1234, Table 1. For a discussion of the consolidation of social services and the organization of the State Bureau of Public Welfare see Sandra Schackel, *Social Housekeepers: Women Shaping Public Policy in New Mexico, 1920–1940* (Albuquerque: University of New Mexico Press, 1992), p. 21.

gram around trained leadership in social work; no member of our field staff has had less than eight years experience in good case work agencies before they came to us and no county worker has had less than five years." Reeves had come to the Bureau of Child Welfare via the Russell Sage Foundation and the Red Cross. The agencies that had trained her workers included the Saint Louis Provident Association, the State Charities Aid Association in New York City, the family welfare agency in St. Paul, and the Medical Social Service Department of Johns Hopkins University.[39] The requirements set by Reeves effectively excluded from social work the women previously attracted to the mission enterprise.[40] Volunteers were welcome to aid in providing relief. The *New Mexico Relief Bulletin* reported in 1934 that some fourteen hundred New Mexican citizens were serving as volunteers on countywide emergency relief committees helping to identify people in need. But their work was subordinated to that of the professional; the final decision concerning one's eligibility for relief rested with a trained social worker.[41]

Mission women could and did serve on these voluntary committees. In Chacón, Eleanor Tilford distributed relief funds to crews who worked building a local road, but if she had been interested in working at the Department of Public Welfare she would not have had the required credentials. The requirements set by Reeves meant that most of the social workers hired did not even come from New Mexico. Only one,

[39] Margaret Reeves to Fred C. Croxton, August 26, 1932, Gov. Hockenhall Papers, 1933–34, Relief Administration in New Mexico, New Mexico State Records Center and Archives, Santa Fe (hereafter NMSRCA). For an overview of Reeves's work see Schackel, *Social Housekeepers*, pp. 141–62. Reeves was born in 1893 in South Dakota and had attended the University of South Dakota and Radcliffe College. Before taking her position in New Mexico, she had worked with the Children's Bureau of Philadelphia, the Seybert Institute in Philadelphia, the American Red Cross in Denver, and the Russell Sage Foundation in New York. She was the director of the State Bureau of Child Welfare in New Mexico from 1924 to 1935 and the State Relief Administration of New Mexico from 1932 to 1935. In 1935 she became the executive secretary of the Milwaukee Council of Social Agencies. She was a member of the Child Welfare League of America (board of directors, 1933–35), the American Public Welfare Association (board of directors, 1932–35), the National Conference of Social Work (child committee, 1932–34, chair of public welfare division, 1934, and third vice-president, 1936). Biographical information is from Durward Howe, ed., *American Women: The Standard Biographical Dictionary of Notable Women* (Los Angeles: American Publishers, 1939).

[40] In this Reeves was simply following standard practice at the time. For a discussion of the way volunteers were knocked out of social work by professionals, see Dorothy Becker, "Exit Lady Bountiful: The Volunteer and the Professional Social Worker," *Social Service Review* 38 (1964): 57–72.

[41] *New Mexico Relief Bulletin*, no. 17 (July 10, 1934), p. 2, NMSRCA.

Emilie Baca, was identified as being from New Mexico originally. Baca was from Las Vegas but had graduated from the University of Missouri, received her advanced training from the New York School of Social Work, and worked at the Brooklyn Cottage Charities before returning to New Mexico.[42] Not only were most of the social workers not from the state originally, but they were placed in charge of several different counties and could not establish themselves in any one community. They constantly traveled over great distances. In a letter to the Reconstruction Finance Corporation, Reeves apologized for not being able to provide the information the federal government required by discussing the problems the geography of the state posed to welfare workers. She wrote that in a territory of "huge distances and poor means of communication," it was "difficult and also very expensive" to collect the data requested. "It would require," she added,

> a corps of field workers and money for traveling expenses . . . . You probably realize that we have counties as large as some eastern states and it is very difficult to reach all points of some of these counties. I am thinking of one county with an area of 6700 square miles and a population of 3281. The county seat is 105 miles from a railroad; there is not even a telephone in the county seat and no telegraph connections. Mail deliveries are uncertain and often the roads, when one leaves the few main highways, make travel very slow and difficult."[43]

New professional standards compounded by distance, both geographical and cultural, rendered the services of these social workers more impersonal, but they were also officially nonpartisan. Reeves required all workers and volunteers who served on the county committees to take a pledge of nonpartisanship, hoping to preclude charges of favoritism and to depoliticize the delivery of social services. She was thrust into the middle of a controversy when she issued a directive reiterating the non-partisan nature of relief. She reminded the chairmen of county relief agencies, as well as all paid employees associated with the New Mexico Relief Administration, that they were "strictly forbidden from paying any assignment of their salary to any political party . . . . No person on

---

[42] Robert O. Brown to Gov. Arthur Seligman, May 29, 1931, Seligman Papers, Bureau of Public Welfare, 1931–32, NMSRCA.

[43] Margaret Reeves to Fred C. Croxton, August 26, 1932, Gov. Hockenhull Papers, 1933–34, Relief Administration in New Mexico, NMSRCA.

the payroll . . . may participate in any way in any political activities. No such person may attend any political gathering whatsoever. You, of course, vote as your conscience dictates, but do not discuss your vote . . . we have no interest whatsoever in how you vote."[44]

Reeves probably believed her directive to be a measure of her own and her staff's professionalism, but the Democratic State Central Committee refused to see these attempts at professionalism as nonpartisan or as being outside the realm of politics. The committee called for Reeves's resignation. Tom Neal, a member of the committee, accused Reeves, a Republican and a Progressive, of preventing President Franklin D. Roosevelt's "friends from assisting in procuring the endorsement of the president's policies by the votes of this state."[45]

The nonpartisan delivery of services as well as the fact that social workers were from out of state created tensions as traditional patronage networks were superseded in distributing relief.[46] The state administration was accused of favoritism, and case workers felt the brunt of villagers' anger. In the case of one worker, identified as Mrs. Knowlton, who was described as having lived in Central America, where she had learned to speak Spanish, and as being "heartily in sympathy with the Spanish American people,"[47] an investigation of the accusation of favoritism determined that there was "a great deal of resentment against Mrs. Knowlton." The investigator concluded that "this resentment extends throughout the county." Although he could not understand why people would not like this woman because she was "well educated," well trained," a "very pleasant person to meet," and "deeply interested in her work," Knowlton's attempts to administer aid impartially had made her unwelcome: "She is not liked and they [the villagers] do not want to like her."[48]

[44] See memo from Margaret Reeves, July 26, 1934, ibid.

[45] Tom W. Neal to John Miles, July 30, 1934, ibid. Reeves eventually lost her job as a result of her attempts to keep her agency out of partisan politics. See Schackel, *Social Housekeepers*, pp. 153–57.

[46] About the confrontation between federal relief administrators and local politicians, William Brock has argued in *Welfare, Democracy and the New Deal* (London: Cambridge University Press, 1988) that the Federal Relief Program was "government by experts at the expense of elected amateurs" (p. 173). He finds that local politicians often resented the power exercised by people who were young and female and "who ignored their wishes, undermined their methods, and questioned their integrity" (p. 335).

[47] See memo from Lillian Franzen, in Gov. Hockenhull Papers, 1933–34, Relief Administration in New Mexico, NMSRCA.

[48] J. A. McBonvery (name is illegible) to Gov. A. W. Hockenhull July 13, 1934, ibid.

Whether because of distance or disagreements over nonpartisanship and favoritism, state social workers did not know their constituents and clients in the way that missionaries stationed for years in one town did. As outsiders providing new services, they faced the same resistance that missionaries had met decades earlier. But the conditions of their work as well as the professional standards it demanded did not allow for the mutual exchange that had developed between missionaries and their neighbors. Asked to speak about the relationship between local social service organizations and state welfare bureaus, Reeves argued, though it is not clear with what evidence, that the people of New Mexico supported the idea that the state had final responsibility in running social service programs. Local organizations were to remain subordinate to the state authority.[49]

As for the conduct of individual social workers, there were debates in the late 1920s and early 1930s about the shape that the work of rural, as opposed to urban, social workers should take. The central question was whether the training received by urban workers and the methods they employed were suitable for rural areas. Should workers be generalists or specialists? Experts concluded that the generalist approach was probably more effective in addressing rural problems, but workers objected, arguing that this approach was too diffuse and did not make best use of their skills. More important, though, was that the generalist approach harkened back to an earlier stage of social service, one associated with a tradition of voluntarism of which mission work had been one part. The new generation of professional social workers were disdainful, seeking to differentiate themselves from that older tradition. This sentiment was perhaps best expressed in a snide poem by one social worker who dismissed the all-encompassing community work engaged in by missionaries:

[49] Margaret Reeves, "The Indirect Responsibility of a State Department for Children: Stimulating Local Organization," *The Family*, 1927, reprinted in *Pioneer Efforts in Rural Social Welfare: Firsthand Views since 1908*, ed. Emilia Martinez-Brawley (University Park: Pennsylvania State University Press, 1980), pp. 134–40. For an overview of the implementation of New Deal social policies in New Mexico see William Pickens, "The New Deal in New Mexico," in *The New Deal: The State and Local Levels*, ed. John Braeman et al. (Columbus: Ohio State University Press, 1975), pp. 311–54. Pickens argues that federal aid "reformed" the New Mexico state government as "social service boards blossomed into professional agencies with substantial support from state revenues" (p. 312), reaching a level of professionalism unknown in earlier years (p. 332).

> . . . i don't wanta be
> a rural case worker
> on account of i don't claim
> to be a superwoman
> or a paragon
> period
>
> † † †
>
> The only women who ought
> to even think of this job
> oughta be old maids
> on account of
> they are the only ones
> who would give a
> lifetime to
> a community program
> and they wouldn't care
> if there wasn't
> any place to go
> when they quit work
> except home
> exclamation mark.[50]

By the mid-1930's, the attributes that had once made missionaries into national heroines—their desire to be "paragons," their willingness to give up family life, to commit themselves to a remote rural location, and to work primarily for spiritual rather than material rewards—were being ridiculed. The organization that had recruited and employed them no longer existed, and its successor, the National Board of Missions, was supporting far fewer projects.

Katherine Bennett had sought to fight the injustices of urbanization and industrialization by encouraging individual women to commit themselves to effecting change. She used her position in the interdenomina-

---

[50] For a discussion of the debate about rural versus urban social work see Emilia E. Martinez-Brawley, "The Nature and Methods of Rural Practice," in *Pioneer Efforts in Rural Social Welfare*, pp. 285–88. Marilla Rettig's poem, "why i do not think i would make a good rural case worker," *Survey*, 1936, is reprinted, ibid., pp. 391–93.

tional organizations in which she remained active to promote the development and passage of social reform legislation. The National Committee for the Cure and Prevention of War, the Woman's Council for Home Missions, and the Federal Council of Churches, organizations of which Bennett was a member, were the vehicles through which she lobbied for change. In 1937, Bennett was appointed by Franklin Roosevelt to serve on his Committee on Farm Tenancy. Mission leaders such as Bennett were able to use their experience within the enterprise as a springboard into higher political circles.

Following Bennett's example, albeit in a more modest fashion, missionaries in the field also broadened their activities, attempting to relieve the worsening conditions of their neighbors. Alice Blake raised money from eastern supporters for a new well and a community laundry. During the Depression, the mission schools that remained open took on extra students when public schools closed for lack of funds to pay teachers.[51] The Brooklyn Cottage Hospital saw its admissions triple and reported that its staff was working harder than ever. "The County has been in arrears in paying the county health officer," it was reported, "and he has not been up in this section of the country during the past year." The county nurse, the report continued, "has such a large area to cover that she depends on the mission to care for this region."[52]

Eleanor Tilford joined the Red Cross and then she served as the local chairman for federal aid work. Dorothy Spencer, a subordinate of Tilford's at the Chacón mission, reported that Tilford spent much of her time working on the local relief project. "They began by giving away supplies," Spencer wrote, "but now they are making them [the local men] work on the roads at $0.15 per hour . . . [the workers] do not get cash. There are close to fifty men to receive aid. Of course they are all poor, and have no cash, but should have enough farm food, if they worked last summer. [Relief work] will supply sugar, flour, lard, coffee, and shoes."[53] Tilford welcomed a former student, Daniel Vásquez, now working with the State Extension Service of the Agriculture Department, back to the town, hoping he could show local farmers new and better ways to make their small parcels of land productive. In 1940, the mission teachers teamed up with the State Health Department to conduct a health

51 "Notes from Alice Hyson Mission," *Women and Missions* 10 (May 1933): 56.
52 "Ever Greater Opportunities," *Women and Missions* 10 (May 1933): 43–44.
53 Dorothy Spencer, Letters from Chacón, December 1, 1932, Menaul Historical Library of the Southwest, Albuquerque (hereafter MHL).

education program to eliminate the threat of typhoid. They also began to promote the Rural Electrification Project, and in 1941 they persuaded the townspeople to join the Mora–San Miguel Electric Cooperative.[54]

Bennett had hoped that the structural changes she initiated would enhance the services provided by the Woman's Board, making the church more responsive to the needs of client groups. Under her direction, the enterprise was "modernized," longtime missionaries expected to acquire new skills and training, and new, more highly trained women were recruited. In the process, the personalistic approach was sacrificed for one that can only be described as more bureaucratic. Bennett had likened the organization to a railroad company, but there was tremendous irony in this comparison as she pushed the organization to emulate the corporate giants which, as bureaucratic structures, showed little concern with social justice and the problems of individuals. Rather than expand missionary activities as conditions in northern New Mexico grew worse, the board curtailed them, preferring, as it had with the schools, not to compete with state programs.

The missionaries who remained protested the curtailment of these programs. In principle, they supported making the organization more efficient, but they objected to the rationalization of mission goals when their own stations were threatened. As the home mission movement declined through the twentieth century, ceding its role to government, those missionaries who remained lobbied relentlessly for their share of mission funds, warning officials that the consequences of closing missions included a loss of faith and commitment on the part of adherents. When Sarah Bowen wrote to protest the rumors she had heard that the board planned to limit its support of the Embudo hospital, she asked how the board could "evaluate in dollars and cents the worth of the Gonzales family, the Vásquez family, the Medinas and many others?" "What is the criteria for judging the value of a life, a church, a school, or a hospital?" she added. Bowen was particularly upset over the board's treatment of local "Spanish-Presbyterians." They had not been consulted in the decision-making process, she noted, and "our Spanish people have been helped lo these many years and now feel left high and dry without a voice in the decisions made or consideration even."[55]

[54] Information File: Chacón Presbyterian Day School, MHL.

[55] Sarah Bowen to Dr. Alexander Sharp, October 6, 1958, Bowen Biographical File, H5, PHS.

Missionaries had accepted the need for more expert skills and training, for new methods and pedagogy, for a heightened emphasis on professionalism, but, as Bowen's comments suggest, they did not completely repudiate the religious principles that had originally stimulated the movement. Sarah Bowen was remembered as a highly competent doctor, specializing in obstetrics and pediatrics but also trained in a wide range of skills required for a rural practice. She was described as the "guiding spirit behind the transformation of the useful, but limited, Presbyterian medical mission in the Sangre de Cristo mountains, from its modest beginnings into a frontier bastion of modern, scientific medicine." She learned to speak Spanish fluently, and she maintained amiable relations with the Catholics in the region. Her work, writes a biographer, "facilitated mutual toleration and even tacit cooperation." Although she believed that her primary duty was to treat the "sick bodies of her patients," she was also "conscious of her responsibilities as a good Presbyterian missionary and established regular religious devotions at both Brooklyn Cottage Hospital and Embudo Presbyterian." Unlike earlier missionaries, she did not go out and proselytize but felt instead that "her personal bearing, character and way of life were the more important elements of her testimony or witness."[56]

In their lives and especially in their work, missionaries moved back and forth between private and public social service. Bowen's successor, Edith Millican, moved on to run a public health clinic in Cleveland, New Mexico, which was organized by the Presbyterians but relied extensively on public funds. When she retired from the Board of Missions in 1961, she started a private practice and remained active in public health work in the region.[57] Home mission activities became one part of the larger welfare structure, and the missionaries themselves helped implement various government initiatives. They continued to think of Christ as their "friend" and "master," but they no longer carried the "word" the same way as did the teachers who had preceded them. Rather than preach the Word of God, they believed, as Edith Millican indicated in her application, that the "best method of making Jesus Christ known"

[56] For a biographical sketch of Bowen see Jake W. Spidle, Jr., *Doctors of Medicine in New Mexico: A History of Health and Medical Practice, 1886–1986* (Albuquerque: University of New Mexico Press, 1986), pp. 185–95.

[57] Ibid., p. 195.

was to "believe in Him so fully that His spirit and love may be seen in my life, in all my actions, in all my relations with people."[58]

Like the women who had preceded her, Millican sought personal salvation through her faith, but the desire to convert "foreigners" was not foremost on her agenda. Her mode of missionizing was much more passive; she would serve by example. In answer to the question, "What do you think is our mission in a country where the prevailing religion is Roman Catholic," she wrote, "to cooperate whenever possible in working for the welfare of the country." She did not "consider race superiority of any significance," preferring to judge individuals "as such." Perhaps most startling, in light of the nationalistic fervor of the early movement, was Millican's response to the question, "How does your loyalty to your own country affect your international ideals," to which she said that she found it "difficult to associate myself with our country. I think I can truthfully say my love for any one country does not affect my international ideals."[59]

This more passive method of missionizing, in which mission women hoped to make converts by the example they set as they worked as doctors, teachers, and social workers, continued to place a high value on the importance of maintaining good personal relations with clients. Missionaries may not have been as concerned with making Protestants, but they continued to believe that they had a crucial role to play in the development of their clients' characters. Poverty could not be eliminated simply by addressing social needs; people must be taught to be independent and self-reliant. Early missionaries believed that conversion signaled this transformation; like their predecessors, later missionaries also sought to address issues having to do with the spirit, though they defined this in broader terms.

Hence mission women believed that they were engaged in a project wherein they did not simply deliver a service or teach practical skills but were also engaged in building character. Reporting on the activities at the Allison-James school, Maud Kinniburgh noted, for instance, that it was important for girls to be trained in more than "reading, 'riting,

[58] Application for Missionary Service, November 4, 1940, Edith Millican Biographical File, H5, PHS.

[59] Ibid. Millican was the child of missionaries stationed in China, and she applied for and was assigned to China before being transferred to New Mexico.

'rithmetic and religion." "She must have well defined standards that will help her in discrimination . . . to weed out the unessentials and conserve the essentials," she wrote, "she needs to be efficient, truthful, straightforward, tolerant of other people's points of view, glad to recognize and utilize the worthwhile regardless of its source and patient in setting forth her own ideas."[60] Another student noted that with the help of her teachers, she had learned to be "brave."[61] Edith Millican apparently served as more than simply a teacher when she trained local midwives. One, Jesusita Aragon, recalled that Dr. Millican saw more in her than a "ranch woman/midwife with little formal education." Not only had she taught Aragon various methods of delivery, but she had also exhibited a "faith" in her student that had "endured for many years." When she retired, Millican gave Aragon her medical instruments, an act Aragon remembered proudly many years later.[62] The rationalization of mission efforts not only curtailed the services offered by the church but also threatened the personal relationships missionaries had built with their clients, believing this to be one of the requirements of their "work."

† † †

By demanding new standards of expertise of their female workers, mission leaders had hoped to alter the very language at the heart of the mission enterprise, to give women workers new status, and to make their work seem more "modern." The language of "domesticity," or "social motherhood," had been an important organizing tool. This was the public and political language used to generate support for the enterprise, but it had not been widely used by mission women among themselves.[63] Indeed, missionaries in the field chafed at the assumption that their work was narrowly confined to women and children. Stressing professional standards and credentials did little to alter gender roles within the

[60] Maud Kinniburgh, "A School on the Tourist Trail," *Women and Missions* 7 (May 1930): 53.

[61] Sofia Romero, "Their Alma Mater—Allison-James," *Women and Missions* 4 (May 1927): 60.

[62] Jesusita Aragon's biography appears in Bobette Perrone et al., *Medicine Women, Curanduras, and Women Doctors* (Norman: University of Oklahoma Press, 1989), p. 116. She refers to Millican as "Millikan."

[63] Barbara Balliet makes a similar argument about the ideology of domesticity being a "public and political" language but not one that women reformers necessarily believed ("What Shall We Do with Our Daughters," pp. 337–38).

church to the benefit of women. Instead, all mission boards were consolidated and a distinctive role for women was lost, as well as a measure of autonomy and power. And as Blake's and Bowen's comments suggest, the women missionaries who remained clearly believed that their work would have been taken more seriously had they been men.

This path, in which an emphasis on personalism gradually gave way to professionalization, was taken by most women's reform organizations at the turn of the century. As Robyn Muncy has shown, female reformers were able to form a "female dominion" in an otherwise male "empire of policymaking" by professionalizing services that had originally been largely voluntary. When these new social service professionals strengthened their connections with government, they relied less on the voluntary networks that had sustained their work. Private voluntary groups continued to be useful insofar as they helped to pinpoint where services were needed, but once this had been accomplished leaders turned to professionals. "They no longer had to rely directly on their non-professional sisters in the voluntary organizations," writes Muncy. "The role of the volunteers reverted to the locale, where many of them aided migratory Sheppard-Towner nurses and sought county funds for the local clinics that leaders recommended."[64] Furthermore, when female reformers identified themselves as professionals, suggests Barbara Balliet, they embraced an ideology of merit and achievement and viewed their careers in "individualist" terms. "Similarly," argues Balliet, "their acceptance of hierarchy meant they could not create a world where work was interesting and fulfilling for women who were not professionals."[65]

These ideals were far removed from those that had guided the home mission movement at its outset. Originally the Woman's Board had defined work to include the labor of all women attached to the endeavor. Work and piety were a reflection of each other, not easily separated. The point had been to enhance women's role in shaping the nation and defining the national identity. A more perfect nation was to be realized by emphasizing personal sacrifice, salvation, and the establishment of personal bonds between different groups and classes.

The mission enterprise tried to stay in the mainstream of reform by adopting a more professional, scientific, and businesslike demeanor. For

---

[64] Robyn Muncy, *Creating a Female Dominion in American Reform, 1890–1935* (New York: Oxford University Press, 1991), pp. xii, 53, 121.

[65] Balliet, "What Shall We Do with Our Daughters," pp. 337–38.

some, the very success of home missions in doing this was the reason for their demise. Entering its sixth decade, the enterprise found that it could not sustain the level of fund-raising that it had enjoyed in the past and was having difficulty recruiting younger women for the mission societies in local churches. One college student, commenting on the problem of securing the support of younger people in the 1930s, suggested that the missions represented the status quo and that many younger people did not believe that the status quo should be maintained. "To many," she wrote, "the church seems part and parcel of the capitalist system . . . the church represents vested interests, and they [supporters] seem to be valued in proportion as they can contribute financially or indirectly secure financial support for its program." She appealed to the board to find a way of "enlisting their services rather than their financial support."[66]

Another writer, also addressing the problem of recruiting young members, suggested that the church presented "too soft a message." The church, she argued, had to stop "talking" about social problems and do something about them. Implicit in the writer's comments was a criticism about the educational role of the mission organizations. She wanted to see a return to an emphasis on service, on work. She surveyed the movements of the late 1930s which she saw as having appeal to young people, namely communism, fascism, and Nazism, and suggested that they were appealing because they were "literally built upon the capacity to endure hardness for a cause." What people were seeking, she concluded, was a creed that would produce a "deep, brutal, implacable revolution of life, which hurts the feelings and burns away soft habits with a devastating fire which reaches into all the ways of life."[67] They were, in other words, seeking an experience of intensity that would engage them completely. The professionalization of the movement exposed a larger debate, which was characterized as theological but had larger political implications. At issue was the role to be played by "faith." What was the ideology, or the faith underlying the enterprise?

[66] Esther Boorman Strong, "That 'Younger Generation' College Woman," *Women and Missions* 14 (September 1937): 195–96.

[67] Mrs. Charles Kirkland Roys, "The So-called Lost Generation," *Women and Missions* 15 (September 1938): 179–81.

Schooled in the evangelism of their day, women missionaries of the latter part of the nineteenth century embarked on their journey to win converts by stressing repentance of sins and dependence on God's grace. Evangelical mores of the day relegated good works to a secondary status; social work was best understood as a "complementary [outgrowth] of the regenerating work of Christ which saved souls for all eternity."[68] Though they worked for an agency of the Presbyterian Church, mission women did not directly engage in the theological debates of their time. They did not, for instance, identify themselves as theological modernists or fundamentalists. Like so many other nineteenth-century Protestants, they probably struggled with contradictory teachings, which, on the one hand, preached that all were born sinners while, on the other, dictated that individuals were "moral agents capable of free choice."[69]

If their belief in the utility of Dwight Moody and Ira Sankey's hymnal, *Gospel Hymns and Sacred Songs*, is any indication of their theological sympathies, mission women might best be described, as George Marsden has described Moody himself, as "pragmatic activists" whose theology was "basically orthodox."[70] Did they believe in biblical infallibility and premillennialism, mediated by a sentimentalism that emphasized "commonality of experience" and a "community of feeling"?[71] Were they more comfortable with Henry Ward Beecher's brand of "evangelical liberalism," which "softened" the orthodoxies of Calvinism, questioning, for instance, the idea of eternal punishment for those who had not been saved, and reconciled the rationalism of science and the morality of religion, seeing in the doctrine of evolution, for example, the Kingdom of God at work?[72] Or were they motivated by Walter Rauschenbusch's

[68] George Marsden, *Fundamentalism and American Culture: The Shaping of Twentieth-Century Evangelicalism, 1870–1925* (New York: Oxford University Press, 1980), p. 91.

[69] Marsden lays out the distinctions between strict Calvinists and adherents of commmon-sense realism (ibid., pp. 15–17).

[70] Ibid., pp. 32–33.

[71] For an analysis of the theological content of Moody and Sankey hymns see Sandra Sizer, *Gospel Hymns and Social Religion: The Rhetoric of Nineteenth-Century Revivalism* (Philadelphia: Temple University Press, 1978). She argues that the Moody-Sankey volume aimed to create a "community of controlled feeling" (p. 130), in which the hymn served as a form of prayer to "emphasize the commonality of experience." These hymns or prayers were optimistic in tone, promoting an image of Jesus as friend. Sizer concludes that the purpose of these hymns was to "transform human society, diffusing the gentle influences of social religion unto the ends of the earth—in such a way as to exert 'influence' on Catholics and other tyrants" (p. 158).

[72] Marsden, *Fundamentalism*, p. 24.

articulation of a Social Gospel that stressed good works and social activism, minimizing the importance of personal salvation?[73]

The church may have placed good works behind personal salvation, but, denied a place in the pulpit and in the theological schools, women could only speculate about the nature of personal salvation privately. Their role, as determined by the church, particularly after the recognition of independent mission agencies, was to see to good works. Hence their own salvation became dependent upon their work, and for much of its history the Woman's Board had reflected an alliance between conservative theology and liberal social concern. Mary James had held the Woman's Board to an evangelical standard, arguing consistently that the organization's goal was a more Christian America. Katherine Bennett suggested that personal salvation could not occur without substantial changes in material conditions. James "envisioned a Kingdom of converted Christians who would serve as a leaven for the rest of society," whereas Bennett, "envisioned a merging of Christianity with the world and hoped that the spirit of Christ would permeate all aspects of the secular order."[74]

This range of theological convictions could be accommodated as long as the organization was willing to embrace any woman who expressed a desire to participate. The move away from religious mission to social work, from voluntarism to professionalization, however, brought with it greater selectivity. By emphasizing medical work over education, for instance, the board privileged women with specialized training and, in the case of women doctors, a group of women who were a minority in their profession. Nor was the emphasis any longer on the spoken or written word, but rather on the work, the actual task, performed by the missionary. Mission work was no longer simply a matter of reading and interpreting the Bible.

Historians have noted that both liberal and conservative Protestants worked together until the second decade of the twentieth century, when they began to encounter deep divisions over the scope of the Social

[73] For a brief discussion of Rauschenbusch's ideas on the Social Gospel and his place in the modernist theological tradition see William R. Hutchison, *The Modernist Impulse in American Protestantism* (Cambridge, Mass.: Harvard University Press, 1976), p. 171.

[74] For the distinction between liberal and conservative Protestant reformers see Ferenc Morton Szasz, *The Divided Mind of Protestant America, 1880–1930* (University: University of Alabama Press, 1982), pp. 61, 44.

Gospel.[75] A fundamentalist challenge emerged to counter the claims of liberal voices like Bennett's that the best policy by which to win converts for the church was to address social problems. Angry that conversion had been deemphasized, fundamentalists reasserted the importance of evangelism, arguing, as did Charles Erdman, that "the primary task of the church was to proclaim salvation to individuals and leave the problems of society to the state."[76] This debate had a particularly divisive effect on the mission enterprise. Fundamentalists wanted to recall missionaries whom they believed were not effectively preaching the Gospel, while liberals remained steadfast in their support for the continuation of social services.[77]

Because of the nature of their role within the church—they could not preach per se, and whatever preaching they did was attached to the delivery of a service, whether medicine or education—mission women found themselves cast into the liberal camp. For many this was a no-win situation; if they emphasized the evangelical aspects of the work, they were accused of neglecting their professional responsibilities, but if they relegated evangelizing to a subordinate role, they were taken to task by conservatives. Most simply attempted to go about their business, continuing to teach or to nurse and doctor. The Gospel remained their motivatation, and when the occasion arose, they would share this information with a student, patient, or neighbor. They turned their attention to the situation at hand and, in the process, earned what William Hutchison has called "a reputation for insular thinking."[78]

---

[75] See Szasz, *Divided Mind of Protestant America*; Donald K. Gorrell, *The Age of Social Responsibility: The Social Gospel in the Progressive Era, 1900–1920* (Macon, Ga.: Mercer University Press, 1988), pp. 230–31. William R. Hutchison, *Errand to the World: American Protestant Thought and Foreign Missions* (Chicago: University of Chicago Press, 1987), focuses more specifically on the impact that this split had on mission activities.

[76] Gorrell, *Age of Responsibility*, pp. 230–31.

[77] In his discussion of the shape this debate took in the foreign missions, Hutchison notes that liberals reiterated their belief that linking humanitarian services and personal evangelism was leading to bad evangelism and second-rate social services. For William Hocking, the dilemma for liberals was the quality of missionaries. Hutchison argues that Hocking, for instance, "advised that where missionaries in the field were ill-qualified for the work of social reconstruction 'they should be withdrawn and only persons of the highest type and quality should be sent out for the future'" (*Errand to the World*, pp. 163–64).

[78] Hutchison points out that this was exactly what happened to foreign missionaries (*Errand to the Wilderness*, p. 13).

† † †

Katherine Bennett had entreated her followers not to become "insulators" when she urged that they adopt a more secular social agenda and commit themselves to the serious social issues of their day such as child labor, poverty, protective labor legislation for women, and the need for old age pensions. She had hoped to align her followers with the Social Creed of the Federal Council of Churches, which held that the Protestant churches must stand for "equal rights and complete justice for all men in all stations of life."[79] Missionaries in the field took this edict to mean that they must broaden the range of services they provided and deepen their loyalties to the communities in which they lived. Though the smaller number of mission stations meant that fewer people were reached, those who did receive services benefited from an enterprise more narrowly focused on addressing day-to-day material needs. But a movement that had been both social and political dwindled, its followers scattered, encouraged to find political solutions elsewhere.

Increasingly Protestants were asked to hold certain principles that were not embodied in a parallel social movement. Although the Social Creed set out a social agenda for Protestant liberals, it did not speak to how these reforms were to be implemented. For political action most Social Gospel Protestants looked to the Progressive movement. Susan Curtis has argued that Social Gospelers hailed the presidencies of Theodore Roosevelt and Woodrow Wilson and saw in Progressive politics the possibility for a new political standard of service and morality. They championed a politics of reform that gave shape to a "domesticated government," which meant that the state "assumed increasing responsibility for the welfare of the American people." Curtis's study suggests, however, that if and when Social Gospelers entered the political arena they did so as public servants, not as candidates for political office. It may be, as Curtis argues, that "progressive politics demanded social gospel Protestantism," yet there remained a distinction between the two movements.[80]

[79] For a discussion of the Federal Council of Churches and its Social Creed see Charles Hopkins, *The Rise of the Social Gospel in American Protestantism, 1865–1915* (New Haven: Yale University Press, 1940), pp. 316–17.

[80] Curtis, *Consuming Faith*, pp. 128–78. Curtis suggests that Social Gospelers put their faith in the Progressive movement only to discover in the aftermath of World War I, after the decline of Progressivism, that the "credit for social welfare went to the state instead of the churches" (p. 146).

Indeed, Donald Meyer has suggested that the very idea of being political and engaging in political activism troubled Social Gospel Protestants. Meyer argues that most social gospel leaders did not believe that politics should play an important role in bringing about a more "righteous" state. The "democracy" that they envisioned "meant a state of being even more than a process; it referred to a type of character more than to a pattern of outward relationships. It meant a type of man. Politics was not seen as in its nature a realm of power, nor political democracy as a particular arrangement or distribution of power."[81] The promise of democracy was not to be found in politics or in political conflict but in the "infinite plasticity of human nature." Class struggle, for instance, would be overcome in the expression of love and "brotherly purpose."[82]

The reluctance of Social Gospel Protestants to engage in politics more directly, their hope that a rhetorical emphasis on love, harmony, and brotherhood would move people to correct abuses, denied women's experiences within the movement. Instead of recognizing the series of contests or confrontations that constituted the home mission endeavor, missionaries and their leaders emphasized an ethic of cooperation. At the point at which it might well have served as the basis for a larger social and political movement, in the 1910s and 1920s, mission activities were curtailed. What remained was a social service organization that did not look substantially different from its secular counterparts.

As the home mission movement shrank, Social Gospel advocates lost one of the arenas in which the possibilities of redemption through love and brotherhood could be realized. In essence, they lost the laboratory for their ideas. The mission enterprise wanted professionals, not women in midst of crisis or women searching for spiritual meaning in their lives. Pastors could preach the importance of love between classes and different groups, but it was easier to understand what they meant when one was forced to confront the differences. Preachers might convert their congregations to the idea of love and brotherly purpose, but what then? How were these new passions to be tapped and used in the realization of a harmonious society if there were fewer opportunities to serve?

---

[81] Donald Meyer, *The Protestant Search for Political Realism, 1919–1941* (Berkeley: University of California Press, 1960), pp. 124–25.

[82] Ibid., pp. 138–39. About the role "love" played for liberal Protestants Meyer quotes from George Coe's *The Motives of Men* (1928): "Love of one another produces a degree of cooperation, which is the massing of human energy, that is impossible to greed, licentiousness, and the lust of power."

Liberal Protestantism had reached an impasse, the reasons for which can be seen in the example of the Woman's Board of Home Missions. Its leaders, supportive of liberal Protestantism, were enamored of professionalism, administration, and rationalization, which pared down the numbers active in the movement. They acceded to the secularization of social services. Although the board advocated the enactment of a variety of social reforms and encouraged a liberal political consciousness among its supporters, it was reluctant to serve as a political vehicle. The result was that the Woman's Board (and later, National Board of Missions) was distanced from its base of popular support, a development that presaged the future of liberalism generally in the United States.

But what of those women who over the years had looked to the mission movement for "useful" work, who had sought a fulfilling spiritual experience? Had they disappeared, been surpassed by a generation of women (and men) at ease with secular standards and the concept of "civic reform"? This study suggests not. We can see in the experiences of individual mission women their ongoing concern with issues of spirituality. They believed, as John McDowell wrote in *Women and Missions*, that "man has needs besides food for his body. He needs bread of life for the soul and spiritual raiment for the higher nature." Hospitals could set broken bones, and schools could teach practical lessons, but "beyond the knowledge learned from books that makes one wise in the affairs of the world, there is a wisdom of the spirit that provides a peace that passes not away." The need of the "spiritual life," concluded McDowell, is "constant."[83] Implicit in these concerns was a critique of the emerging welfare state, particularly those aspects that would appear increasingly bureaucratic and impersonal. Indeed, in the fundamentalist backlash within the major Protestant denominations in the 1920s, which singled out the mission groups for going far beyond their original mandate to spread the word of the Gospel, lay the beginnings of a backlash against big government. It is doubtful that those women working within the movement would have wanted to curtail the variety of services they performed and return to the fundamentals of preaching the Gospel. But the backlash contained a focus on individual belief in God and voluntary action that they would have approved.

---

[83] John McDowell, "Our Country Needs the Church," *Women and Missions* 8 (January 1932): 375–77. McDowell's article was apparently a rebuttal to attacks leveled at the church "for what is called its inability to cope with present economic and social emergencies."

Bibliography

Manuscript Sources

The principal manuscript sources used, those cited in the footnotes, are as follows. At the Department of History and Records Management Services, Presbyterian Church (U.S.A.) in Philadelphia (referred to in this work as PHS), Record Group 51, Woman's Board of Home Missions Correspondence, Papers and Reports, 1879–1925, Boxes 1–4, and Record Group 105, Woman's Board of Home Missions, 1878–1948, Boxes 1–6. These two collections contain letters to and from missionaries in the field, reports of the Woman's Executive Committee, and, later Woman's Board of Home Missions, minutes of annual meetings, office conferences, and so on. Also consulted were the Biographical Files (designated as H5), which contain applications and performance and medical reports, as well as additional correspondence between missionaries and the board.

The Menaul Historical Library of the Southwest in Albuquerque, New Mexico (referred to as MHL), proved a valuable source of manuscript materials elaborating the interaction between missionary and client. Organized into Information Files, the materials include newspaper clippings, unpublished biographies of missionaries and students, class lists, reports and studies done on different mission schools, church membership rolls, and letters of missionaries and students. In addition, the New Mexico State Records Center and Archives in Santa Fe (NMSRCA) is the repository for the Arthur Seligman Papers and Andrew Hockenhull Papers, as well as the *New Mexico Relief Bulletin*, all sources pertinent to my discussion of the professionalization of social work. Other manuscript sources appear under "Published and Unpublished Primary Sources."

Periodicals and Newspapers

Home Mission Monthly
La Aurora
Las Vegas Daily Optic
Las Vegas Gazette
La Voz del Pueblo (Las Vegas, New Mexico)
Our Mission Field
Presbyterian Home Missionary
Raton Weekly Independent (Raton, New Mexico)
Revista Católica
Revista Evangélica
Rocky Mountain Presbyterian
Women and Missions

Oral Histories
(Tapes deposited at the Menaul Historical Library)

Angelina Badger
Ruth Barber
Cosme García
Dora Vásquez

Government Documents

Congressional Globe. 32d Cong., 2d sess. January 10, 1853, Appendix 104.
U.S. Bureau of Census. *Religious Bodies, 1916.* 2 vols. Washington, D.C.: U.S. Government Printing Office, 1919.
U.S. Department of Interior, Bureau of Education. "Biennial Survey of Education, 1918–1920." *Bulletin,* 1923, no. 29, pp. 40, 48, 104, Tables 9, 11, 12, 16.
——. "Private High Schools and Academies, 1917–1918." *Bulletin,* 1920, no. 3, pp. 42–55, Tables 10, 12, 13, 14, 15, 21.

——. "Public and Private High Schools." *Bulletin,* 1912, no. 22, pp. 14–36, 192, Tables 4, 10, 14, 22, 35.

——. "Statistics of Public High Schools, 1911–1922." *Bulletin,* 1924, no. 7, Tables 7, 9, 27.

——. "Status of State School Systems, 1917–1918." *Bulletin,* 1920, no. 11, pp. 8–10, 42, 93–99.

U.S. Serial Set. Various documents from 34th through 63d Congresses, 1856–1915, Parts I-VII, microfilm.

Published and Unpublished Primary Sources

Addams, Jane. *Twenty Years at Hull House.* 1910. Reprint, New York: New American Library, 1981.

Alcott, Louisa May. *Work: A Story of Experience.* 1873. Reprint, New York: Schocken Books, 1977.

Atkins, Carolyn, ed. *Los Tres Campos, The Three Fields: A History of Protestant Evangelists and Presbyterians in Chimayo, Cordova and Truchas, New Mexico.* Albuquerque: Menaul Historical Library of the Southwest, 1978.

Austin, Mary. *Land of Journey's Ending.* London: George Allen & Unwin, 1924.

Bandelier, Adolph. "New Mexico: Why It Does Not Flourish." *Nation,* January 28, 1886, p. 70.

Barker, S. Omar. "Trementina: Memories of a Mission Village." *Albuquerque Journal* 23 (September 1980): 10–12.

Bethany Institute for Woman's Christian Work. *Annual Report,* 1873–74, 1876–85, 1887–88, 1890–91. New York Public Library.

Blake, Alice. *Home Life in New Mexico.* New York: Woman's Board of Home Missions of the Presbyterian Church of the U.S.A., n.d.

——. "Memoirs of Alice Blake: Interviews with Missionaries, Teachers and Others in Northern New Mexico." Manuscript. Menaul Historical Library of the Southwest, Albuquerque.

Bliss, Edwin. *The Encyclopedia of Missions.* New York: Funk and Wagnalls, 1891.

Bohannan, C. D. "Report on Survey of Chacon, New Mexico, Community." Made under the auspices of the Board of National Missions of the Presbyterian Church in the U.S.A., unpublished report, 1927. Menaul Historical Library of the Southwest, Albuquerque.

Brown, Milton. *Educational Work in New Mexico.* New York: Board of National Missions, Presbyterian Church, U.S.A., 1957.

Bibliography

Cabeza, Fabiola de Baca. *We Fed Them Cactus*. Albuquerque: University of New Mexico Press, 1954.

Caruth, J. A. *Business Directory of Arizona and New Mexico for 1897*. Las Vegas, N.M.: Daily Examiner Printing and Binding, 1897.

Cather, Willa. *Death Comes for the Archbishop*. New York: Vintage Books, 1971.

Chavez, Fray Angelico. *My Penitente Land: The Soul Story of Spanish New Mexico*. Albuquerque: William Gannon, 1979.

Clark, E. P. "Twenty-two Years Ago." *Nation*, April 30, 1896, p. 337.

College Settlements Association. *Annual Report*, nos. 3–7 (1891–96). Sophia Smith Collection, Smith College, Northampton, Mass.

Colorado, New Mexico, Utah, Nevada, Wyoming, and Arizona Gazeteer and Business Directory, 1884–1885. Chicago: R. L. Polk, 1884.

Craig, Robert. *Our Mexicans*. New York: Board of Home Missions of the Presbyterian Church in the U.S.A., 1904.

Crowell, Katherine. *Our Mexican Mission Schools*. New York: Woman's Board of Home Missions of the Presbyterian Church, 1914.

Darley, Alex M. *The Passionists of the Southwest, or the Holy Brotherhood: A Revelation of the "Penitentes."* 1893. Reprint, Glorieta, N.M.: Rio Grande Press, 1968.

Darley, George. *Pioneering in the San Juan: Personal Reminiscences of Work Done in the Southwestern Colorado during the Great San Juan Excitement*. Chicago: Fleming H. Revell, 1899.

Davis, W. W. H. *El Gringo: New Mexico and Her People*. 1856. Reprint, Lincoln: University of Nebraska Press, 1982.

Defouri, James H. *Historical Sketches of the Catholic Church in New Mexico*. San Francisco: McCormick Brothers, 1887.

Durán, Julian. "Our Relation to Mexico." *Sandstorm Yearbook, 1920*. Albuquerque: Menaul School for Boys, 1920.

Editorial. *New York Times*, February 6, 1882, p. 4.

Esquibel, Alfonso. *Vaquero to Dominie: The Nine Lives of Alfonso Esquibel*. Las Vegas, N.M.: N.p., 1978.

Fry, C. Luther. "Changes in Religious Organizations." *Recent Social Trends in the United States: Report of the President's Research Committee on Social Trends*. New York: McGraw-Hill, 1933.

George, Henry. *The Complete Works of Henry George: Social Problems*. New York: Doubleday Page, 1904.

Grainger, Jane Atkins, ed. *El Centenario de la Palabra: El Rito Presbyterian Church, 1879–1979*. Albuquerque: Menaul Historical Library of the Southwest, 1980.

Bibliography

Gregg, Josiah. *Commerce of the Prairies*. 1884. Reprint, Chicago: R. R. Donnelley & Sons, 1926.

Hall, G. Stanley. "Mission Pedagogy." *Journal of Race Development* 1 (October 1910): 127–46.

Hodgin, Charles E. *Early School Laws of New Mexico*. Albuquerque: University of New Mexico, 1906.

Home Mission Council of North America and Council of Women for Home Missions. *Annual Report*. New York: Home Mission Council of North America, 1908–40.

Interdenominational Conference of Mission Teachers in New Mexico. *Program*. Albuquerque: Menaul Historical Library of the Southwest, 1913.

Jackson, Sheldon. "Scrapbooks on Woman's Home Missions, 1875–1884." No. 62. Presbyterian Historical Society, Philadelphia.

Jaramillo, Maria Cliofes M. de. *Shadows of the Past*. Santa Fe, N.M.: Seton Village Press, 1941.

Lummis, Charles F. "The Penitente Brothers" (1893). In *Land of Poco Tiempo*, pp. 77–108. Albuquerque: University of New Mexico Press, 1966.

McFarland, David. *A Plea for New Mexico*. N.p., 1867. New York Public Library.

Mackey, Druzilla. "The Protestant Missionary and the Social Worker." In Minutes of the Thirteenth Annual Meeting, Interdenominational Council on Spanish-Speaking Work in the Southwest, Department of History and Records Management Services, Presbyterian Church (U.S.A.), Philadelphia.

Morris, Samuel L. *At Our Own Door: A Study of Home Missions with Special Reference to the South and West*. New York: F. H. Revell, 1904.

Morse, Hermann N. *Toward a Christian America: The Contribution of Home Missions*. New York: Council of Women for Home Missions and Missionary Education Movement, 1935.

New Mexico, Arizona, and Colorado Missionary Association. *Annual Report with Constitution and Lists of Officers and Members*. New York: N.p., 1869.

New Mexico Business Directory. Denver: Gazeteer Publishing Co., n.d.

New Mexico (Terr.) Department of Education. *Education Directory of New Mexico, 1909–1910*. East Las Vegas, N.M.: Optic Publishing Co., 1910.

New Mexico Education Association. *Annual Meeting Program*. N.p.: N.p., 1901–20.

New Mexico (Terr.) Superintendent of Public Instruction. *Annual Report*. N.p.: N.p., 1891–1911.

Odom, Harold W. "Public Welfare Activities." In *Recent Social Trends in the United States: Report of the President's Research Committee on Social Trends*, pp. 1224–34. New York: McGraw-Hill 1933.

Park College. "Charter." Record Group 32, Box 22, Folder 3, Department of History and Records Management Services, Presbyterian Church (U.S.A.), Philadelphia.

Park College. "The Story of Larger Things." Manuscript, 1907. Record Group 32, Box 22, Folder 5, Department of History and Records Management Services, Presbyterian Church (U.S.A.), Philadelphia.

Presbyterian Church in the U.S.A. *Minutes of the General Assembly.* New York: Presbyterian Church of the U.S.A., 1870–1925.

Presbyterian Church in the U.S.A. Board of Home Missions *Annual Report.* New York: Presbyterian Church in the U.S.A., 1874–1920.

Presbyterian Colleges. New York: College Board of the Presbyterian Church in the U.S.A., 1913.

Prince, Le Baron B. *A Concise History of New Mexico.* Cedar Rapids, Ia.: Torch Press, 1912.

——. "New Mexico: A Defense of the People and Country." *New York Times,* February 28, 1882.

Rankin, Melinda. *Twenty Years among the Mexicans: A Narrative of Missionary Labor.* St. Louis: Christian Publishing Co., 1875.

Read, Benjamin M. *A History of Education in New Mexico.* Santa Fe, N.M.: New Mexico Printing Co., 1911.

——. *Illustrated History of New Mexico.* N.p.: Published by author, 1912.

Reeves, Margaret. "The Indirect Responsibility of a State Department for Children: Stimulating Local Organization." In *The Family,* 1927. Reprinted in *Pioneer Efforts in Rural Social Welfare: Firsthand Views since 1908,* edited by Emilia Martinez-Brawley, pp. 134–40. University Park, Pa.: Pennsylvania State University Press, 1980.

Rendón, Gabino, as told to Edith Agnew. *Hand on My Shoulder.* New York: Board of National Missions, Presbyterian Church in the U.S.A., 1953.

Rettig, Marilla. "why i do not think i would make a good rural case worker." Originally in *Survey,* January 1936. Reprinted in *Pioneer Efforts in Rural Social Welfare: Firsthand Views since 1908,* edited by Emilia Martinez-Brawley, pp. 391–93. University Park, Pa.: Pennsylvania State University Press, 1980.

Ritch, William, ed. *The New Mexico Blue Book.* 1982. Reprint, Albuquerque: University of New Mexico Press, 1968.

Romero, Benigno. "Bolshevism." *Sandstorm Yearbook.* Albuquerque: Menual School for Boys, 1920.

Romero, Cecil V., trans. "Apologia of Antonio José Martínez." *New Mexico Historical Review* 3 (1928): 327–46.

Salpointe, J. B. *Soldiers of the Cross. Notes on the Ecclesiastical History of New*

Mexico, Arizona, and Colorado. 1898. Reprint, Albuquerque: Calvin Horn, 1967.

Sandstorm Yearbook. Albuquerque: Menaul School for Boys, 1914.

Sergeant, Elizabeth Shepley. "God's Country." *Nation,* July 10, 1920, pp. 39–40.

Spencer, Dorothy S. "Conquistadores Hoy Dia or Folklore and Customs of the Spanish Americans in New Mexico." Unpublished paper, 1945. Menaul Historical Library of the Southwest, Albuquerque.

Stelzle, Charles. *A Son of the Bowery: The Life Story of an East Side American.* New York: George H. Doran, 1926.

Stewart, Robert L. *Sheldon Jackson.* New York: Fleming H. Revell, 1908.

Stowell, Jay. *The Near Side of the Mexican Question.* New York: Home Missions Council, 1921.

——. *A Study of Mexican and Spanish Americans in the United States.* New York: Home Missions Council and Council of Women for Home Missions, 1920.

Stright, Mary. "Diary, October 1882–January 1883." Manuscript. Menaul Historical Library of the Southwest, Albuquerque.

Strong, Josiah. *Our Country.* New York: Baker & Taylor, 1885.

Taylor, Graham. *The Social Application of Religion.* Cincinatti: Eaton and Mains, 1908.

Tenney, Henry. *The Schauffer Missionary Training School.* 1912. New York Public Library.

Twitchell, Ralph Emerson. *The Leading Facts of New Mexican History.* Vols. 1–5. Cedar Rapids, Ia.: Torch Press, 1917.

Union Missionary Training Institute. *Eighth Annual Report.* N.p.:N.p., 1893. New York Public Library.

Vásquez, Dora Ortiz. *The Enchanted Dialogue of Loma Padre and Canada Bonita.* N.p.: N.p., 1983.

——. *Enchanted Temples of Taos: My Story of Rosario.* Albuquerque: Menaul Historical Library, 1982.

Wald, Lillian. *The House on Henry Street.* 1915. Reprint, New York: Dover, 1971.

Walker, Mrs. Calvin. *Woman's Board of Home Missions: A Historical Sketch.* Philadelphia: Presbyterian Church in the U.S.A., 1902.

Walker, Syndor H. "Privately Supported Social Work." In *Recent Social Trends in the United States: Report of the President's Research Committee on Social Trends.* New York: McGraw-Hill, 1933.

Walmsley, Myrtle. *I Remember, I Remember Truchas the Way It Was, 1936–1956.* Albuquerque: Menaul Historical Library of the Southwest, 1981.

Bibliography

Willard, Frances E. *Glimpses of Fifty Years: The Autobiography of an American Woman.* N.p.: H. J. Smith & Co., 1889.

Woman's Board of Home Missions. *Annual Directory of Schools and Stations Supported by the Woman's Board of Home Missions.* New York: Woman's Board of Home Missions of the Presbyterian Church in the U.S.A., n.d.

Woods, Robert. *The Settlement Horizon: A National Estimate.* New York: Russell Sage Foundation, 1922.

Works Progress Administration. *New Mexico: A Guide to the Colorful State.* New York: Hastings House, 1940.

Wright, Julia McNair. *The Complete Home: An Encyclopedia of Domestic Life and Affairs.* New York: Charles Drew, 1879.

Index